SONS OF THE EMPIRE

Sons of the Empire

The Frontier and the Boy Scout Movement, 1890–1918

Robert H. MacDonald

UNIVERSITY OF TORONTO PRESS
Toronto Buffalo London

© University of Toronto Press Incorporated 1993
Toronto Buffalo London
Printed in Canada

ISBN 0-8020-2843-8

Printed on acid-free paper

Canadian Cataloguing in Publication Data

MacDonald, Robert H.
Sons of the Empire : the frontier and the Boy
Scout movement, 1890–1918

Includes bibliographical references and index.
ISBN 0-8020-2843-8

1. Boy Scouts – History. 2. Frontier and pioneer
life. 3. Baden-Powell, Robert, Baron, 1857–1941.
I. Title.

HS3312.M23 1993   369.43'09041   C93-093285-4

This book has been published with the help of a grant from the Canadian
Federation for the Humanities, using funds provided by the Social Sciences
and Humanities Research Council of Canada.

Contents

Acknowledgments / vii

Introduction: A Scheme to Save the Empire / 3

PART ONE
Scouting for Men

1
The Legion That Never Was 'Listed / 31

2
Buccaneers: The War Scouts / 62

3
The Wolf That Never Slept: A Scout at Mafeking / 88

PART TWO
Scouting for Boys

4
Zulu Warriors or 'Red Indian' Braves? The
Frontier Spirit in *Scouting for Boys* / 117

5

The Laws of the Jungle: Teaching Boy Scouts
the Lessons of Good Citizenship / 145

6

Mrs Britannia's Youngest Line of Defence: Militarism
and the Making of a National Symbol, 1908–1918 / 176

Conclusion: Scouting and Myth / 203

Notes / 211

Bibliography / 225

Appendices / 243

Index / 255

Illustrations following pages 16 and 168

Acknowledgments

This book began when I strayed from a reading of Kipling's verse, 'The Law of the Jungle' (in the *The Jungle Book*), to search out other texts that gave lessons to boys on obedience. I discovered *The Wolf Cub's Handbook*. I became interested in the ways social myths worked, and took a look at the hero worship of Baden-Powell at Mafeking. Then came the Boy Scouts, then the myth of the frontier. That was in 1981, when an earlier form of chapter 3 appeared as an article in the *Dalhousie Review*.

My debts are numerous. I am especially grateful to those fellow workers in the field who shared their knowledge, particularly John Springhall, who gave me the benefit of a lively correspondence, and Geoffrey Pocock, who most generously showed me his work on the Legion of Frontiersmen. I would like to thank my two research assistants, Christine Brown and Claudia Baker, who helped me with bibliographical work, and my colleagues, Anna Wurtele, Parker Duchemin, Alan McLay, and Ben Jones, who read and criticized all or part of the text. My thanks too to those who fed me information: Naomi Griffiths, Larry McDonald, Don Beecher, Barbara Gabriel, Faith Gildenhuys, and the Gordon Wood clipping service.

The staff at Scouts Canada, Ottawa, allowed me the run of their extensive archives; Pat Evans and Bob Milks were very helpful. I benefited from the knowledge and goodwill of many others: Graham Coombe, Scout Association Archivist, Baden-Powell House, London; Stan Horrall, RCMP historian, Ottawa; Malcolm Wake, director of RCMP Museum, Regina; Captain Bill Guscott, curator of the Princess Patricia's Canadian Light Infantry Museum, Calgary; Doug Cass, assistant chief archivist of the Glenbow Museum, Calgary; Jill Shefrin and Dana Tenny, librarians, Osborne Collection, Toronto Public Library, and the staff at the inter-library loans desk of Carleton University's MacOdrum Library. Thanks too to Guy Mayson, who alerted me to the National Film Board of Canada's film on Baden-Powell.

Finally, the thanks which are the most heartfelt of all: to Diana, to Sally, and to Stephen, for home truths and criticism when they were most needed.

I gratefully acknowledge the financial assistance of the Social Sciences and Humanities Research Council in the form of a travel grant, and in various smaller subventions administered by the Dean of Arts and the Dean of Graduate Studies and Research, Carleton University.

SONS OF THE EMPIRE

'Count, are we feeble or few? Hear, is our speech so rude?
Look, are we poor in the land? Judge, are we men of The
  Blood?'

RUDYARD KIPLING, 'The Song of the Sons'

Introduction

A Scheme to Save the Empire

When Lieutenant-General Robert Baden-Powell launched the Boy Scout movement in 1908, he needed a hero his boys would respect. Like many others, he thought that Britain was in danger, for it seemed certain that she would soon be in the middle of a European war, and she was far from ready to fight. Her army was small and her navy under-equipped. Worse still, Baden-Powell worried that young Englishmen would prove themselves weaklings: he feared, in the language of the day, that they would fail 'the supreme test of manhood' in battle. He hoped that Scouting would make things right. He would teach the soldiers and sailors of the coming war – the present boys of Britain – to be real men; becoming healthy and strong, and understanding their duties as citizens and patriots, they would be the saving of the country. For the movement's hero he offered himself, not as a soldier, but in the character of that up-to-date invention, a scout of the Empire.

In the years before the First World War there was a widely accepted understanding that Britain was losing ground in the race with her competitors; her once confident political and mercantile superiority was threatened by her rivals, her markets were shrinking, and the economy appeared to be weakening. Even the country's military strength was vulnerable: the Boer

War had rattled the public's trust in its army, and Germany's new navy was exposing the inadequacies of Britain's older capital ships. As a sympathetic American commented, John Bull was failing at the 'far more scientific game that Germany, Japan and America are now playing ... The sun that never sets is setting.'[1] Britain no longer effortlessly dominated the world.

To some pessimists, the country's difficulties were part of a larger problem, for civilization itself seemed to be rotten. Europe was sick in mind and body. The proofs were everywhere; the middle classes were worldly and selfish, the working classes degenerate, society had become immoral, modern literature and art quite decadent, everyday life selfish and materialistic. The old countries were dying, and there was a general loss of will and vitality. Rider Haggard put it all down to an absence of faith, and worried about the decline of European populations. He had heard that the French were refusing to propagate themselves.[2] The civilized nations were heading toward 'race suicide.' Softness and selfishness seemed to be the characteristic vices of an over-pampered society.

In Britain the condition of the working class occasioned great anxiety. Perhaps the most alarming phenomenon was the depopulation of the countryside and the overcrowding of the inner cities, a migration which was spawning a new type of degenerate – the weak, stunted, over-excited, and too often diseased slum-dweller. Weakness and vice showed up in the behaviour of slum children: apprentices, 'street arabs,' delivery boys, loafers, and 'corner boys' led apparently undisciplined and aimless lives; they amused themselves at football matches and in the music halls, they smoked and loitered round the public houses, and read the penny dreadfuls. From their ranks sprang the hooligans, who terrorized the streets at night. They could only be cured by a healthy dose of the cat o' nine tails. These were middle-class fears, directed against the half-known and not-to-be-trusted working class; but even the middle class seemed to be losing its way, and thought its youth at risk.

The root of the problem seemed to be the failure of modern society to produce men who were strong, both morally and physically, and to some concerned patriots such as Baden-Powell, the solution was obvious. If civilization itself was to blame, with its materialism, urban problems, and moral temptations, then the country should look to the younger countries, where life was simpler, and where the battle for existence was real. How could manhood be tested? At home there were few challenges, and the weakest, surviving easily enough, set the tone for the rest. The nation was suffering from a loss of energy; it had to pick itself up, put aside its self-indulgent pastimes, and look to its future. Civilization sapped a man's strength: as Baden-Powell put it some years later, 'with its town life, buses, hot-and-cold water laid on, everything done for you,' it tended 'to make men soft and feckless ... God made men to be *men*.'[3] The middle class had to lead the way, and take a lesson from the Empire. The colonists risking their lives in Canada, Australia, New Zealand, or Africa had strength and initiative; in contrast to the bored or indifferent or pleasure-seeking islanders, they were *real* men.

This book argues that the frontier, and its stereotypical hero, the war scout, provided British society at the beginning of this century with an alternative ethic, answering this general fear about the condition of the nation's virility. Though in hindsight we might think that the period of imperial expansion was over by the turn of the century, the idea of the frontier was still potent and romantic to many Edwardians, and it came to symbolize an attractive solution to a set of increasingly complex problems at home. War was on the horizon; to make sure the future combatants were virile and strong seemed the only way to keep the peace.

The frontier myth supported the frontiersman as a cult figure, it used 'primitive' races such as the 'Red' Indian and the Zulu as examples of martial virility, and, in Baden-Powell at Mafeking, it made the imperial scout a national hero. The outward symbols of the frontiersman – his cowboy hat, his flannel shirt and neckerchief, and perhaps most oddly, his short trousers (as used by Baden-Powell in India and on the South African veld) – dramatized through the Boy Scout movement the call to a revitalized manhood. These symbols spoke of the difference between restraint and freedom: the Edwardian boy, who was buttoned up, stifled in heavy clothes, and too often under orders to behave himself, now had the chance to put on a Boy Scout uniform. Dressed up in frontier clothes, flannel shirt, 'cut shorts,' and stetson hat, he could play the exciting game of 'man-hunting' under the leadership of the most charismatic hero of the day. For many of the first recruits to Scouting the effect was liberating. In its first fresh years the movement promised something new; it came with a breath of adventure, with the trappings of an exciting life lived on the edge.

What is attempted in the following pages is neither social history nor biography, but a study of masculinist ideology and the work of social myth, telling the story of the war scout, describing the birth of the Boy Scout movement from the frontier enthusiasm, and showing the subsequent evolution of the Boy Scout to the status of a patriotic symbol. That Scouting's inventor was at the same time determined to make good citizens of his boys is part of the story. In fact, the tension between adventure and discipline, between escapism and the moral lesson, was also at the centre of Scouting: while Scouts might enjoy themselves learning the skills of the frontier, their parents would approve of lessons in citizenship. The mix was powerful, and by the time the First World War began, when its first recruits were reaching military age, the Scout movement had become a national institution, ready to stand beside the army and the navy in the defence of Britain and her Empire.

The first part of Baden-Powell's manual, *Scouting for Boys*, was published on 15 January 1908. To a young reader, the picture on the cover might suggest a story. Concealed by some rocks, a boy lay watching the sea; a short way out was what looked like a warship, on the beach below were some figures, and a boat. Had the warship landed a raiding party: was this an invasion? The boy on the cover was dressed in a peculiar way, for his trousers were cut off at the knees. Was this what boys who scouted wore? Beside him lay a cowboy hat and a stick: were these what boys who scouted used? Everyone knew what scouts were. Red Indians were scouts. Buffalo Bill was a scout. The Boers had been scouts, but they had been beaten at their own game by our scouts. The book said it was 'Part I,' and it cost fourpence, a considerable sum, four times the price of a weekly magazine like the *Boy's Own Paper.*

Scouting for Boys came out in six fortnightly parts from 15 January onwards; the complete edition was published on 1 May 1908. Baden-Powell, late inspector general of cavalry, was well known as the hero of the siege of Mafeking in the recent South African War. The first cover, and the first part, were both typical of his direct approach to boys: the use of his own nickname 'B.-P.' and his own famous hat, the hint of being at the centre in the serious business of stopping an invasion, the invitation to learn scouting, which was the 'game' that was played on the frontier, and was the most exciting war skill of all. But *Scouting for Boys* was something more than simply an exciting invitation, for Baden-Powell had as his sub-title 'A Handbook for Instruction in Good Citizenship.'

Scouting for Boys was an immediate success, and Scout troops were started all over Britain. At first it had been Baden-Powell's intention to encourage boys to scout from within existing youth movements such as the Boys' Brigade or the Church Lads, but such was the demand from unattached boys that the idea was soon abandoned. By the end of the first year Scout committees had been set up to regularize the selection of scoutmasters, the bureaucracy of Scouting was in place, and a number of firms had been appointed official suppliers of uniforms and equipment. The movement spread in the year of its founding to Canada, Australia, and New Zealand, and by 1909 to India. It even had an appeal beyond the Empire: it was taken up almost at once in Chile, Argentina, and Brazil. As early as 1910 Baden-Powell crossed the Atlantic for his first tour of Canada, where the governor general, Earl Grey, who had known Baden-Powell in South Africa, agreed to become the first Chief Scout of the Dominion. That same year the movement started in the United States, prompted by a Chicago publisher, William Boyce, whose experience of a helpful, friendly, and unselfish Boy Scout in a

London fog made him determined to encourage Scouting in his own country. In the spring of 1910 Baden-Powell, then in command of the Northumberland Division of the Territorial Army, decided to resign his commission to devote himself full-time to Scouting.

It is difficult now to put Scouting into its original context, uncontaminated from its subsequent history and the gradual evolution of its aims. The movement developed a moral code which seemed at the centre of the liberal, humanist system. Consciously non-denominational, interracial within limits, and bridging the classes, it favoured hard work, selflessness, and universal brotherhood. It became, in time, the spirit of cooperation and peace, a League of Nations for the young. Yet in its initial form, Baden-Powell's handbook was correctly understood by most of his interested contemporaries to be the work of a general who was worried about the next war. Addressed in the first place to a generation of mostly urban boys and their middle-class scoutmasters, *Scouting for Boys* expressed the middle-class values of the public school code and the Protestant work ethic. Its ideology was conservative and defensive, seeking to find in patriotism and imperialism the cure for an apparently disintegrating society. Its orientation was aggressively masculine, its mission to save boys from the sapping habits of domestic and urban life.

The originality of the Boy Scout scheme was that its concept of service was inspired by the imperial frontier. In Baden-Powell's eyes, the men who were building the Empire were models of virility: they were accustomed to life in the open, they could live rough, they were hardy, self-sufficient, and practical. If a boy could only be induced to follow their example, he might be turned away from idleness and uselessness, and the country would be saved. As Baden-Powell repeated again and again in the speeches he made to advertise his scheme, the downfall of Rome had been caused by a decline in good citizenship, by the want of energetic patriotism, by the growth of luxury and idleness, and by the exaggerated importance of party politics. These were precisely the conditions that threatened Britain. The hope of the future lay with the rising generation. If young boys could only be trained to be 'peace scouts,' and take for their model the men of the frontier – pioneers and trappers of Northwest Canada, explorers and hunters of Africa, prospectors, drovers, and bushmen of Australia, and above all the men of the Canadian North-West Mounted Police, the South African Constabulary, Royal Irish Constabulary, and other colonial police forces – then the country might be saved. These were the men 'whose manhood was strong and rich, and whose lives were pure.' A boy trained to be a peace scout would be certain to develop character and manliness, honour, endurance, and patriotism.[4]

Scouting for Boys thus presented the frontier life both as an adventure and as a discipline, an escape from the enervating, feminine atmosphere of the home to a place where pure masculine character could be shaped. Ironically, as the first cover hinted, this vision of the frontier was, in its soul, inward-looking. The program of regeneration it advised was set within a defensive frame, between one war past – Mafeking – and one to come.

The rapid growth of Scouting was remarkable, but it was not, as several of the Scout histories later represented, miraculous, for it combined a shrewd marriage of public service and good business. Baden-Powell's own position in national life, together with the patriotic nature of the enterprise, gained the movement considerable 'official' support from the start. Baden-Powell was conscious of the importance of a 'name'; he managed to persuade important people to lend their formal approval, and he agreed to let the conservative paper, the *Daily Telegraph*, adopt the Scouts (the paper pledged £4,000 a year towards Scout headquarters). More considerably, he worked with the backing of the newspaper magnate, Arthur Pearson. In Pearson's hands, Scouting was in fact a lucrative scheme to be run in the first place with an eye on the till. Pearson treated Scouting like any other commercial enterprise or circulation raiser: he lent Baden-Powell one of his editors to help write the handbook – the easy-reading formula that had worked for the popular *Pearson's Weekly* and *Tit-Bits* would work well with *Scouting for Boys*; he publicized Baden-Powell's lectures to create a market for the parts as they came out; he used the momentum to launch a weekly paper *The Scout*, which to Baden-Powell's disgust turned out to be as trashy as any 'ordinary boys' paper.' Pearson put his own senior manager, Peter Keary, in control of the business side of Scouting, and it was not until seven months had passed that Baden-Powell managed to set up a separate organization. The financial arrangements between Pearson and Baden-Powell were unequal and very much to Pearson's advantage.[5]

The practice of the marketplace and the ideals of the movement may often have been at odds, but together they made a powerful combination. By the end of 1909 there were some 60,000 Boy Scouts registered in Britain alone; by 1910 the number had risen to 107,000, by 1913 to 152,000, and by 1917 to over 194,000.[6] A rally of Scouts was held at the Crystal Palace in September 1909. King Edward VII sent the boys a message, telling them that he took the greatest interest in them, and that he knew that the training they were receiving now would help them do their duty as men, should danger threaten the Empire. A second and much larger rally was held in Windsor Great Park two years later; this time Edward's son, now George V, inspected the Scouts. Each succeeding rally was more ambitious than the last: 11,000 Scouts had come to the Crystal Palace, 26,000 were at Windsor; these were one-day affairs. When the third gathering was held in 1913 in Birmingham, 5,000 Scouts were in camp for a week. This, the Imperial Scout Exhibition, was a public demonstration of Scout activities and skills from life-saving to carpentry to cooking, and it was brought to a climax with a huge rally attended by His Royal Highness Prince Arthur of Connaught. At the Imperial Exhibition too there were Scouts from across the Empire and around the world, from Europe and the United States, from Gibraltar, India, and China. After the war these international meetings would be known as jamborees.

The movement began to meet the particular needs of special Scouting constituencies: the Sea Scouts were formed in 1910, the Girl Guides in 1912 (though 'Girl Scouts' had appeared unofficially as early as 1909), and by 1914, the group for younger boys, the Wolf Cubs, was planned. As David MacLeod has argued, writing of the history of the Boy Scouts of America, the business of Scouting would eventually turn into Scouting's own expansion. By the 1920s even Baden-Powell, at the head of an increasingly authoritarian bureaucracy, was to feel that the spirit of scouting might be lost as the organization grew ever more formalized.[7]

The success of the movement had limits. Scouting, as it turned out, recruited in Britain mainly from the lower middle class and the upper working class. Lower working-class lads could hardly afford Scout uniform and equipment;[8] more significantly, they disliked Scouting's insistence on discipline and often found its middle-class morality patronizing. They identified Scouts as 'stuck up,' and jeered at Scout troops in the street. Scouting, one social worker put it, would 'deal with a class of boy who is as a rule higher up in the social scale than the boy of the slum.' For those who were working with street corner boys, Scouting was not much good, and the boys' club, which stressed neighbourhood, friendship, and the individual attention of adults, seemed a better idea.[9] Yet Scouting was to exert an influence on British society far out of proportion to its actual enrolments.

The youth movements that were founded in Britain, the British Empire, and the United States at the end of the nineteenth and the beginning of the twentieth century had their origins in complex social forces. Essentially they represented an attempt by the dominant middle classes to rescue and impose good order on what seemed the most vulnerable and potentially the most dangerous section of the lower classes. The founders of the most successful boys' movements – in Baden-Powell's word the 'uncles' – were William Smith of the Boys' Brigade, Ernest Thompson Seton of the Woodcraft Indians, Daniel Beard of the Sons of Daniel Boone, and Baden-Powell himself. None of these men was an intellectual, none of them had a systematic philosophy of education and youth training. They reacted to the ideas of their time, and the success or failure of their work depended more than anything else on their ability to respond to what was in the air, to voice public concerns, suggest popular solutions, and institutionalize topical enthusiasms. The youth movements preached virility, discipline, love of nature, Christianity, patriotism, imperialism; they were a mission to save a generation of *boys* from godlessness and degeneracy. Their success depended on the sugar round the pill: on the images each movement projected, on their uniforms, on the adventures they inspired, on the models of manhood they paraded and made glamorous. It is to be doubted if ideology in the raw has much power until it is somehow turned into narratives which may seduce the imagination. Each of the youth movements, in its own way, found it needed to make the bare ideas exciting and accessible to boys, and, at best, to give them stories to believe in. Their success was greatest with the classes which shared their ethic; ironically, the working class, most in need of 'saving,' was the most resistant to the message.

William Smith started the Boys' Brigade in Glasgow in 1883. Though it was rooted in Presbyterian evangelical Christianity, both in aims and means it was characteristic of later youth organizations. Smith was a businessman, a member of the Young Men's Christian Association, and a spare-time officer in the 1st Lanarkshire Volunteers. He was much influenced by the work of the American revivalists, Moody and Sankey. He decided that he would teach the street-corner boys of Glasgow the kind of Christian manliness then so much in favour in the English public schools, and he thought of mixing the drill of the Volunteer Force with the Sunday school teaching of his evangelical church, the Free College Church. He gave his boys, who were mostly the sons of artisans and small shopkeepers rather than the 'hooligans' he had first considered, a uniform, a dummy rifle, a haversack, and a pill-box cap, and drilled them in companies, splicing military discipline, outings, and patriotism to religion. The mixture was attractive, and by 1890 the Boys' Brigade had over eleven thousand members in Scotland, and five thousand in England and Wales.[10] Other church-sponsored organizations imitated Smith's beginning, such as the (Anglican) Church Lads' Brigade, the Jewish Lads' Brigade, the Catholic Boys' Brigade, the Boys'

Life Brigade. The army and the navy, with less success, continued to encourage and sponsor cadet corps. Outside of the churches and the military, by the 1890s there were many other organizations recruiting boys for a variety of good causes – for the Empire, for teetotalism, for purity, for non-smoking.

The story in Canada and the United States was much the same. The early organizations were church-sponsored, and in many cases were little more than Sunday schools and youth clubs. In the United States Ernest Thompson Seton had started his Woodcraft Indians about 1902 (the movement was variously called the Woodcraft Movement or the Seton Indians), based on the ideal Indian and the study of woodcraft. Daniel Beard took the American pioneer as his model, and in 1905 founded the Sons of Daniel Boone. Both organizations had only a limited success. In 1910 the Boy Scouts of America, patterned on Baden-Powell's Scouts, recruited both Seton and Beard as joint 'uncles'; their philosophies clashed, and Seton's non-militaristic internationalism eventually succumbed to Beard's aggressive patriotism. Seton however had a powerful influence on the Scout movement, especially on those of Baden-Powell's officers who were opposed to militarism.

The social ideas that informed and inspired the youth movements can be simplified, but they were by no means simple; Scouting cannot be understood without some summary of its historical background. Both it and the other youth movements reflected and were a response to several quite different influences: popular imperialism, social Darwinism, the crisis of masculinity and the search for 'national efficiency,' social concerns about poverty and slum conditions, new theories of education, and the value of fresh air. All the ideas were topical in 1908 and contributed to shape Baden-Powell's invention.

From the 1890s on, popular imperialism was a dominant force in British social life; it pervaded public consciousness through a dozen media, as John MacKenzie has shown.[11] In juvenile texts, school readers, popular histories, and the boys' magazines, the ideology of imperialism was announced to the young in straightforward and obvious terms: might was right, England was strong, what she had she held. The moral justifications followed behind, with the bringing of Christianity to the pagans, and the imposition of law on the unruly. After the missionary and the soldier came the merchant; trade created prosperity. Across the seas from the mother country were the daughter colonies establishing British forms of government, and beyond them, strange lands of outer darkness, places of disorder, and, probably, places of impurity. In time the Empire might claim even these. The duty of each British citizen was to guard against those foreigners who coveted the riches of the British colonies, who envied, who plotted, and threatened. *Scouting for Boys* itself reflected this simple imperial doctrine; Baden-Powell's view of history was nothing if not a confident summary of contemporary attitudes.

The Edwardians also had more complex thoughts about imperialism.* Lord Milner, fresh from his term as governor of the defeated Boer republics of the Transvaal and the Orange River Colony (1902–6), summed up his vision of a Greater Britain as 'one united family,' exercising a 'decisive influence' for peace, and promoting a common civilization. He believed the words 'Empire' and 'Imperialism' were much misused; the true imperialist favoured neither domination nor aggrandizement.[12] John Buchan, one of Milner's young men in South Africa, describing the intoxicating effect of the imperial idea, reiterated its essential idealism.

> I dreamed of a world-wide brotherhood with the background of a common race and creed, consecrated to the service of peace; Britain enriching the rest out of her culture and traditions, and the spirit of the Dominions like a strong wind freshening the stuffiness of the old lands. I saw in the Empire a means of giving to the congested masses at home open country instead of a blind alley. I saw hope for a new afflatus in art and literature and thought. Our creed was not based on antagonism to any other people; we believed that we were laying the basis of a federation of the world. As for the native races under our rule, we had a high conscientiousness.[13]

*The discussion here does not reflect the complexities of political opinion and allegiance; support for imperialism cut across political party lines, and was complicated by other political issues, such as tariff reform.

In constrast, the liberal thinker J.A. Hobson considered imperialism reactionary. He argued that the landlords, financiers, and factory owners liked jingoism (or knee-jerk patriotism) because it distracted the public; governments that supported social reform were an expensive threat to making money.[14] Other radical liberals, such as L.T. Hobhouse, attacked what they saw as the grossness of imperial ambitions, and deplored the excesses of an imperialist Tory government, typified by Joseph Chamberlain's tenure at the Colonial Office (1895–1903), Cecil Rhodes's land-grabbing ambitions in southern Africa, and by the scandal of the abortive Jameson raid which did so much to provoke the Boer War.

The war, which for its opponents produced the worst excess of unthinking patriotism, returned the Conservative (and pro-imperialist) government to office, but soon the imperial cause seemed to its opponents to waver. By 1905 the liberal polemicist Charles Masterman was pronouncing the death of the imperial 'illusion' and the loss of power of its leading writers, Rudyard Kipling and W.E. Henley, whose collective genius so perversely inspired what he called the 'Reaction' against liberal humanitarian principles. The Reaction had set itself against the old ideals of liberty, equality, brotherhood, and universal peace.

> It revolted always against the domination of the bourgeois. It estimated commerce as a means of conflict and a weapon of offense. It clamored for the ancient Barbarism; and delighted in war; and would spread an English civilization, not by the diffusion of its ideas but by the destruction of its enemies. It was a message of vigour and revolt congruous to a nation wearied of the drabness of its uniform successes; with the dissatisfaction and vague restlessness which come both to individuals and communities after long periods of order and tranquillity. To the friends of progress the dominance of such a spirit seemed of the elements of tragedy. Literature, after its long alliance with the party of reform, had deliberately deserted to the the enemy.[15]

The epitaph was premature, at least in terms of popular feeling. Though in 1906 the Liberal party won a huge majority on an anti-imperial platform, the spirit this victory expressed seemed to wilt: in the years before the First World War, popular imperialism marched on. Military competition with Germany became a fact, nationalism had its resurgence. Anti-imperialism was, in the essence, an intellectual and rationalist belief; imperialism a powerfully emotive force. As such, it was an effective weapon in the hands of those who were calling for preparedness and the training of youth.

Popular imperialism fed on images of heroism and military triumph. It spoke of conquest, it used a myth of history to justify the inevitable progress of Empire. This ideology reached into all corners of late-Victorian and Edwardian life, colouring dozens of activities, from big-game hunting to athleticism. Children, and boys in particular, were obvious targets; a vast patriotic literature was directed precisely at them. Healthy boys needed tales of action; stories should be 'manly,' and 'red-blooded.' Boys' magazines like *Chums* exploited the excitement of military action, history was presented as a 'Romance of Empire,' and innumerable fictions detailed a repertoire of heroic deeds.*

Fears of a weakening virility were widespread by the end of the nineteenth century. If men were becoming soft, women, perversely it seemed, were turning aggressive. The public appearance of male homosexuality in the 1890s, culminating in the notorious trial of Oscar Wilde, was sufficient evidence of something deeply wrong with English manhood. At the same time the challenges of the 'New Woman,' now demanding the vote and freedom from patriarchal control, appeared to destabilize middle-class order even further. Industrialization or a widened franchise might be blamed: each could be the source of male alienation or female activism. One response to this apparent crisis was for 'real men' to seek out ever more robust forms of masculinity, in shooting and big-game hunting, on the playing fields, in the misogyny of Clubland.[16]

---

*Bertrand Russell, in his notorious letter to *The Nation* of 15 August 1914, linked the masculine spirit of imperialism with the boys' books when he claimed that the mad rush into war was a 'blood lust,' a reversion to 'atavistic instincts,' which had been encouraged by that 'whole foul literature of glory,' and by 'every text-book of history with which the minds of children are polluted.'

1 Sitting Bull and William Cody, 1885

2 Superintendent James M. Walsh, North-West
Mounted Police, photographed in the late
1870s wearing frontier dress

3 The Legion of Frontiersmen in Regent's Park, London, summer 1906

4 Jerry Potts, the North-West Mounted Police's Métis guide and interpreter, late 1870s

5 Burnham escapes after shooting the priest of the M'Limo

6 'Mafeking – Waiting' by Charles Robinson, March 1900. The drawing illustrates the verse 'We wait, we wait ... but helpless bairns lie murdered at the gate.'

Saturday, May 26th, 1900.

UNDER THE
UNION JACK

Vol. II.—No. 29.

FROM "CALEDONIA, STERN AND WILD."
One of Lord Lovat's Special Corps of Highland Gillies.

7 A Lovat Scout, 1900

8 Baden-Powell at Mafeking. Drawing by R. Caton-Woodville, June 1900

The 'crisis in masculinity,' as it is sometimes called, encompassed a wide range of social concerns, but it is nowhere more evident than in the words of the founders of the youth movements. They spoke of binary oppositions between 'men' and 'women': men were strong, women were weak, 'real' men were vigorous, other men were 'half men, half old women.'[17] Where would the boys of Britain stand – with the real men, or with the women? The polarity extended to the separate spheres of the two sexes. The world of action, of the military, the Empire, and commerce, was male, the world of home and childhood, was female. Now the influence of the feminine seemed to pervade society, eroding masculine character, gendering civilization itself. How could young boys be saved? The public school solution, separating boys from their mothers before too much damage was done and subjecting them to a spartan regime in a world without women could hardly be attempted for the whole country. Yet the influence of the home had to be resisted, and boys had to be trained to be hard and self-disciplined. The frontier might be the last hope for the manhood of Britain. There, nature, in its most pristine state, was left still uncontaminated.

The debate about national efficiency, the idea that Britain compared badly with other better organized states, also focused on the state of the country's manhood. One pamphlet, which summarized alarmist opinion, and which attributed Britain's difficulties to a lack of energy, particularly impressed Baden-Powell. In *The Decline and Fall of the British Empire*, Elliot Mills, a backbench Conservative MP, suggested that there were social-Darwinian causes for the country's problems: the nation was losing its vitality, and in a competitive world only the fittest would survive. The British now preferred the town to the country, they were forsaking the sea, indulging in luxury and vulgarities, watching games instead of playing them, losing faith in God, and were paying too many taxes. Mills pretended that his pamphlet was printed in Tokyo, and was a Japanese report to the government of Japan. Young men of Britain's declining empire, the mock report said, were left without direction.

There existed among them no respect for parents, no reverence for old age, nothing but an insane insistence that every sorry child of sloth and ignorance had an unreasoning right to do what he pleased. Four months under canvas, and a sound education in the most bracing of all schools, the school of war, would have given a new tone to the community, and compelled every man to realize what it meant to be the citizen of an Empire which strove to direct the aspirations of the world.[18]

Compulsory military training, Mills went on, besides being the best insurance against war, would crush 'the spirit of Jingoism and unchristian militarism,' and turn the man in the street into 'the most peaceful of beings.' Such ideas expressed very well the position of those who, like Baden-Powell, despised the easy patriotism of the popular press, yet were looking for ways to keep Britain and her empire strong.

Throughout the Edwardian decade the search for national efficiency went on. Japan and Germany were seen as model progressive states able to organize their economies and their citizens towards national goals. The lessons of the Boer War were mulled over; as early as 1906 a European war seemed possible. Lord Roberts, the grand old hero of the army, became president of the National Service League. In this position he was seen as a natural ally of those who were proposing various schemes to prepare the country: cadet forces, athletic programs, training in marksmanship, the formation of a volunteer, part-time army. By 1910 para-military organizations such as the Legion of Frontiersmen and the Legion of Scouts were recruiting to defend the Empire. The newly crowned George V coined the slogan 'Wake up, England!' The enemy was now identified, and the rebuilding of the navy became a race with Germany.

Germany was not merely a commercial and political rival, but was supposed to be rehearsing an invasion of England. The German ambition was exploited by National Service League supporters; by 1908 German invasion plans were widely believed and widely feared. In that year, addressing officers of his new Territorial Army command, Baden-Powell caused a stir by arguing that the coming German invasion was aimed at the heart of England, the industrial Midlands. The invasion would come when England least expected, probably on the August Bank Holiday. The best defence was preparedness; that was the purpose of the new Territorial Army.[19] Erskine Childers in his 1903 thriller, *The Riddle of the Sands*, had first described the discovery of German intentions in the North Sea. He wrote to rouse the public from its lethargy, considering unpreparedness a national disease. Other popular writers exploited the invasion scare, and invasion stories flooded the popular and juvenile press.

The health of the nation's children was linked to the debate on national efficiency when Parliament, alarmed by the quality of the Boer War recruits, set up a committee to investigate the extent of the problem. Reporting its findings in 1904, the Interdepartmental Committee on Physical Deterioration, having interviewed a wide variety of witnesses, cited the slum conditions of the industrial cities as the root of the problem: air pollution, bad housing, unhealthy workplaces, long working hours, poor and insufficient food, dietary ignorance – pickles and strong tea with everything – bad milk, alcoholism, all made for an unhealthy and diseased working class. The juvenile population was particularly hard hit. The committee heard evidence of an appalling infant mortality rate and of schoolchildren so undernourished they could barely keep awake in class. Cigarette smoking was widespread. As one of its many recommendations, the committee urged that 'some grant should be made from the National Exchequer in aid of all clubs and cadet corps in which physical or quasi-military training, on an approved scheme, is conducted.'[20] The future of the country obviously rested on the health of its children. Youth clubs, the committee noted, were of some help, taking children off the streets, helping them to exercise and reach the fresh air.

The poor health and poorer prospects of working-class children were described in several social and polemical essays which Baden-Powell read (and recommended to potential scoutmasters in *Scouting for Boys*): Robert Sherard's *The Child-Slaves of Britain*, Leslie Cornford's *The Canker at the Heart*, Sir John Gorst's

The Children of the Nation, Samuel Keeble's *The Citizen of To-morrow.* W. Blackburn Fitz-Gerald, contributing to Keeble's collection of essays, claimed that 'the strength of the nation is being undermined at the foundations.' Citing the studies of Charles Booth and Seebohm Rowntree, he estimated that between ten and fourteen million people lay below the poverty line – that is, had neither enough to eat nor sufficient clothes to keep themselves warm. In Sherard's 'pathetic book,' Fitz-Gerald found the statistic that at least half a million children of school age, the youngest five years old, were 'engaged in wage-earning labour.' Quoting Cornford, he noted the problem of the legion of errand boys and unskilled lads who, automatically discharged by their exploitative employers when they reached the age of eighteen, sank into manhood, 'ill-fed, unhelped, and desperate ... into the irreclaimable.' These problems could only be solved by radically improved social conditions; in the meantime, as Keeble and other evangelical Christians believed, much could be done to help the victims through charitable work. Fitz-Gerald was encouraged by the efforts of the boys' clubs, and pointed to the United States, where, using the latest psychological theories, Ernest Thompson Seton and others were organizing the boys' own instincts for play.[21]

To an extent, Scouting was a direct response to the debate about national efficiency, but in the larger context it expressed vaguer conservative or reactionary fears. The masses in their millions seemed foreign, godless, uncontrollable; they were awkwardly independent, and at times almost lawless; they threatened good order with continual strikes and riots. The spectre of degeneration rattled its bones: slum dwellers were probably polluting the race through mental deficiency; the new science of eugenics explained the process. 'The shape of the face gives a good guide to the man's character,' Baden-Powell said in *Scouting for Boys*, driving home the point with a sketch of a firm-jawed, long-headed Boy Scout, flanked by two examples of bad breeding. The working-class 'loafer' or 'shirker' came out looking like a degenerate, wearing a cloth cap and a muffler – the uniform of the typical hooligan. A more dangerous thought still was that the hooligan was at least tough, and that the middle-class was soft, and perhaps even effeminate.[22]

One cure for physical and moral deterioration was in nature. It was in the open air, away from the corruption of the cities, that the youth movements looked for new life. The Boys' Brigades had camps, the Church Lads excursions, while the Scouts took to the outdoors and practised their woodcraft. Fresh air was the cry. There was wholesomeness and health in the fields and under the stars. As the liberal social reformer R.A. Bray argued, in an essay which summarized progressive contemporary theory on the subject, the children of the town had to be removed from their half-life of the streets, and allowed to experience 'the beauty of sunrise and sunset, the changes of the seasons, the fresh green of spring and the red gold of autumn, and all the loveliness of the night.' Only then was it possible for moral training to begin. An annual country holiday for each child might open a window to the great mystery of life.[23]*

A romantic appreciation of nature had deep roots in nineteenth and early twentieth-century British middle-class society. The countryside in its beauty was opposed to the grim and ugly city; the countryside meant harmony, peace, and ease; whatever man had not made, whatever was natural, seemed superior to the work of man's hand. Nature was innocent, and unspoiled, as was the child until corrupted; put the child back in nature, and the child's response was a measure of his pureness of heart. Nature was a moral test.

These feelings were echoed by a generation of nature writers, by George Borrow, Richard Jefferies, and Kenneth Grahame; they had at least part of their inspiration in the writings of the German and English romanticists, in Ruskin, and in the works of the transcendentalists. The man in balance, Emerson said, was the man whose senses were in harmony with nature, 'who has retained the spirit of infancy even into the era of manhood.'[24] The mystery of life was waiting for the young in the English

---

*Arthur Pearson, the newspaper magnate and sponsor of Scouting, publicized in his papers the Pearson Fresh Air Fund, which sent slum children on holiday to the country or the seaside.

countryside, in the Black Forest, or in the tangles of the Connecticut woods.

Climbing mountains or walking in the countryside were physical recreations with a spiritual dimension; to camp outdoors was to return to nature. In the United States the outdoors clubs and the societies for the preservation of the wilderness, the enthusiasm of outdoorsmen as different as Teddy Roosevelt and John Muir, the several wildlife publications (*The Interior, The Outing Magazine,* or *Forest and Stream*), all spoke about the important place of nature in American culture. To go back into the woods, as William Gray, one-time editor of *The Interior,* said, was to return to paradise. The way to the hearts of boys, those 'little barbarians,' was through allowing them the joy of building 'a mimic camp-fire.'[25] Perhaps the most influential of the American outdoors writers was Stewart Edward White, whose books, such as *The Forest, The Mountains,* and *Camp and Trail* were both practical guides to, and appreciations of, the wilderness. The youth movements, and in particular Scouting, were touched by this American dream of the wilds and the outdoors. Baden-Powell was to quote from and recommend White's books in several of his works for Scouts and Rovers.

Love of nature also had an important place in contemporary educational theory. Utilitarian learning by rote – satirized by Dickens in *Hard Times* in the person of Mr Gradgrind – was a system which was pervasive in the public education of the late nineteenth century, but its inadequacies and inhumanities were apparent to many liberal thinkers. The advocates of 'progressive' education, in which the child's sense of discovery and play were cherished, returned to the theories of the 'German school' of the late eighteenth and early nineteenth centuries. Pestalozzi, Froebel, and Herbart, following Rousseau, had emphasized the importance of kindness and love in school, and the place of play in development. Pestalozzi, working intuitively, had encouraged his children to be observant; Froebel had stressed the good environment, inventing the school in a garden, the *kindergarten.* Another ally of progressive educators was the social-Darwinian philosopher Herbert Spencer, who had argued that children should be introduced to science through nature study; they should be trained to observe. These theories were enjoying a revival by 1908, and they were used by some youth leaders to confirm their own understanding that participation and fun in the outdoors were good for children.

The teacher Charlotte Mason was an influential English popularizer of the progressive ideas, and a firm advocate of the place of nature in the training of the child. Baden-Powell read her books, and recommended them to scoutmasters in *Scouting for Boys*. In *Home Education* Mason told parents of the importance of the outdoor life, and the absolute value of the school of nature. 'Never be within doors when you can *rightly* be without,' she said, arguing that training began with watching the crops, the flowers, the animals, the bees, the seasons. 'The Sense of Beauty comes from Early Contact with Nature.' Nature study taught a child science, a landscape in miniature explained geography. Mothers should be silent, and let their children talk to nature.[26]

Mason had an enthusiasm for outdoor play, and was one of the first to see that it could include the latest game from the frontier. She came across Baden-Powell's little pamphlet *Aids to Scouting* just after its publication in 1899, and made the discovery that military scouting fitted nicely into modern educational theory. Baden-Powell, she said, 'set us on a new track. Hundreds of families make joyous expeditions, far more educative than they dream, wherein scouting is the order of the day.' In bird-stalking, 'all the skill of a good scout comes into play. Think, how exciting to creep noiselessly as shadows behind river-side bushes on hands and knees without disturbing a twig or a pebble till you get within a yard of a pair of sandpipers.' Every family, Mason said, 'should possess *Scouting* in default of the chance of going on the war-path with a Red Indian.'[27]

Whatever their specific goals, the youth movements held in common that they could drive out the bad by bringing in the good, and so turn the loafer or hooligan into the Christian boy or the good Scout. In line with contemporary educational theory, habit was the key: a good habit supplanted a bad. Drill, exercises, competitions all served to make good behaviour second nature. Of all the virtues in the training of young people obedience was the first.[28] These quite orthodox ideas seem to have been generally accepted by the founders of the youth movements.

If nature was a moral influence on the child, more obviously, it was good for a child's health. Its appreciation was coupled with the movement to liberate the body, called by the Germans *Leibeskultur* or 'body culture.' Its influence was marked in a variety of contemporary phenomena, from the movement to revive the classical Olympic Games to the fashion revolution which freed women from corsets. Open-air schools, an experiment started in Berlin in 1904, were quickly imitated in both Britain and the United States; it was realized that fresh air, good food, and exercise made a startling difference to the health of slum children.

The fresh-air theory fitted in easily with the goal of national regeneration, and connected both to the imperial program and to the idea of the frontier. The boy who would soon defend the Empire was now called the 'open-air boy.' In 1901 the boys' magazine, *Young England*, commissioned a book in its patriotic and imperial series for this new kind of boy, so necessary to the health of the nation. Its author, the Reverend C.M.A. Hewitt, a master of Winchester College, wrote that 'wild life has irresistible charms,' and contrasted the 'bonds of civilization' to the joys of camping in the open, sleeping on the ground, swimming in country ponds, cooking for oneself, and reverting, in essence, 'to a state of primitive savagery.' A boy introduced to this life was a 'Young Campaigner,' practising the skills that would make him a good soldier.[29] The editor of Hewitt's book made the connections clear: he linked the imperial program to the ethics of games and the outdoor life, and to the spirit which had produced 'the heroic deeds of our countrymen.' Eight years later the idea was still timely. 'General Baden-Powell and Mr. C.B. Fry [the famous cricketer, who was also involved in youth schemes and lent his name and talents to the *Outdoors Magazine*] are beloved of the youth of the realm,' said the *Graphic* in 1909, 'and they are both taking an active and useful part in the evolution of the Open-Air Boy.' Here the newly popular pastime of camping came into its own.

Camping had long been practised, for soldiers had to camp, as did explorers and big-game hunters. By the Victorian years an urbanized middle class had moved outdoors for much of its enjoyment. Bourgeois myth-makers such as Kenneth Grahame lovingly described the symbols of the free life and the open road: picnics, the gypsy caravan, 'messing about' in boats. As early as 1886 illustrators in the *Boy's Own Paper* were showing boys on their summer holidays camping out, lying at ease in front of a well-organized tent, boiling an egg for breakfast on a camp stove, fishing, swimming in the river, using a sleeping bag, fighting off insects. Eight years later Dr Gordon Stables, the ubiquitous writer for boys, was describing a 'Camp Life for Boys' based on his own practice – although this, coming as it did with a semi-permanent cabin, complete with man-servant, was hardly roughing it. Camping made for hardiness in his eyes. 'I do most firmly believe that there is a bit of the Crusoe in every really manly boy who livesand breathes,' he said. There was 'nothing like a bit of camp life in summer for making boys men.'[30]

That camping was a novel and rather daring activity is plain from the words of its advocates, who seemed to feel that their first business was to defend it as both safe and character-building. Camping was educational, since it allowed boys to get about and see things; it encouraged resourcefulness and strengthened the bonds of friendship. It was virile. Its enthusiasts spoke at length on the healthiness of fresh air, and calmed fears of the cold and the damp. The camping life was 'enlightened Bohemianism.'

Behind all these remedies for a tougher and better Britain was the idea of nature as the stern arbiter of life, whose laws of breeding had to be obeyed, who spoke of survival and extinction, who demanded that the fittest live while the weak went to the wall. The Darwinian theories had made their way into popular consciousness; they were being applied not only to the lower species but to human society. If only the fittest survived, then young people had to be fit; if nature was competitive, then young people had to compete.

Young boys may have been in need of direction at the turn of the century in Britain and the United States, or they may not; what is important is that in contemporary eyes they appeared to be in danger, and their condition suggested a national crisis. This is not so much a relativist argument as a reminder that the idea is stronger than the fact. The Scout movement was a success because it answered so many hopes and anxieties: it was both 'progressive' and reactionary, responding, on the one hand, to a number of liberal ideas in education and social theory and, on the other, to a wide range of conservative, imperialist, and militarist opinion. It was a novel solution to the worries of an age, and though it incorporated many different idealisms and gave its recruits a wide variety of experience, its initial stimulus, to use its Founder's own emphasis, was the need to BE PREPARED, and that, in essence, meant making *real* men.

Without the frontier myth the movement might have appealed to adults as a sensible and worthy institution, but it would have made little impact on its intended recruits or their scoutmasters. Here Baden-Powell's own heroic status was crucial: he was, to the movement, both hero and scout, proof of his own frontier argument about virility. His peculiar energy and charisma added an almost irresistible impetus. He put boys first, and let them join him in his 'game'; he was interested in character, but he knew he had to appeal to their imagination. He had, as his biographer Tim Jeal reminds us, the Peter Pan gift of never growing up. The frontier was the place of adventure, and by reliving its excitements he could teach boys to imitate his heroic life.

The Boy Scout movement escaped academic study for its first half-century, but thrived on in-house memoirs and uncritical biographies of its founding hero. In the last twenty years a number of historians have turned their attention to Baden-Powell's

life-work and, recognizing its importance as a social phenomenon, have raised and debated questions of its origins and nature.
Was it just a happy episode in the lives of thousands of youngsters, or was some serious indoctrination going on? Did it touch
the working class? Was it a militarist organization? A machine to
reproduce carbon copies of good citizens? An expression of
patriotic fervour? Did it come about because the country was
experiencing a crisis in masculinity? John Springhall, in his
Youth, Empire and Society (1977) laid the groundwork for much of
the subsequent discussion. Michael Rosenthal, in his polemical
The Character Factory (1986), argued for social indoctrination;
Tim Jeal, in his massive biography *Baden-Powell* (1989), made a
detailed and persuasive psychological study of the founder's life,
providing the ammunition for future debate and analysis. There
have been other significant contributions, but none has fully
explored the connections between the idea of the frontier and
the Boy Scouts, or given due weight to the movement's most
obvious yet important inspiration, military scouting.

In the early editions of *Scouting for Boys* Baden-Powell added
to each chapter a list of books he recommended to Scouts and
their scoutmasters (see Appendix 2). These have acted as a stimulus for the research of this study. They have provided a surprisingly substantial introduction into the mind-set of the period,
and have given focus to an interpretation of the movement itself.
Baden-Powell, in his military career, was the author of a number
of books, on military scouting, on his military campaigns, and
on sport. These have also been useful as a source of attitudes
and language, revealing in their usage of the discourses of popular imperialism. Other contemporary texts, especially newspapers and periodicals, filled in the gaps. My aim has been to
illustrate the original context of Scouting, using Baden-Powell
and his handbook as a point of entry into the Edwardian age.
This is necessarily a discussion of the male world; the influence
of the frontier on women and the girls' organizations, and the
ways in which they negotiated and appropriated masculinist ideology, is a separate study.

The first part describes how the imperial frontier was imagined, and how its 'reality,' reported in the media, came into public consciousness; the second part shows the way in which the myth of the frontier was used to launch the Boy Scout movement.

PART ONE
Scouting for Men

CHAPTER ONE

The Legion That Never Was 'Listed

When two old comrades meet, perchance to fight again in Rhodesia, or one to help the other out of trouble on some beach in the
Southern Seas, or to dine together dressed up like ridiculous wait-
ers, the bond of the blood is strong between us still. The news told
then of the old troop begets no laughter: A. deserted; B. shot himself; C. died of typhoid; D. of bad liquor; E. has disappeared; F. is
supposed to have fallen at the Yalu; G. was found frozen to death
in a coal-shed at Medicine Hat; but for the rest, spirits are calling
across the deep from all the continents and all the oceans.

(Roger Pocock, *The Blackguard* 97–8)

For the hundreds of thousands of young men who went out to
the imperial frontier, life was rarely quite what they expected.
Conditions were harsh and the climate usually extreme; they
might be confined to a life in barracks for months at a time, or
isolated in a cabin throughout a cold, dark winter; they might
have to endure the hardships of jungle heat and its awful humid-
ity, or risk thirst in the desert. Wherever they went, it seemed,
they were plagued with flies or mosquitoes; scorpions and
snakes shared their beds. They would be lucky if they stayed
healthy: food was often scarce, or monotonous (corned beef or

sardines three times a day); eating canned food they might get ptomaine poisoning, missing fresh vegetables they might come down with scurvy. Patrolling the Canadian prairies, say, with the North-West Mounted Police, these would-be adventurers risked frostbite, going into the Sarawak jungle they were almost certain to get malaria or worse. The typical frontier community, such as a mining camp in Rhodesia in 1900, was likely to be a brutal and sordid place, the women, if any, whores and derelicts, the men going to the devil – a process which began with not shaving and not washing, and ended quickly enough with the whiskey bottle. At worst, such places were soddenly drunken, and in their misery the young adventurers lost their self-respect, 'took to kicking Kaffirs,' and cursed the day they thought to leave home. If they managed to get back to England, they might well regret that too, for middle-class society, hidebound in its conventionality, gave cold comfort to the black sheep that returned to embarrass it.

Yet in the popular imagination the frontiersman was a colourful figure at the beginning of the twentieth century: Australia had her bushmen, Canada her trappers, equatorial Africa explorers and hunters, southern Africa prospectors. The United States, before all, invented the frontiersman, in the pioneer, Indian scout, or cowboy. The American ideal set the image of the Anglo-Saxon adventurer: a stetson hat and a cowboy neckerchief marked his uniform, and the frontiers of the world, from the Philippines to the plains of Patagonia, were his testing ground.

Though this image was quintessentially American, by 1908 it had entered popular British culture. The explorer, the miner, and the frontier policeman belonged to a brotherhood whose loyalty to the clan was testament of loyalty to the Empire, whose very wanderings were token of the Empire's far-reaching bond. He seemed to revive the spirit of the Elizabethan seaman; he was virile, a true Englishman, one of the 'sons of a roving breed.' His adventures filled thousands of fictions for men and for boys, and in the hands of writers such as Rudyard Kipling, Rider Haggard, Robert Service, and John Buchan, he began to symbolize the imperial dream. Fact fed on fiction, history turned into myth:

the frontiersman became a type that carried the meanings of a world still in flux. He proved his courage by panning gold in the Klondike, fighting pirates in the South Seas, running guns in South America, or killing Zulus in South Africa – and he came home to yarn about his experiences with other old frontier hands in the cosy camaraderie of London's Savage Club. The legend was to have as short a life as the Empire itself: when Grey Owl wrote in 1931 of the *Men of the Last Frontier,* he mourned their passing, and recorded that 'on the outskirts of the Empire this gallant little band of men still carries on the game that is almost played.'

This chapter is the story of the frontiersman as he was imagined, of his evolution and, most importantly, his meaning. It begins to answer the question of why Baden-Powell chose the frontiersman, in the form of what he was to call the 'peace scout,' as the ideal example for boys, as *the* model of manhood for his Boy Scouts.

In fact each of the 'uncles' of the movement found inspiration on the frontier. For his Sons of Daniel Boone (and later for the Boy Scouts of America), Dan Beard favoured the 'buckskin man,' a perfect specimen of Anglo-Saxon manhood, a blond giant standing six foot two in his moccasins, slender, powerful, and erect. This '*he-man,*' in Beard's judgment, had all 'the reckless, rollicking fun of Robin Hood with the rugged morals of Abe Lincoln': he was an individualist, an explorer, a patriot, honest, honourable and true. Ernest Thompson Seton, in contrast, despised Beard's inspiration. He thought the scouts of the plain and the men of the mountains were 'almost without exception, treacherous, murderous, worthless, without the shadow of a claim on our respect but this: at best, measure of dull brute grit.' But Seton also dreamed of ideal men, and looking west, put his trust in the frontier's aboriginal people, the noble and stoical Indians.[1]

In *The Educated Imagination*, Northrop Frye draws a simple distinction between two worlds: the real world, in which we spend our day-to-day existence, and the world of the imagination, which informs the way we live. The world we construct, or dream, is the realm of myth, and of literature; it is an improvement on the real world, for it is more ordered, more dramatic, more satisfying than everyday life.[2] If history records the details of life, myth encourages the facts of history to arrange themselves in convenient and understandable patterns. Myth simplifies, but above this, myth makes the story told seem inevitable and natural, a complete and obvious justification of the values of society. Myth in fact is ideology dramatized and disguised in fables and examples whose 'meaning' is self-evident: in anecdotes such as Drake's game of bowls, Bruce's lesson from the spider, Lincoln's log cabin; in heroic types like the Elizabethan adventurer or the dashing musketeer. When these stories are told they circumvent history and create a presence stronger than fact. Here, the metaphorical reality plays its part: things are not alive until they have been imagined.

To understand what prompted Baden-Powell and his contemporaries in their dream of the frontier, Rudyard Kipling is the most obvious authority. Kipling imagined the Empire, and expressed its most enduring myth. His readers responded, accepting Kipling's reality as their own. The myth made heroes of the young men who went looking for adventure, it spoke of their courage and sacrifice, it celebrated their lust for life. To take Kipling's poem 'The Explorer' as illustration: the explorer leads the adventure of Empire, he is the pathfinder for the pioneer and the settler. He stands for innocence and another Golden Age; he will discover the new world, he will cross the river into the promised land. His summons are the lines whispered by the voice of imperial destiny:

> Something hidden. Go and find it. Go and look behind the
>   Ranges –
> Something lost behind the Ranges. Lost and waiting for you. Go![3]

What was waiting was 'white man's country past disputing,' the sites of future cities, a virgin wilderness ripe for what we still call development. The frontiersman, thus imagined, denied the weakness or indifference of the mother country. He was bringing the dream of the frontier home. But Kipling was not alone, nor was he the first in his inventions.

To reach the original meaning of the frontiersman and his myth we have to return to the first half of the nineteenth century, to discover why in 1907, in Baden-Powell's words, this was the type 'whose manhood was strong and rich,' whose life was 'pure.' This point should be in fiction, for the historical fact seems to have no impact until it enters the imagination, and it should be American, for that was the ideal frontier of the nineteenth century in the English-speaking world. Fenimore Cooper is the author, his hero Natty Bumppo the first important frontiersman. With his Leatherstocking hero Cooper created a figure of mythic power, one who, like Robinson Crusoe, passed into public possession, serving to define for a while the dream-wish of the western world.

In *The Pioneers* (1823), the first novel of the Leatherstocking saga, Natty Bumppo appears as an old man, but a man whose thin face has 'every indication of the most robust and enduring health.' He is dressed in deerskins – his buckskin breeches give him the nickname of Leatherstocking – and he carries with him everywhere a long rifle. His first prominent scene is a shooting match, which he wins by shooting the head off a turkey at a hundred yards. In the later novels, which take us both forward and backwards in time, we learn the history of this man of the woods, of his upbringing by the Delaware Indians, of his actions as a scout in the Indian wars, his conflict with the settlers, his removal ever farther west to his death among the friendly Pawnee beside the Rockies. Natty is man stripped to elemental virtue: he is strong, hardy, courageous, intrepid, honourable; he is the personification of his well-earned epithets, Deerslayer, Hawkeye, Long Rifle, the Pathfinder, the Trapper. He is the Scout above all scouts, the Hunter above all hunters, Indian friend and Indian killer.

The wilderness it turns out is Natty's Garden of Eden, shared by his fellow savages, noble and ignoble. There he has all he needs, his to kill or be killed. The serpent in this garden is not the wicked Indian Mingo, for the bad savage acts only according to his nature, but rather the settler, whose clearing in the woods announces the coming of the profane world. When Natty, now living on the edge of the settlement, cuts the throat of a deer out of season, and so runs foul of the game laws, his simple, pre-lapsarian world is confronted by the sordid values of the new order. In a society of property-owners there is no room for the dreamlike freedom of the wilderness. 'You've brought in the troubles and divilties of the law,' Natty says at his arrest, 'where no man was ever known to disturb another.' Towards the end of his life he reconciles himself to the inevitability of change, but his words sound as a requiem for lost innocence:

How much has the beauty of the wilderness been deformed in two short lives! My own eyes were first opened on the shores of the Eastern sea, and well do I remember that I tried the virtues of the first rifle I ever bore, after such a march, from the door of my father to the forest, as a stripling could make between sun and sun, and that without offense to the rights, or prejudices, of any man who set himself up to be the owner of the beasts of the fields. Natur' then lay in its glory along the whole coast, giving a narrow stripe between the woods and the ocean to the greediness of the settlers. And where am I now! Had I the wings of an eagle, they would tire before a tenth of the distance, which separates me from that sea, could be passed; and towns, and villages, farms and high ways, churches, and schools, in short, all the inventions and deviltries of man are spread across the region![4]

The story of Cooper's frontiersman allows of no simple reading; its richness and its power set up a complex web of meanings. Natty Bumppo's simple life is a celebration of the primitive, and an attack on the corruptions of civilization. D.H. Lawrence put his finger on the utopian dream of the novels, which in their return to Natty's youth yearn for innocent beginnings, and dream of an America young once more. The suggestion that civilization is wicked, and that only in nature is there purity and strength, is something of a subversive myth, as Henry Nash Smith has argued. But it is none the less powerful for that.

The Leatherstocking was the 'symbol of the national experience of adventure across the continent.' His peculiar relationship with the Indian, both as fellow-scout and fierce enemy, has been read as a working out of white American guilt, an imaginative simplification of the horror of genocide. In the words of one critic, 'a sordid fact of American history was purified when the woodsman killed the noble savage in this idyll of death in the midst of unspoiled nature.' Natty's soul-friendship with Chingachgook set in place the type for a whole genre of American romance – the pairing of the cowboy and the Indian, the Lone Ranger and Tonto. As Leslie Fiedler pointed out, Cooper invented the Western.[5]

To posterity, Cooper's frontiersman was the archetype of the free man whose independence was earned not only by his courage, his coolness, and his hardiness, but by his rifle. Leatherstocking is the adventurer living by his own law (his law is nature's law, but he has taken it as his own); his code is simple and admits of few shades of grey. He exists only in the uncomplicated world of romance, where sex is an unnecessary interruption, and every problem can be solved by the knife or the gun. These simplicities gave him mythopoeic power: he is the very embodiment of American adventure, a hunter forever scouting the savage Indian in the wild woods, the model for an everlasting boyish game. Natty's archetypal scene is the moment in *The Deerslayer* when he outdraws and kills the Huron on the banks of Lake Glimmerglass, fixing the simple idea that the best man was the man with the truest aim, the quickest finger on the trigger. Since he is an honourable man we trust the morality of his actions, but, Natty is a killer.

By the time of Cooper's death in 1851 the image of the frontiersman was in place in the American imagination, and history hurried to catch up with the pattern. Cooper had, perhaps, taken his inspiration for Natty Bumppo from the supposedly autobiographical history of Daniel Boone, which appeared in 1784 in John Filson's *Discovery, Settlement and Present State of Kentucke*. Here Boone is presented as the founder of Kentucky, bringing civilization to the wilderness; but Boone was to conform in later accounts and in popular history to the image of the solitary hunter, seeking independence and happiness in a state of nature. His heroic legends were opposed to the comic stories of Davy Crockett; both displaced the earlier image of the frontiersman as a savage and perhaps depraved outlaw. Boone epitomized the man of few words, Crockett the teller of tall tales. But it was in Crockett's vulgarity, in his aggressively folksy voice, that Cooper's patrician values found their answer. Natty was always aware of his social inferiority; the next generation of heroes thought themselves better than anyone.[6] A crowd of democratic buckskin boys joined Boone and Crockett: Kit Carson, Hugh Glass, Jim Bridger, Buffalo Bill, mountain men and scouts, names and lives which soon passed into folklore. But D.H. Lawrence's words for Natty apply equally to these historical figures: 'a man who turns his back on white society. A man who keeps his moral integrity hard and intact. An isolate, almost selfless, stoic, enduring man, who lives by death, by killing, but who is pure white.'[7]

Not all recorders of actual frontier life subscribed to a celebration of the frontiersman; military men, in particular, seem to have been sceptical. Colonel Richard Dodge listed various types of frontiersmen according to their degree of decadence. The first, and least harmful, were the trappers, but they were surpassed by the Indian traders – 'nowhere could be found a more utterly debased and worthless set of men' – and by the 'squaw men,' those white men who had chosen to live with the Indian tribes, and who, in Dodge's opinion, exploited the natives, earning their admiration only by their capacity for 'lying, stealing, drinking, treachery, and debauchery.' Miners were hardly better, buffalo hunters were the lowest of the low, cowboys were rough and ready at the best. All in all, the frontier received the scoundrels, ruffians, and con men of civilization, whose main ambition was to grab what they could before the law interfered. Dodge noted one particular type, the outcast, who had chosen the frontier as a refuge from justice. 'Almost all were extremely inquisitive and suspicious, but many had humane and hospitable habits, while others were as savage and dangerous as their Indian neighbors.'[8]

Yet by the middle of the nineteenth century the frontier was romanticized in both art and fiction. The West was the source of novelty, the picturesque, abundance, and the magnificent. George Catlin had painted the Indian in the 1830s; his *Letters and Notes on the Manners, Customs, and Condition of the North American Indians* was published in 1841. He was followed by other artists; for the rest of the century the West was a popular subject. American soldiers wrote memoirs of their Indian campaigns on return to barracks; British novelists such as Mayne Reid and R.M. Ballantyne hurried to set their stories in the new land of wonder. All contributed to an idea of this Wild West, this country of heroic savages, of oceans of buffalo, of daring men on spirited horses. The frontier became the perfect setting for the adventure story, where a set of stereotypical characters in stereotypical adventures owed as least as much to Cooper's conventions as to western geography or history. Whatever the historical reality, the mythical meaning of the frontier was stronger.

The westward progress of the pioneer became the course of destiny, of empire. The poets understood: to both Whitman and Thoreau the west was vital, the east dead and tame. In 1893 the historian Frederick Jackson Turner put forward the thesis that the frontier itself had formed American character, that a new American had emerged – democratic, self-sufficient, individualistic, nationalistic. The very fact of pioneering had altered American behaviour: plentiful resources made the settlers wasteful, isolation made them inventive, space encouraged them to wander, hard conditions forced them to be materialistic. The myth-makers took Turner's argument and the settlement of the frontier became 'The Winning of the West,' a chapter of Manifest Destiny, a hymn to Anglo-Saxon progress. Theodore Roosevelt, paraphrasing Turner, claimed that 'as the frontiersmen conquered and transformed the wilderness, so the wilderness in its turn created and preserved the type who overcame it.' The frontiersman was now a distinctively American type, one who, like

Boone, was independent, whose nature was rough and bold, in whose soul 'the fierce impatience of all restraint burned like a fire.' He was heart and core American, for Roosevelt claimed the successful pioneers 'were almost exclusively native Americans.' Thus the myth, self-enclosed and self-justifying, repeated and praised itself. Speaking of Cooper's characters, Roosevelt saw in them a prescient forecast of imperial strength: they were 'uncouth, narrow, hard, suspicious, but with all the virile virtues of a young and masterful race, a race of mighty breeders, mighty fighters, mighty commonwealth builders.'9

In sum, by the beginning of the new century the frontiersman in America was a potent symbol of masculine fantasy, who would be reproduced in a number of variations throughout popular American culture. His rifle stood for the freedom to bear arms – that American dream asserted as constitutional right – his scouting and hunting in the woods as a ritual of male initiation. Like so many of his heroic successors, he was on the run from women and sexuality itself: domesticity and its responsibilities might unman him. And now he was seen as an image of imperial destiny.

Roosevelt was writing in the last years of the century, when the American frontier was thought to be closed; as memory of the western conquest receded the frontiersman became a fixture in the popular imagination. In 1869 a hack writer of romances who called himself 'Ned Buntline' had gone west in search of a hero, and found in Nebraska William Cody, a scout and buffalo hunter. On his return Buntline wrote a serial in the *New York Weekly* titled 'Buffalo Bill, the King of the Border Men,' and so began the legend of Buffalo Bill Cody, the 'King of the Scouts.' Buntline and his successor Prentiss Ingraham turned out hundreds of Buffalo Bill stories, dime novels and plays, and Ingraham helped Cody write an autobiography. What they created had only a passing connection with Cody's own experiences, but with Cody's enthusiastic help the distinctions between fact and fiction were soon blurred beyond all recall. Buffalo Bill became the slaughterer of forty thousand buffalo, the survivor of countless gun duels, the killer and scalper of hundreds of Indian braves, the friend of General Philip Sheridan and General

George Custer, the faithful son of a brave mother, the mightiest hero of them all.

The legend would hardly have amounted to so much if Cody had not agreed to be his own publicist, first to act a part in the plays that Buntline wrote, and then to be manager of his own show, the 'Wild West,' which he launched in 1883. In the early 1870s Cody was appearing in theatres as the hero of 'Scouts of the Prairie' and 'Scouts of the Plains,' two crude melodramas which had scouts, trappers, and cowboys fighting Indians. There was a girl to be rescued, 'a beautiful Indian maiden with an Italian accent and a weakness for scouts,' as a Chicago critic put it.[10]

Cody returned from time to time to the frontier itself to improve upon his heroic past; in his autobiography he recalled one incident, when after Custer's defeat at the Little Big Horn in 1876, he killed the Indian chief Yellow Hand. The two had unhorsed each other, and had fired their rifles at each other, when Cody ended the duel with his knife. 'Jerking his war-bonnet off, I scientifically scalped him in about five seconds.' As the soldiers came up, Cody 'swung the Indian chieftain's top-knot and bonnet in the air, and shouted: "The first scalp for Custer".' This exciting and symbolic moment was re-enacted for years in the 'Wild West' show. It was said however that Cody had bought his scalp from a soldier for five dollars.[11]

What Cody and his partners did in the 'Wild West' was to reinvent the frontier. His circus, complete with a herd of buffalo and with Indians recruited off the reservation, toured round eastern North America, and in 1887 crossed the Atlantic to begin a series of visits to London, Paris, and Berlin. The show was novel, sensational, entertaining, and drew huge crowds. Cody himself, dressed in the fanciest of outfits, his hair long and curled, riding on a white horse, seemed the most romantic of heroes, and his Indians – he had Sitting Bull on show for one tour – were the genuine article. On Cody's death in 1917, Zane Grey claimed that Buffalo Bill had done something few men had ever done: given a new game to the children of the world.[12] This was a fair judgment on the nature of Cody's 'Wild West'; it was not a staging of history, but a play of cowboys and Indians.

When Cody took the 'Wild West' to England in 1887, Victoria

broke her mourning seclusion of twenty-six years and left Windsor to see a command performance in London. The Queen graciously rose and bowed as 'Old Glory,' the American flag, was paraded; she was afterwards presented to Red Shirt, the senior Indian chief, and two Indian women with their papooses. The Prince of Wales and four kings (Denmark, Belgium, Saxony, Greece) took a ride in the Deadwood coach, and Cody joked that he had a royal flush in hand.[13] The royal party saw bands of Sioux and Arapahoe, cowboys, scouts, and Mexican vaqueros riding, as the advertisements said, '200 Native American Bronco horses.' They saw shooting, lassoing, and hunting, and watched an attack on the Deadwood coach and another on the settler's cabin. They were entertained by buck jumpers, a cowboy band, and the sharp-shooting of Miss Annie Oakley and Miss Lillian Smith (only sixteen). A high point was Buffalo Bill's duel with an Indian impersonating Yellow Hand. *The Times* reported that 'Colonel Cody may be induced to show Yellow Hand's scalp and the knife with which he cut it off.'[14]

Cody was well aware of the meaning of his entertainment, and made sure that the press would explain it to European audiences. He pointed out that though the Indians were picturesque, they were savages; though their fate was a tragedy, it was inevitable. His frontiersmen were proof of American innocence and American strength, they were 'children of nature.' (Cody's people lived in camp while the show was open, and they ate their own 'frontier' food – barbecued meat, cornbread, and beans.) At the same time these 'conquerors of the wilderness' showed off American organization: they constructed a wilderness in Earl's Court in ten days, dumping seventeen thousand railway carloads of rock and earth on the exhibition site; they planted trees, and lived in a 'state of nature.' Darwinian theory worked, Cody said: both the frontiersmen and their broncos demonstrated the selectivity of the frontier, and proved that only the strongest survived. This was a lesson for the effeminate products of civilization.[15]

In the 1893 'Wild West' program a new frontier hero came into public view, when the usual turns were augmented with a

'Congress of Rough Riders of the World,' which, though they included riders dressed as English and German soldiers, Cossacks, and Argentine gauchos (and a hundred Sioux Indians), gave pride of place to the cowboy. When the circus first began, its sham fights featured scouts driving off Indians; now the Deadwood coach was rescued by Buffalo Bill and 'his attendant Cowboys.' It is possible to guess why this change came about. The frontier had disappeared; scouts were longer in active service; a new frontiersman was needed, and the cowboy, or roughrider, was to hand. The 'Wild West' commercialized legend, not history; cowboys, too, were picturesque. There was only one scout, Buffalo Bill, but there could be many cowboys.

Though he appeared late in the myth of the frontier, the cowboy was to prove the most enduring symbol of American masculinity. His distinctive character and behaviour, his love of freedom, sense of dignity, loyalty to his friends, his laconic speech, easy slouch, quick action, his 'whooping up,' were soon all accepted as conventional. His Texan uniform – open vest, bandanna, buckskin gloves, chaps, and revolver – came to mean the West itself. His stetson especially was the mark of the frontiersman. As romantic hero, he was given a certain kind of dandyism – a rattlesnake skin for a hat band, a leather cord decorated with poker chips to hold his hat on in a wind (caught round the back of the head, not under the chin). If he was in the money he might sport silver spurs and a gold-embossed saddle, and give the rattlesnake on his hat diamond eyes. For the working cowboy on a Texas or Wyoming ranch, the reality might be less exotic, though the tough-man image was supported by popular lore, and even encouraged by the commercial studio photograph. The cowboy's story, grafted onto the plot of pioneer versus savage, realized a classic form of the romance, an expression of simple good defeating evil.[16]

The first serious fiction of the cowboy's imaginary world appeared long after his appearance in the dime novels. Alfred Henry Lewis's *Wolfville* (1897) made the cowboy larger than life, but Owen Wister's *The Virginian* fixed the archetype and established the Western plot. Wister's Virginian was a gentleman in the rough, chivalrous and laconic; he was man enough to lynch a friend turned cattle thief, and he was man enough to risk losing his girl by killing his enemy in a duel. In the scene that was to become a classic of the Western, his cool response to an insult at the poker game was to lay his pistol on the table, 'and with a voice as gentle as ever, the voice that sounded almost like a caress' to drawl 'when you call me that, *smile*!' True to the genre, Wister's novel described the West as Paradise Lost: his cowboys, whose every action, even to a close and easy acquaintance with death, was 'clean' compared to the vice of the east, were living in a country that would not be long fit for men. Women, children, and wire fences, each 'struck cold on the free spirits of the cowpunchers.'[17] Wister's eastern snobbery, his racist Anglo-Saxonism, and his anti-democratic sympathies – his novel supports the ranch-owner against the settler in the range wars – did not seriously disturb what were to become the classic dispositions of the genre, with the cowboy, representing 'true' values, saving the community from its villains.

Two artists added to the myth, even as the cattle ranges were closed off with barbed wire. Charlie Russell, the 'Cowboy Artist,' published his *Studies of Western Life* in 1890, and for the next thirty years his paintings made the West picturesque. Frederic Remington took his subjects from the historical 'Old West,' the dream West of noble Indians, the first explorers, scouts, the army,' but it was the cowboy whose image he served best. In his vision the cowboy was 'The Last Cavalier,' the heir to a chivalric tradition of now vanishing horsemen, determinedly Anglo-Saxon. To Remington, as to Wister, the ideal was racial purity. There was no room for 'Jews, Injuns, Chinamen, Italians, Huns' in the clean lands of the West.[18]

In his various personae the American frontiersman had become a powerful symbol of energy, innocence, independence, and strength, of a code of honour, and of an assertive nostalgia for a simpler way of doing things. He proved the truth of Darwinian theory, and he offered a solution to the weakness of civilization. The Western myth flourished as an image of a 'preindustrial, rural society,' serving to compensate a largely urbanized audience for 'the loss of community and nature in their real lives.'[19] It should be added that this audience was male, and the specifically masculine expression of the frontier cult demanded the repression of the feminine. In a culture that took cowboys for its heroes, women and their values were a very real threat.

The British Empire had its own frontiers, and here the Wild West was borrowed and modified. In Canada, almost from their establishment in 1873, the North-West Mounted Police took on an heroic image, for their task of policing a remote, unmapped, and almost boundless territory seemed herculean. There were few settlements between Manitoba and the Rockies; somewhere in the vast western territory the Métis – the people of aboriginal and French and Scots descent whose attempt to set up their own republic on the Red River in 1869–70 had been put down – were opposed by only a few Canadian settlers; somewhere wolf hunters, mostly American, were killing the Assiniboine they suspected of stealing their horses; somewhere in their forts by the border traders were selling whiskey to the Blackfeet. In Ottawa the prime minister, Sir John A. Macdonald, was at last persuaded to form an armed force and to send them west to establish law and order, to assert Canadian authority over the territory. Soon the North-West Mounted Police were 'The Riders of the Plains,' distinctively Canadian heroes, as some verses by one constable claimed:

> Our mission is to plant the right
> of British freedom here –
> Restrain the lawless savages,
> And protect the pioneer.
> And 'tis a proud and daring trust
> To hold these vast domains
> With but three hundred mounted men –[20]

From the beginning, in the Canadian mind the Mounted Police were opposed to the image of the American wild west, to

American disorder, to lynch law, to murder, violence, and injustice. The Mounties did ride in 1874 from Fort Dufferin in Manitoba to the Belly River in what is now Alberta, they did close Fort Whoop-up and stop the whiskey trade, they did build Fort Macleod and Fort Calgary. Their early history became a proud legend, their march west of 781 miles an epic, the Canadian frontier made safe for settlement, and the force an emblem of imperial order. The legend insisted on the Pax Britannica: the mounted policeman was a model of courtesy, patience, modesty, and courage, whose very presence made wild cowboys tame, who sent bad men scurrying back to their hideouts in Montana. The Indians recognized his mysterious power, and became peaceable subjects of the Great White Mother across the sea. The mark of the Mountie was that he went alone into danger; indeed, he was able to do things single-handed that took other police forces whole troops to accomplish. The typical Mountie tale is at the expense of the Americans:

> A whole column of American cavalry escorting an unruly tribe was relieved at the border by three policemen.
> 'Where's your escort for these Indians?' asked the American commanding officer.
> We're here, Colonel,' answered the Mountie Corporal.
> 'Yes, yes, I see. But where's your regiment?'
> 'We're here,' the Corporal said again.
> 'Yes, I know. But aren't there any more of you?'
> 'Oh, yes, sir, Colonel,' said the Corporal. 'There's a fourth chap, but he's back up in the hills frying a mess of trout for our breakfast.'[21]

Other details became part of the legend. No matter what it took, no matter how far he had to travel, the Mountie got his man. He never fired first; restraint and discipline was his code. His law was fair to all, but relentless in its execution. His territory was peaceful. The Klondike proved the point. Dawson was quiet and orderly, and the miners could go about their business without fear of violence; Skagway, over the American line, was a hell on earth, ruled by the bad man, 'Soapy' Smith. In hundreds of popular fictions, the Mountie was described as a peculiarly imperial hero, a man whose character was moulded by the best of Anglo-Saxon virtue. He might be an English lord or a ne'er-do-well, a younger son from across the Atlantic or the hired man off an Ontario farm, but it was certain that he was only to be found in the best of company, a hardened veteran of a dozen trails or campaigns. With his fellow adventurers he had come from the ends of the earth to the Canadian prairies to prove his manhood.

In fact the mounted policeman shared the glamour of the other riders of the plains, and his uniform gradually evolved into the standard frontiersman's kit. A change of clothes marked his membership of the frontier brotherhood, just as it distanced him from his old association with the British army. By 1895 the force was replacing British issue pill-box hats and white regulation helmets with the stetson, which was both a symbolic and a practical measure, for the old headgear offered little protection from the sun and rain. One trooper reported that the caps were 'utterly useless out on the burning plains,' and the helmets were 'far too heavy.'[22]

In other parts of the Empire the spirit of the frontier played an equally powerful role in defining the values of colonial society. The pioneer who hacked his farm out the bush was mythologized as the ideal New Zealander; he was tall, strong, honest, and above all, virile. He expressed the ideal of a powerful and exclusive masculine mystique: he was a 'mate.'[23] In Australia the bushman became the culture hero – anti-authoritarian, independent, democratic, again the very spirit of 'mateship.' The isolation of Australia seemed to encourage the fixing of this type early; the democratic and republican tradition (celebrated in the bush ballads), was actually hostile to English sensibilities. And Australian virility was second to none: when Cody's rival, Texas Jack, toured Australia with his roughriding act, the popular poet, Henry Lawson, suggested the American saddle was just too secure, and the cowboy himself, compared to Australian bushmen, was close to effeminate:

Texas Jack, you are amusin'. By Lord Harry, how I laughed
When I seen yer rig and saddle with its bulwarks fore-and aft;
Holy smoke! In such a saddle how the dickens can yer fall?
Why, I seen a gal ride bareback with no bridle on at all!...
How I'd like ter see a bushman use yer fixins, Texas Jack;
On the remnant of a saddle he can ride to hell and back.[24]

Whether the cowboy in his North American form or in his antipodean variation was the more virile could never be settled; luckily for the myth there was another place of adventure. Africa by the 1870s was the latest British frontier, *the* place to explore, to paint red on the map, to colonize. The search for the source of the Nile became a symbol of white progress; the wanderings of the missionaries, with David Livingstone at their head, became an image of Christian self-sacrifice. The exploits of the big-game hunters, shipping home quantities of heads and skins from the plains and jungles of the continent as proof of their prowess, represented an elaborate enactment of imperial conquest.[25]

By the end of the century the men who joined Cecil Rhodes in South Africa were seen empire-building, mining the gold and diamonds of a Lost Continent, planting farms in the wilderness, perhaps even securing for England an unbroken road from the Cape to Cairo. The pioneers of Rhodes's new territories – Mashonaland, Matabeleland – could take pride that they served 'an empire excelling all others in extent and power, and a civilization that stands first and foremost in the universe.'[26] They could relive on this last frontier the glories of the American West, and for the hostile Indian they could substitute the fighting Matabele.

Some contemporary accounts of this frontier of the 1890s are prosaic, describing life in everyday terms. The writer was there, and he records what happened, but he sets down the events without a sense of a larger context: he has no imaginative framework for his story. Other writers, in contrast, subscribe to the dream, and, with each contribution, amplify it and give it credit. Yet others resist, and in their resistance, erect an anti-myth.

Most of the first-hand reports from the South African frontier subscribe to the same vocabulary, picturing the 'opening up' of the country as a last great adventure, and the pioneers as the last heroes of the Empire. Life imitated art; those on the spot in Bulawayo dressed up as actors in the drama. The would-be frontiersmen, as one old Africa hand said mockingly, 'paraded the town in sombreroes, revolver upon each hip, wristlets crammed with revolver cartridges, open shirts, an appearance of piratical daring that would have done credit to a modern bioscope.'[27] Others recognized a social elite when they saw one. Bulawayo, said a Canadian traveller, was a community of gentlemen where 'a stranger pauses to ask himself if he dreams, or if the Household Brigade, the Bachelor's Club, and the Foreign Office have depleted themselves of their members, and sent them, disguised in broad-brimmed hats and riding-breeches, to hold the capital of Matabeleland.' 'Young men of the most eligible kind,' he added, 'are everywhere.' It had been much the same around Salisbury as early as 1892, and the young Percy Fitzpatrick, South African born, was disgusted by the parade. 'I don't believe that anywhere on the face of the globe has been collected such a crowd of grass-green Johnny-come-latelies as the titled pioneers of Mashonaland ... They glint and glisten in the sunlight with burnished cutlery and silvermounted revolvers. You can scarcely put your hand on a part of their bodies where there isn't something that will "go off" – some artifice for attack or defence ... Round the campfires at night the gossip and scandal of London society was a recognized thing.'[28]

The romantic image was what mattered. These adventurers were content with their growing reputation as careless, happy-go-lucky fellows, more or less the imperial heirs to those other men of action, Drake and the Elizabethan privateers. The radical journalist Henry Labouchere might label them 'buccaneers' in the hostile pages of *Truth*; they knew their imperial history, and could take pride in sanctioned piracy. Sympathetic accounts of their grasshopper days insist on the symbolism of imperial strength, on its freebooting past, its cartridge belts, revolvers, and stetsons, its good fellowship, its gold. Though they honoured much from the American west, if these buccaneers discounted anything, it was innocence.

These meanings are confirmed in the fictions that took Africa as their subject. 'There was a Boy who went to seek his fortune,' Fitzpatrick began *Jock of the Bushveld* (a South African story which Baden-Powell was to recommend to his Boy Scouts), in a soulful and mysterious preface. Fitzpatrick was trying to capture the mystery of initiation: what was it that would drive the Boy towards the testing ground, towards adventure, away from all the safe sure things of home? The Boy can only tell his dog his dreams:

> There was something stronger than the things he knew, around, without, beyond – the thing that strove within him: that grew and grew, and beat and fought for freedom: that bade him go and walk alone and tell his secret on the mountain slopes to one who would not laugh – a little red retriever; that made him climb and feel his strength, and find an outlet for what drove within. And thus the end was sure; for of all the voices none so strong as this!

The Boy has to prove he is worth his keep, that he has the right stuff in him, that he is a Man. He is passed from one trekker or prospector to another, till the moment comes when his manhood, no longer in the balance, is finally realized. Fitzpatrick's popular novel catches the *fin-de-siècle* nostalgia for the wilderness and its challenge. The tenderfoot, escaping from the decadent city, is answering the call of the wild. He is looking for the clean white man's country, so often to be found, as in Jack London's case, only in the pure northern snows, or in some far place which will surely be the testing ground of his true self. The frontier is the site of initiation; the old, 'salted' frontiersman the high priest of its rites of passage.

In Africa, history was turned into fiction almost before it was made. Rider Haggard, whose experience in the colonial service provided the background for his African bestsellers, took the famous big-game hunter Frederick Selous as a model for his hero Allan Quatermain. (Selous's tally of elephants shot and lions bagged makes startling reading in an age more conscious of conservation.) Haggard's Quatermain, the narrator of *King Solomon's Mines* and several of Haggard's other fictions, comes across as the wiry, grizzled, tough white hunter, who pretends to a becoming modesty and a quite unbelievable timidity. He leads two intrepid English adventurers, Sir Henry Curtis and Captain John Good, RN, into the depths of the mysterious continent. Haggard's yarns begin typically with this fraternity of honest Englishmen together sensing that something is dead in the dreary December of England, and that life is to be fought for in the 'wild land' of Africa. 'The thirst for the wilderness was on me,' Allan says in one such prelude, romantic words for the impulse that propelled colonial conquest.[29] The white hunter was to be the advance guard of thousands of young recruits to Rhodes's Chartered Company, and he would serve, both in fact and in fiction, as their example and avatar. To a large extent the imperial idea was created in its fiction.

It is impossible to say at which precise moment an imaginative identity is formed, but in the making of the imperial frontiersman one event seemed to crystallize his meaning in the public mind. At the Queen's Diamond Jubilee in 1897 the Empire assembled to march past:

Canada had the advance guard – age before beauty, Australasia the rearguard, while in the mainguard Negroes, Chinese, Malays were nursed by white Yeomanry from the tropics, by the Indian army, and South Africa. From the east and the West, from the Arctic tundras and the swamps of the Blackwater Fever, we of the Blood and our Brothers, frontiersmen of the Empire, and our fellow-savages, were rank and file, shoulder to shoulder, marching from Portsmouth Town to Southsea Hard, with the tramlines underfoot, the cheering in our veins, the streaming flags above us; six hundred guests of the Great Mother going to see her fleet. There had been no such gathering of the clans, no such assembly of the Legion, no like pageant of Empire since the world began.[30]

These were the words of Roger Pocock, self-professed frontiersman, rider of the trails of life, one-time tenderfoot, one-time
Mountie, prospector, missionary, cowboy, and scout, recording
the moment when his fraternity of imperial adventurers was recognized and given its pride of place. The frontiersman, in
Pocock's eyes, was a member of a rare breed, an outcast (except
among his own) from an effete and corrupting homeland, yet
inspired with the old spirit of England.

The language of Pocock's dream – the 'Blood,' our 'Brothers,' the 'Legion' – came from Kipling. In 'The Song of the
Sons' from 'A Song of the English' Kipling had claimed sonship
of the Great Mother for the colonial. 'We that were bred over-
seas,' Kipling said, are men too, and our gift is 'Love without
promise or fee.' 'Mother, be proud of thy seed!' he told
England. 'Judge, are we men of The Blood?'[31] Kipling's vision
of the unity and brotherhood of the Empire led him to make
much of those he saw unjustly neglected, not only colonials, but
common soldiers, officer outcasts, those in the savage lands who
carried the burden.

In the verses of 'The Lost Legion' Kipling celebrated the
imperial frontiersman, and in so doing gave him a name and an
identity. The Lost Legion (like those of that other not so different legion, the Gentleman Rankers), are damned; theirs the
thankless task of Empire, and the dirty job without reward. Leaving the safe comforts of home, they go to the ends of the earth,
to hunt, prospect, and explore, to 'chivy the slaver,' to adventure
wherever adventure is found. The Legion that never was 'listed
(that is, enlisted) will never be acknowledged, or thanked:

> There's a Legion that never was 'listed,
> That carries no colours or crest,
> But split in a thousand detachments,
> Is breaking the road for the rest.
> Our fathers they left us their blessing –
> They taught us, and groomed us, and crammed;
> But we've shaken the Clubs and the Messes

To go and find out and be damned
(Dear boys!),
To go and get shot and be damned.[32]

The paradox of this legion is that though its men are 'lost men,' they are the *crème de la crème* of the Empire, and the Empire cannot do without them. They are brothers to all the Great Mother's other lost sons, the younger sons, the remittance men, the misfits, the black sheep. These legionaries are beyond the pale of civilized society, a 'wholly unauthorized horde' as Kipling describes them, yet they are 'dear boys,' 'good men,' 'Gentlemen Rovers' who know their own special worth, and who acknowledge their own special brotherhood. As Kipling's misogynistic novel, *The Light That Failed*, puts it, they have the 'go-fever' in them, they long for 'the old hot, unregenerate life,' for the freedom to 'scuffle, swear, gamble, and love light loves.' A respectable female is the worst thing that can happen a man such as these: 'she'll waste his time, and she'll marry him, and ruin his work for ever ... and – he'll never go on the long trail again.'[33]

Kipling's praised these men for their virility, adventurousness, loyalty, and brotherhood. He saw these virtues as the strength of the Empire, made plain in the independence and pride of the Canadian, the Australian, the New Zealander, the South African, the colonial men who had the *real* English spirit – 'Truly ye come of The Blood!' He gave this insight expression both in formal dedications of imperial unity such as 'A Song of the English,' and as occasional hymns to some part of the same spirit: military adventure on the frontier, the fraternal associations of the banjo, the smell of woodsmoke, the intimacy of the campfire.

Kipling's Lost Legion thus gave an imaginative reality to the imperial frontiersman; the image was accepted, treasured, and popularized.* Robert Service in his Klondike verses played varia-

---

*See, for instance, John Mackie, *The Life Adventurous* (1907), dedicated by the author 'to any old comrades of the great Lost Legion who may read these lines' (p. 9), or the works of Colonel G. Hamilton Browne, *With the Lost Legion in New Zealand* (1911), *A Lost Legionary in South Africa* (1912), and *Camp Fire Yarns of the Lost Legion* (1913).

tions on the theme: the Yukon was a demanding mistress who destroyed weaklings, who could only be won by 'men with the hearts of Vikings, and the simple faith of a child.' Her law was a straightforward law of Darwinian survival: 'surely the Weak shall perish, and only the Fit survive.' The younger son – 'he's building Britain's greatness o'er the foam' – was the type of bold spirit the Empire needed, superior to his unadventurous brother in the army or the church. As with Kipling, the man of the 'Legion Lost' was a rolling stone, a man 'never meant to win.'[34] The frontier was romanticized in these hymns of manhood proved and innocence redeemed, these tales of outcasts from the feast, of lives sacrificed to the greater cause.

There is no more striking example of this imperial development of the myth than a volunteer organization started in 1905 called the Legion of Frontiersmen. Composed in the main of a collection of rolling stones returned home to defend the Mother Country from her foes this was the Lost Legion come to life. The Legion of Frontiersmen thought of itself as a 'corps of scouts, pioneers and guides,' 'men already trained by a rough life in outlying parts of the Empire,' holding themselves 'ready for military service if called upon by the State.'[35] The Legion was something of a curiosity in its simplicity, a creation which reflected the force of the idea of the frontier at the ebb tide of Empire, and, in several ways, which stood as a peculiar adult version of the Boy Scouts.

The Legion was the invention of Roger Pocock, who had led the sort of life the best frontiersman might lead. Pocock wrote a letter to the London newspapers, and then enlisted the rather cavalier assistance of Lord Lonsdale, the highly popular 'sporting Earl' – boxer, jockey, racehorse owner, dare-devil – himself an explorer, hunter, and eccentric on the grand scale. Lonsdale had had exciting times among the Indians and Inuit of the Arctic back in 1888, and had returned to Lowther Castle with an impressive collection of trophies. He rather fancied leading the Legion, and agreed to be its president.

Pocock had the idea that there were many old frontier hands

with the sort of training that would come in useful in time of war. They might for one reason or another not be eligible for regular service in the armed forces and be better suited for the independent work of scouting than the drill of an army regiment. They would be united by good fellowship, by their common experience in the school of hard knocks, and by their readiness to defend the Empire from her enemies. Their uniform was something that each man was likely to wear on his own frontier: stetson or slouch hat, silk scarf, flannel shirt, gauntlets, breeches, high boots, spurs, cartridge belt, revolver.

The organization soon formed commands in England and throughout the Empire. In London its members began their public life by parading in Hyde Park, and going on a test ride in a heat wave to Brighton. They preferred, quite illegally, to keep their revolvers and bandoleers about them. Pocock saw that they were in the news, reminding the world that 'Frontiersmen form a great natural brotherhood, all hunting for trouble, and burning for service.' They would soon, he said, 'become the swiftest mounted force on earth.' 'Any white Britisher ... who wishes to serve the Empire, and who has worked, hunted, or fought in wild countries or at sea, may join the Legion at once by sending half a guinea to the secretary.'[36] Five thousand men, he stated, had already accepted his invitation.

The history of the Legion is wrapped in veils of legend, mostly of Pocock's manufacture. Its London commandant, Manoel de Herrera Hora (*né* Melville Hora), though popular with the legionaries, was something of a loose cannon, and had to be relieved of his command when he insisted on flogging the Legion bandmaster on parade. De Hora claimed he was the son of a Latin-American father and a Red Indian mother (his family was in fact English, his father, Whinfield Hora, a London wholesale druggist), that he had fought in a South American revolution, had commandeered the Peruvian battleship *Huascar*, and, pirating coal from a British steamer, was torpedoed by HMS *Shah*. Pocock afterwards put it about that de Hora had been a Boer spy, had escaped into the South African desert, turned up in

Johannesburg, kept order when the Boers retreated, and surrendered the city to Lord Roberts. For a moment before his exposure he was a hero of the Empire.[37]

In these early days the Legion seems to have taken some pride in its piratical beginnings, and its historians, following Pocock, numbered gun-runners, adventurers, and men 'gone native' among its first and most distinguished members. Charles Mason helped Sun Yat-sen overthrow the Manchu dynasty; a Captain Salisbury, while on a raiding force in the Congo, was forced to flee for 2,500 miles 'pursued by cannibals with filed teeth'; and Pocock himself had some exciting times spying on Russian naval bases in the Black Sea, passing the information on to Admiral Prince Louis of Battenberg.[38]

After its initial success, the affairs of the Legion languished. Its leaders took to quarrelling among themselves, the rank and file became discouraged, there was a shortage of money, and Lord Lonsdale returned to his real love – breeding racehorses. Finally in July 1909 there was a 'night of the long knives': a new general council was elected, and Lieutenant-Colonel Paddy Driscoll was appointed London commandant. This saved the Legion from collapse. Driscoll had been the commanding officer of Driscoll's Scouts in the Boer War, saluted by the press in his heyday as the 'King of Scouts.'[39] *Vanity Fair*, honouring his new command, and remembering the 'undying glory' that his Scouts had once gained for him, drew his portrait over the title of 'An Old War Horse' in its February issue. Under Driscoll and the commandant-general, Sir William Serjeant, the finances of the Legion were put in order, and support from influential quarters returned.

By 1910 the Legion listed on its councils and committees the names of several prominent imperialists: the Earl of Meath, Sir Francis Vane, Admiral Prince Louis of Battenberg, Admiral Arden Close, the Earl of Onslow, the sportsman Sir Claude Champion de Crespigny, and the popular novelists Sir Gilbert Parker and Cutcliffe Hyne. That year Roger Pocock brought out *The Frontiersman's Pocket-Book*, a *vade-mecum* for the legionary; he was able to include contributions from Fred Selous the white hunter, from Sam Steele of the Royal North West Mounted Police, from Erskine Childers, Edgar Wallace, Ernest Thompson Seton, and Baden-Powell. Rider Haggard was a supporter, as were Conan Doyle, Arthur Pearson the newspaper owner, and C.B. Fry. In later years Pocock claimed several other imperial names as members of the Legion: Jan Smuts, John Boyes the 'king' of Kenya, 'Cape-to-Cairo' Grogan (Captain E.S. Grogan, the first to walk the length of the continent), and 'old Baden-Powell' himself.

The qualifications of some of the contributors to Pocock's *Pocket-Book* give a fair measure of the Legion's sense of itself:

- Late Chilean Navy, Master Mariner, Explorer, Expert in Signalling, etc.
- Soldier, Prospector, Mining Engineer, Trader, Freighter, eight years in Yukon Territory and Alaska, etc.
- Soldier, Explorer, Prospector, mining Engineer, Mail Rider, Freighter, Cowboy, Horsebreaker, Rancher; Veterinary Surgeon, Canadian Government and Canadian Mounted Rifles; Staff Scout to Lord Roberts, etc.
- Cowboy.
- Horsebreaker and Hunter, Indian Service.
- Australian expert with the stock whip.
- Seaman, Cowboy, Irregular Soldier, and Pioneer in many countries; a Chief of Scouts forGeneral Hutton's Division, S.A. Field Force, etc.

And so on. The *Pocket-Book* gave practical advice on survival skills, on taking care of man and horse, on scouting, signalling, and demolition. It included a section on morale, with a dedication from Bishop H.H. Montgomery (the father of Monty, the future field-marshal), who compared the Frontiersmen to the Knights of the Round Table, and awaited 'The Idylls of the Legion.' It repeated the idea that the Frontiersman was a special kind of imperial soldier whose frontier life made him unfit for 'parade-ground psychology,' but had ideally shaped him to much more arduous and challenging duties. 'The expert Frontiersman represents the survival of the fittest'; he could not be produced 'by artificial means.'[40] The Legion, however, did attempt its own training. Two Frontiersmen, Captain Pete Morgan and Evelyn ffrench – a man Pocock referred to as the greatest horseman of the age – set up the Imperial School of Colonial Instruction at Shepperton, where ffrench demonstrated his skills with the stock whip. Sir Francis Vane recruited boys for the Legion's Cadet Yeomanry.[41]

By 1911 the Legion had over six thousand members, and when war began in 1914 Commandant Driscoll was able to count off over one thousand men for inspection on Horseguards Parade. The East Cheshire Troop (with their horses) crossed the Channel at their own expense and offered their services to Belgium, reaching the continent two days before Britain declared war on Germany. Attached to the 3rd Belgian Lancers, they went into action on 16 August, a week before the British Expeditionary Force fought the battle of Mons. In 1915 the 25th Battalion of the Royal Fusiliers was formed entirely from Frontiersmen; it fought in East Africa, and among its number was Selous (who was killed in action aged sixty-seven).

The Legion was strong in several parts of the world, particularly New Zealand and Newfoundland, and it had great success in the western provinces of Canada. There recruitment was high, and it ran a vigorous campaign for official Dominion recognition. In its literature the Legion claimed that when the Princess Patricia's Canadian Light Infantry was raised in 1914, six hundred men of the Legion joined in a body, and so enabled the regiment to be the first Canadian regiment in battle.* For a time the Royal North West Mounted Police were 'officially' connected to the Legion and seem to have regarded it as their military branch.[42] The Legion raised the 210th (Frontiersmen)

*The importance of the Legion's contribution to the Patricias is discounted by the regiment's archival curator, Captain Bill Guscott. The founding charter for the Princess Patricia's Canadian Light Infantry was signed on 10 August 1914. Very soon afterwards some three thousand volunteers were interviewed; of these, 1,098 were enrolled. The regiment's records show that of those selected only eighty-three claimed any connection with the Legion of Frontiersmen.

Infantry Battalion, and carried out security duties with the Mounted Police throughout the war.

The significance of the Legion of Frontiersmen lies not in its military importance, but in what it represented. It came into being in a time of crisis, and it reflected both the deepest anxieties and the most quixotic solutions of that crisis. Its first leaders were raffish, self-advertising romantics with a vision of the Empire under threat; they told their yarns to show off their intimacy with adventure. They and their fellow frontiersmen were a proof of imperial virility, cheerfully theatrical in dress, not to be trusted after dark. Living on the fringe of 'gentlemanly' society – Pocock was frequently embarrassed by his lack of a military commission, and suffered under a rumour that he had murdered or 'lost' a fellow Englishman on a Klondike expedition; de Hora had done a term in prison in New South Wales for horse-stealing – their response was to create a world of their own, more masculine, more fraternal, in which the 'real' values of manhood were appreciated. In other ways, too, the Legion was of its time. It engaged with enthusiasm in the spy fever and invasion alarms of the pre-war years; Pocock thought of his men, reporting from all quarters of the world, as the eyes of a blind Empire. Driscoll kept up the good work, passing on intelligence reports to the War Office, whose attitude to the Legion swung between lukewarm support and embarrassment. R.B. Haldane was listed as an early member, but as war secretary 1905 to 1912, he was careful to avoid giving the Legion official backing.* The Legion, accustomed to going its own way, carried on in the same general enterprise as Baden-Powell: 'Being Prepared.'

The Frontiersmen used the symbols of the imperial frontier to make their cause meaningful. Their badge was the cross of St.

---

*At the end of its first year the Legion asked the War Office for approval. Haldane replied by expressing his 'sympathy with the aims and objects of the Legion,' but 'recognized it as a purely private organization, in no way connected with any Department of State.' The Legion then proclaimed that it was 'officially recognized.' The War Office was left to deny that it had recognized the Legion, and asked that instead the phrase 'take cognizance of the Legion' be used in all correspondence.

George within a laurel wreath, their motto 'God Guard Thee,' copied from the signet ring worn by General Gordon when he fell at Khartoum.* Their letterhead was a lion, with the names of the countries of the Empire forming its mane: 'The Glory of a Lion is his Mane.' Their frontiersman uniform linked the parts of their tradition together, their neckerchief and shirt of black serge reminding them of Baden-Powell's South African Constabulary,[43] the 'Boss of the Plains' stetson and the Strathcona boots of the North-West Mounted Police, the Sam Browne belt of the new army, their shoulder chains of the 'knights of old.'[44] They claimed Kipling as their poet laureate, and took his 'Lost Legion' as their formal hymn, enlarging the numbers of the damned to suit their own more ambitious ranks. Their own song described their mission in down-to-earth terms and spelled out the Legion's patriotic program. It had for its chorus these words:

> Out from the woods of the great North-West,
> Under the Austral sky,
> From the south and the north
> They'll come forth
> At the sound of the Mother's cry!
> And each at his post, where the danger is most,
> Will stand as a sentry then;
> Britishers all, to stand or to fall,
> The Empire's Frontiersmen![45]

In hindsight, the Legion was something of a sideshow in the great imperial drama, an example of the reactionary, romantic, militarist impulse of the pre-war years. But its determined creation of itself illustrates clearly enough the role myth can play in the construction of a self-enclosed reality.

For those who wrote for boys, or who made it their business to

---

*Roger Pocock also owned a silver cigarette case which he claimed had been found on General Gordon's body after his death, listing it among the bequests in his will (information from Geoffrey Pocock).

instruct boys, the frontiersman was an obvious model. He had a distinguished pedigree stretching back through a variety of romantic types: the Indian fighter, the prospector, the cowboy, the mounted policeman, the pioneer. He could be presented as the heir to a tradition of Anglo-Saxon adventurers, a brother to Charles Kingsley's Elizabethan hero Amyas Leigh, one with the heroic empire-builders of the ages. The image was clear and powerful: it spoke of simple adventure, of energy above all else; of loyalty, of a cause greater than self. It was free from the complexities of life in the real world of commerce, free from the responsibilities of domesticity, or the complications of sex. Frontiersmen lived in a boys' world in which all problems could be solved by a sharp eye and a quick finger on the trigger. And whereas Natty Bumppo was a loner, the new frontiersman found joy and strength in the fellowship of his kin. The comradeship of the Lost Legion would come to be part of the mystique of the Boy Scouts, the magic of the campfire would be one of their own symbols, and 'Who hath smelled wood-smoke at twilight?' – Kipling's verse from 'The Feet of the Young Men' – would be recited at Scout sing-songs.[46] To the founders of the boys' movements the frontiersman seemed an image of themselves, and his place of action, the outdoors, a sufficiently safe retreat from the enfeebling presence of the feminine. Taking the boys to the next best thing to a frontier would remove them from mother, sisters, and the home. In the woods they could then become real men.

CHAPTER TWO

Buccaneers: The War Scouts

It has been suggested that Major-General Baden-Powell's unrivalled skill as a cavalry scout forms quite a remarkable instance of heredity, seeing (says the *Chronicle*) that he is descended from Pocahontas, the American Indian Princess.

(Newspaper cutting, *c.* 1900)

On 23 May 1896 Baden-Powell was on his way to the African frontier, riding in the Mafeking-Bulawayo coach, which as he wrote in his diary, was 'a regular Buffalo-Bill-Wild-West-Deadwood affair.' With him were his commanding officer, Major-General Sir Frederick Carrington, and two of Carrington's staff. They were headed for Matabeleland, where the Matabele (or Ndebele) were at war with the white settlers. The coach, a boneshaking vehicle drawn by ten mules, lurched and pitched over the rocky track, the sun was hot, the flies 'thick as dust,' the mules pitifully weak. Baden-Powell was cheerful, for, as he said, the tedium and hardship of the trip were 'compensated for by the splendid climate, the starry night, and the "flannel-shirt" life.' He was thirty-nine years old, ready to enjoy six months of scouting, 'the best sport in the world.'[1] On the African frontier in the last years of the nineteenth century the disciples of Natty Bumppo and William Cody were to have their last brief fling.

Baden-Powell had long been a captive to Buffalo Bill and all his works. Back in 1887 his regiment was stationed in the north of England. It was the year of the Queen's Golden Jubilee, he had volunteered to run the military tournament in Liverpool, and he had just seen Cody's 'Wild West'. Inspired by the circus frontiersmen, he orchestrated his troopers in spectacular scenes of riding, shooting, and scouting, with, as a climax, machine gun driving at high speeds.[2] What more happy climax to his own life could he wish for than riding nine years later to a frontier war in a Wild West Deadwood coach?

Bulawayo was full of the excitement of war. Baden-Powell met and immediately liked the veterans of the campaign of '93, the swashbucklers and bearded buccaneers, old frontier hands like Fred Selous, good soldiers like the 'dandy lancer' Micky MacFarlane, and the hero Maurice Gifford.* They put on the style; they affected puttee leggings and hunting stocks, they dressed up in cowboy clothes. Baden-Powell admired their 'wide-awake' hats, the bandoleers across their chests, the revolvers on their hips. 'The strong brown arms and sunburnt faces,' he said, 'all show them soldiers, ready-made and ripe for any kind of work.'[3]

The Matabele War of 1896 was in its second stage: a local field force was ready to disband, and an imperial relief force, commanded by officers of the regular army, was about to begin a systematic pursuit of the still defiant Ndebele. Baden-Powell's duties were at headquarters. He organized everything from food and medical supplies to the supply of remounts, and he attempted, between bouts of office work, to join his fellow officers on the veld.

His first sight of the enemy came when he took part in a skirmish against more than a thousand Ndebele fighters. He was

---

*The Honourable Maurice Gifford was a well-known soldier of fortune and imperial adventurer, who had served as an amateur scout to General Middleton in the Second Riel Rebellion in the Canadian west. In Matabeleland Gifford raised Gifford's Horse from local volunteers. He had his arm amputated after being shot in a skirmish, and was decorated the next year by the Queen at the Diamond Jubilee in recognition of the bravery of the Rhodesians.

shot at; he charged the enemy; he had a 'close shave' – a man up a tree fired down on him, but missed. A week later he went on a reconnaissance trip with the American scout Frederick Burnham; between office duties, he managed in the next few months six more expeditions into the Matopos Hills. These made up what he called in reflection 'the joyous adventure of my life.'[4]

He had fallen in love with the easy, unbuttoned days in the open, with the frontier kit of the old hands from the American West, with the thrill of tracking spoor, with the whole romance of it all. 'What was it made me go to the extravagance of subscribing to *Harper's*, but Remington's sketches of Cowboy Life?' he asked his diary. Writing of his experience afterwards in England, he longed to be back in Africa. 'I used to think that the novelty of the thing would wear off, that these visions of the veldt would fade away as civilized life grew upon me. But they didn't ... somebody in the next room has mentioned the word saddle, or rifle, or billy, and off goes my mind at a tangent to play with its toys ... I can't help it if my toys take the form of all that has to do with the veldt life, and if they remain my toys till I drop.' In a rare moment of introspection he wondered if he should not be making his reputation as a 'sensible, well-informed man,' instead of running off to play by the campfire, but he reassured himself with Oliver Wendell Holmes: 'most of us are "boys all our lives,"' and perhaps in our toys, he thought, we come to know God.[5] He thought that frontier life had all the elements which should appeal to a real Englishman: 'hard work, adventure, general discomfort and genuine fun.[6]

If imperial scouting had its golden age it was surely in Matabeleland, for it was here in the 1890s that the two most famous scouts of the Empire made their reputations, and it was here that the mystique of the imperial frontier reached its height. Baden-Powell arrived in time to catch the second half of the second war, and in time to describe his adventure in the most exciting terms; the American Fred Burnham scouted in both Matabele wars, and became a imperial hero. Matabeleland had everything: a white man's climate, a brave native warrior race, the Ndebele (related to the Zulus), well-bred colonists, the promise of gold, land to ranch.

Writing of the country as it was in 1893, Fred Burnham claimed that the pioneers were engaged in one of the last great adventures of Empire:

> One of the joys of life on this frontier was the mingling of the adventurous and hardy from every corner of the world. If there was a single colony of the British Empire that was not represented, I have yet to hear of it. There was a brave contingent from Australia, placed by mutual consent under the command of their greatest and best-loved prospector, Thomas. His heroism, his whimsicality, and his almost impossible doings became a tradition ... We had Americans with the nasal Yankee twang and the soft Southern drawl as well as the Western slang, to match the quaint lingoes of the Britishers. Added to all was the large Dutch element, so similar to the men from our own West. The Honourable Sirs and Lords who joined us, fought with us, starved with us, and died as men should, doing their bit, were the least materialistic of all and often generous to their own undoing. Even our rotten wasters and ne'er-do-wells became for a time heroic and dependable.[7]

The frontier in imagination thus transformed the worst into the best: it encouraged democracy and camaraderie, it nourished freemasonry. It belonged to youth, and Burnham, in a comment that reveals the easy assumptions of imperial conquest, remarked on the laughing, careless, casual way in which the young men of this 'young man's land ... assumed control of this part of the continent.'[8]

Burnham had arrived in Matabeleland as a colonist, just before the outbreak of the first rebellion, in 1893. He had made his way up from the Cape with his wife and young daughter by mule team. Bulawayo was surrounded, and in the siege, his daughter Nada died, weakened from privation.* He blamed her

---

*Nada was named after Rider Haggard's heroine in *Nada the Lily* (1982). Haggard's romances were a powerful influence on the idea of imperial adventure in southern Africa.

death on the Ndebele, and at once offered his services to the settlers' forces. He was assigned to a group of scouts under the general command of Major Allan Wilson.

Burnham was that most necessary article on a new frontier, a scout from the American West, a man moreover who had fought Indians. He had learned his craft from scouts who had scouted under Kit Carson, or who had served under General Crook, old scouts whom he claimed were inspired by 'deep romantic and philosophical ideals.' This was the essential pedigree, to be the heir in an unbroken tradition of the old mountain men, to be an initiate of the school of Indian teaching. He had learned when he was still little more than a boy to study his enemy, to harden his mind and his body to 'stoical endurance,' to relax in the midst of danger, to develop each of his five senses. Scouting was knowing, thinking, understanding: knowing that the Apaches roasted mescal, studying the air currents of their canyons, smelling the odours of their fires, following the scent to their secret hiding places.[9]

Burnham was at once sent out on scouting sorties against the Ndebele, and his ability to find his way around the difficult country, even at night, and to avoid capture again and again, proved the superiority of his training. He might be surrounded by the enemy, or even lost, but he had only to search his brain 'for all the lore of the great scouts' of the American West to come up with an answer. His companions might trust to the compass, but he would use only 'memory pictures' of the countryside, Indian fashion. He entertained his English friends with 'frontiersman's tricks,' killing a duck on the water without a wound, firing underneath it. His friends found it hard to credit his tales of sharpshooting, even though all were perfectly true accounts of the frontiersmen's skill with the muzzle-loading rifle, how they 'drove nails, snuffled candles, barked squirrels, split bullets on ax blades, and occasionally shot mugs of whisky from one another's heads ...' His knowledge helped him survive: he alone knew the old Indian trick of eating brains, the only nourishing part of a starved horse. But even he learned a few new scouting habits in Matabeleland: instead of signalling with

animal cries, the African colonists used the Australian call 'coo-
ee.'[10] It seems, too, that Burnham brought with him some of the
less acceptable customs of the western frontier, for a fellow scout
found him one day 'carrying a whittled stick with several pairs of
ears stuck on.' He was told to bury them before Major Wilson
saw him.[11]

In an episode which was afterwards to become one of the
founding legends of Rhodesia, Burnham was with Wilson's
troop in its heroic last stand at the Shangani river. Wilson was in
pursuit of the Ndebele king Lobengula and the treasure he was
reputed to carry. But his party rode too far, too fast; they were
surrounded by Ndebele. Burnham was one of three men who
escaped from the slaughter – a fact that afterwards threw a
shadow of cowardice over his reputation, for the code of gallant
behaviour stipulated that a man must stand and die with his
comrades. By his own account, he said he had been ordered by
Wilson to break through the Ndebele horn formation and go
for help. He took with him another American scout and an Australian; the three forced their horses through a thicket, the only
spot the Ndebele had left unguarded. They were immediately
seen and followed. Using 'a trick that would never have worked
with Apache Indians' – they backtracked their horses through a
muddy stream – they evaded the Ndebele, and repeated the tactic several times before they escaped.[12] The Ndebele, Burnham
claimed, recognizing his prowess as a scout, had already named
him He-Who-Sees-in-the-Dark.

In the second Matabele War of 1896 Burnham again played a
highly visible role. He was appointed chief of scouts to the commander of the imperial relief force; his exploits were written up,
and his picture was in the illustrated papers. The uprising had
been partly triggered by the removal of the white police force to
the Transvaal; at first the colonists had only themselves and volunteers from the Cape to rely on in opposing the Ndebele. They
formed various irregular forces – the Rhodesia Horse Volunteers, the Afrikander Corps, the 'Cape Boy Corps' of native
troops – all generally organized as the Bulawayo Field Force.
The Ndebele killed isolated settlers and burned their farms, so

the Field Force went on raids to retaliate. It was much like Indian war on the American frontier, and Burnham again found his scouting methods in demand.

Throughout 1896 the 'Matabele campaign' was reported in the British press, and it stood as a adventurous contrast to the trials of the current Sudan campaign against the 'rebellious Fuzzy Wuzzies.' In northern Africa British soldiers, clad in their sun helmets and khaki tunics, were marching through the desert in the search for the Madhi's forces. The illustrated papers repeated a scene, '105 degrees in the shade,' that showed British officers sweltering in their tents. At the same time, in the 'white man's country' of Rhodesia, there were the irregular troops of the Field Force, dressed in their cowboy hats and bandoleers, riding out to hunt down the Matabele, or 'Charging the Rebels in Thick Bush.'[13] Of all the heroes, none were so fine as Grey's Scouts, a 'picked body of men' who showed 'splendid gallantry and devotion to one another.'[14] The work of individual scouts was also celebrated; Baden-Powell, as was his usual practice, sent sketches and copy back to the illustrated papers in England. Burnham was pictured tracking the witch doctor of the god M'Limo to his lair in the hills, shooting him and making his escape. As it later transpired, Burnham had killed the priest of a friendly clan; to the public it hardly mattered, given the 'halo of romance shed around the incident.'[15] Fred Selous was mentioned in reports, and when he published his account of the first months of the rebellion while the issue was still in doubt, the heroism of the colonists was made plain.*

For Baden-Powell, the Matabele campaign was a succession of hot days and cool nights on the high veld, scouting the Ndebele, tracking their spoor, spying on their positions, escaping their ambushes, killing them in their caves. His first act of faith had

*The radical journalist and MP, Henry Labouchere, had claimed that 'the natives are being shot down like game at a battue, with apparently as little danger to the shooters as to those killing hares and rabbits' (Selous, *Sunshine and Storm* 226–7). Selous disputed this, and gave details of Ndebele atrocities. He and Labouchere were old enemies, and when Labouchere attacked the actions of the Chartered Company in 1894 in *Truth*, Selous sued him.

been to exchange his army uniform for the 'working kit' of the veld. He found the cowboy hat more practical than the army helmet, the flannel shirt with the soft collar better than the stiff-necked army tunic. A handkerchief round the neck prevented sunburn. His service revolver could be carried in an open 'cowboy' holster, wearing one spur 'colonial' fashion had much to recommend it, and the colonial military saddle was more useful than army issue.[16]

He preferred to be alone when he was scouting, taking with him only 'my one nigger-boy, who can ride and spoor and can take charge of the horses while I am climbing about the rocks to get a view.' This man was called Jan Grootboom; he had worked for both Selous and Burnham, and he was to teach Baden-Powell much about scouting. Burnham compared him to Rider Haggard's Zulu hero Umslopogaas, and Baden-Powell came to trust his devotion and admire his bravery. He was, he said afterwards, 'a white man in a black man's skin.'[17] In the Matopos hills Baden-Powell learned the necessity of studying his enemy, using the landscape, and the importance of camouflage. For leaping about on the boulders his india-rubber boots were essential, and for fast retreats down the hillside it was as well that he knew how to skirt-dance.*

Observation and deduction were the essence of scouting; Burnham had the edge in observation, but Baden-Powell was a master at deduction. Burnham called him Sherlock Holmes (or 'Old Rubber Shoes'). Scouting itself, Baden-Powell said, was like reading a book, and all the little signs that had to be interpreted were the letters on a page. The scout was the man who could read, and his craft was a mystery only to the illiterate. Everything had meaning: 'a few grains of displaced sand here, some bent blades of grass there, a leaf foreign to this bit of country, a buck startled from a distant thicket, the impress of a raindrop on a spoor, a single flash on the mountain-side, a far-off yelp of a dog'

---

*Skirt-dancing was a craze of the 1890s. Performed in a long, loose skirt by female dancers, it was popular in the theatres and music halls. Classes were offered to respectable young ladies (see *Pall Mall Budget* 10 May 1894, p. 15). As one of his turns, Baden-Powell skirt-danced at regimental concerts.

– all details were there to be made sense of, all facts were clues to the astute detective.[18] Grootboom – in a deduction that Baden-Powell afterwards took as his own – came across a strange leaf on the ground close to the trail. It was damp; it smelt of Kaffir beer. It told the story of Ndebele women carrying beer to their men, of their men drinking it while it was fresh, of becoming drowsy and comfortable, of forgetting to keep watch. It told the scout he could reconnoitre in safety.

Scouting was thus a science, no longer an inbred sense peculiar to the native. Burnham had found that he could outtrack the Hottentots and the Masaruas even at their best, and Baden-Powell discovered that though the Ndebele were clever in many little ways, they rarely took the trouble to cover their own spoor, and they were useless in the dark. The civilized scout could answer intuition with logic, and meet nature with science. Sherlock Holmes was an obvious model. Memory could be trained as Houdini trained his son, 'to recapitulate the contents of a shop window after a single look at it' (this became 'Kim's game' in *Scouting for Boys*, after Kipling's novel). All in all, the English would make the best scouts. Using the American, frontier sense of woodcraft – the knowledge a man needed to survive in the wilderness – he claimed for himself and his fellow-countrymen a privileged status: 'We English have the talent of woodcraft and the spirit of adventure and independence already inborn in our blood to an extent to which no nationality can lay claim, and therefore among our soldiers we ought to find the best material in the world for scouts.'[19] What the frontier represented was now within the reach of Englishmen. They had the 'real stuff'; they too could be *men*.

There were two styles of frontier scouting in the 1890s, each at odds with the other. One, in the tradition of Fenimore Cooper's Natty Bumppo and Chingachgook, was tracking, and took inductive skills; the other, after the fashion of the Indian fighter, was rougher and readier, where scouts were little more than an advanced patrol. In the imperial army and on its fringes it was now the fashion to be a scout for the glory of the thing; so highly regarded had the skill become, Baden-Powell remarked in 1899, that Light Infantry skirmishers had taken to calling themselves scouts. Tracking was for the purist, skirmishing for the rough-rider. Both styles would be practised in the Boer War, and both would contribute to the prestige of scouting.

Armies need information about the enemy; a system of patrols and scouts, which obtains and passes back information, is essential to military health. Though the recent experience of the imperial army had been in small wars against subject peoples, in the late nineteenth century British military theorists were still drawing lessons from Napoleonic battles, with the American Civil War and the Franco-Prussian War as recent variations. Their textbooks showed reconnaissance as a necessary but not very important part of war. Colonel Cornelius Clery in *Minor Tactics* (1874), using European examples, defined scouting only as a patrol, and limited it to reconnoitring, its object the discovery of the enemy's whereabouts.[20]

Military orthodoxy at the end of the century still tended to favour traditional tactics, with armies of massed infantry arranged in squares or regular formation, supported by guns in the centre, and cavalry on the flanks, or cavalry concealed in the square, waiting to pursue the enemy. This was the arrangement, for instance, in the Sudan campaign of 1898, where the battle of Omdurman was a classic set piece in the desert beside the Nile. Such scouting as had to be done was performed by patrols, often detached from a cavalry unit. Even in conditions that demanded caution, such as the Maori wars of the 1860s (conducted in the fern forests and heavy bush of the North Island), units of the regular army employed close formation and frontal assaults, and left the scouting up to the irregulars. As one imperial frontiersman said, speaking of the equally badly managed Zulu campaign of 1879, 'the ordinary British officer was as ignorant ... of scouting as a chimpanzee is of skating.'[21]

The typical colonial war was a small affair, against a disorganized opposition fighting guerrilla fashion. It was not always possible to 'butcher and bolt' – as officers on the Northwest Frontier put it – and regular army units were sometimes surprised and ambushed in their confident ignorance. The native levy of scouts was one solution, but the quality of that levy depended too much on the fighting inclination of the native. In practice the imperial army had been in the habit of using scouts as a forward fighting force, and it recruited scouts wherever possible from friendly natives. As early as the 1840s corps of Guides were formed in India; by the end of the century it was usual for any colonial expedition to enlist the services of a troop of irregular 'scouts.' On the Ashanti expedition of 1895–6, for instance, a native levy was used to scout ahead of the army. Baden-Powell was its commander. He outfitted his men with a red fez, and told them they were the eyes to the body of the snake as it crawled through the jungle. He called them 'B.-P.'s Scouts,' but he found them lazy, stupid, and cowardly.[22]

There was a running debate about how useful such corps were, and whether they had talents that regular soldiers lacked. Major Charles Callwell, in his *Small Wars* (1896), said that the Gurkha scouts on the Northwest Frontier should not be called scouts at all; rather, they were skirmishers, trained soldiers using scouting methods. Scouts, properly, did not engage the enemy, and he considered the true scouts those used in bush warfare, as in the Ashanti jungle. These were native levies, and indeed it was probable that only natives were fit for this sort of duty: 'The lithe savage can swarm up trees to obtain a look out, a very necessary precaution at times; and if blue-jackets have vied with the aborigines on occasion in power of climbing, it must be admitted that the true soldier does not shine at such work.'[23] There was thus something of a military understanding that scouting was best left to those whom nature had designed for scouting, while the true soldier fought in the way a white man fought. It was on the American frontier that this understanding changed, as white men imitated the 'racial' skills of the Indian.

To an extent, American professional soldiers shared the bias of their European fellows, though in the field they might have to take what they could get. During the prolonged Indian wars of the American frontier the United States army employed scouts as supernumeraries; some were white trappers and mountain men, some were of mixed race, some were friendly Indians. Their first duty was to track and follow hostile Indians, but they were often given the task of hunting game, particularly when units were moving through buffalo country. Scouts were not intended for fighting (in spite of Buffalo Bill's stories), though there were no non- combatants on the frontier. Professional soldiers had mixed views on scouts: some admired them, some abominated them, and others found them useful. General George Crook, in particular, employed large numbers of scouts on his expeditions against the Sioux and Apache, and even recruited from the tribes he was fighting. One of his officers reported on the 'curious ethnographical collection' of Indian, Mexican, American, and half-breed scouts gathered for one campaign – 'some were good, and others were good for nothing.'[24]

The mobility of the Indian tribes and the guerrilla nature of their attacks made scouting an important branch of war in the West, and led to a wider use of scouting techniques. The army began to do its own scouting: units on reconnaissance were called scouts, and search and destroy expeditions were also called scouts. 'There is an old saw in the army,' one of Crook's officers, Captain John Bourke, wrote of the campaigns in the 1870s, 'that you can never know a man until after having made a scout with him in bad weather.'[25] Yet the usual meaning of a scout on the frontier rested with the auxiliary – that is, he was a man hired for the length of the campaign to track, follow, and possibly engage the enemy.

The American scout's reputation was earned by his skill, bravery, and hardiness, mentioned first in the memoirs of army officers, and then publicized by the dime novels. Some scouts wrote of their own adventures, or, like Cody, had their adventures written for them. Readers in the east learned what scouts did, how they escorted the immigrant trains across the plains, how they could shoot from a gallop, how they signalled to each . other in Indian style, imitating the cries of coyotes. Some of the frontier scouts had operated against the Indians as a body: Bill Hamilton, who published his memoirs in 1905 at the end of a long life, recalled his years as an Indian killer in a gang of scouts which offered its protection to the miners of Nevada and California in the 1850s. They called themselves the Buckskin Rangers; they took scalps, but they had a code of professional ethics, sparing women and children.[26] Baden-Powell, incidentally, recommended Hamilton's memoir to the Boy Scouts.

Even while the North American frontier was still open, the scout was judged, in some lingering sense, by the degree he met the ideal, and the ideal of the collective imagination was in essence a model from fiction. Behind the popular sense of the scout lurked his literary archetypes, Natty Bumppo and Chingachgook.

The perfect scout was an Indian, a 'child of nature,' a savage. Chingachgook's refined senses, his persistence and courage, his powers of endurance, were nothing beside his 'natural,' instinctual gifts. No enemy could skulk in the woods but he knew it, no fugitive could evade his pursuit. The classic scene of scouting is Cooper's description in *The Last of the Mohicans* of Chingachgook and his son Uncas tracking the prints of the fugitives, seeing the faint depression of the heel in the grass, reading the moccasin marks, noting the branches pulled aside, sensing the message until they discover its meaning. Natty Bumppo himself can do no better than interpret, and keep his blundering fellow whites from spoiling the trail: '"Now the whole secret is out," he says, seeing his Indian friends at their work, "and all is plain as the north star at midnight. Yes, here they have mounted. There the beasts have been bound to a sapling, in waiting; and yonder runs the broad path away to the north, in full sweep for the Canadas."'[27]

With this literary pedigree almost always at the back of the public mind, the scout became a colourful figure in popular culture. Officers traded stories of scouts that could track a single Indian across miles of rock and desert; generals had their own favourite scouts in their entourage, to add to their own heroic image. The impression a scout made was what mattered. General Custer chose a man called California Joe as his chief scout because he looked the part – slouch hat, long hair, and pipe –

but Joe was not up to his command, and got drunk on his first patrol.[28] On the imperial frontier against hostile natives the scout was no less necessary. The North-West Mounted Police in the Canadian west relied on their Métis guides, who, as interpreters, made known to native Indians the force's pacific intentions. Their most famous scout was Jerry Potts, the son of a Scots father and a Blood mother, 'short, bow-legged, with ill-set black eyes and a long straight nose ... given at times to much strong drink.' Potts had the distinction of coming to the rescue of the Mounted Police on their march west in 1874, when they were well and truly lost near the end of their journey; he became a 'character' in their history, noted for his taciturnity. Potts was incorporated into the Mountie legend, becoming, as one romantic historian put it, the 'spirit of the plains itself,' his uncanny sense of direction the instinctive attribute of his Indian blood. In Australia, too, aboriginal trackers seemed to have uncanny scouting skills; they were used to hunt down bush-rangers. In New Zealand the Maoris were equally adept; irregulars in the Maori wars learned to imitate them, even to taking off their trousers and using a shawl as a kilt, all the better to move easily through the wet fern forests.[29]

By the end of the century, military units all over the Empire began calling themselves scouts.[30] It was the name of choice for any irregular mounted corps: in the Riel Rebellion of 1885 Major Sam Steele of the Mounted Police, stationed in Calgary, was ordered to raise a corps of police and civilian horsemen, mostly cowhands. His recruits became Steele's Scouts. In the same conflict were Boulton's Scouts, French's Scouts, and the Moose Mountain Scouts. Steele took pride in his recruits, saying 'the cowboy has no superior in the world, and in spite of his free life he takes to the order of military experience as if he were born to it.'[31] As the cowboy followed the scout in the 'Wild West' show, so the irregular trooper was the cowboy given a uniform and some drill.

In the United States fighting frontiersmen made the headlines in 1898 when a 'cowboy' corps, the First us Volunteer Cavalry, was recruited for the Spanish-American War. These were the 'Rough Riders,' whose exploits were tied from the beginning to their founder and chief publicist, Theodore Roosevelt. The idea for a force of fighting cowboys was apparently given to Roosevelt by Baron Hermann Speck von Sternburg, afterwards German ambassador at Washington; Roosevelt's admiration for things western, and his own experiences on his ranch in North Dakota, made the suggestion attractive. Roosevelt first floated the idea in 1886, when a war with Mexico seemed likely; his scheme was not needed. When war came with Spain, he saw his chance. He left his political post in Washington where he was assistant secretary to the navy, and devoted his considerable energies to raising the regiment. He recruited cowboys and stockmen from the western states and territories, and in the east he found men who wanted to be cowboys. These included lawyers, clerks, and college boys. The press soon named the corps the 'Rough Riders,' and publicized their song:

> Rough, rough, we're the stuff,
> We want to fight, and we can't get enough,
> Whoo-pee!

William Cody himself volunteered to lead the way to Cuba.

Roosevelt's enthusiasm for the fighting cowboy is a useful example of the power of a popular idea. In the hysteria of the first months of the Spanish-American War all sorts of wild opinions were flying around, both inside and outside the military: one of Roosevelt's rival cavalry commanders, also raising cowboys, considered that all he had to do was 'to give each of the boys two revolvers and a lariat, and then just turn them loose.' Roosevelt saw that more was needed; he had in the recruits the makings of good soldiers, but some training was in order. His Rough Riders were 'accustomed to the use of firearms, accustomed to taking care of themselves in the open; they were intelligent and self-reliant; they possessed hardihood and endurance and physical prowess; and, above all, they had the fighting edge, the cool and resolute fighting temper.'[32] Cowboys came with most of the skills that made good cavalrymen, and all that had to

be added was enough drill to enable them to fight in an organized body. When the Rough Riders reached Cuba, Roosevelt,
showing much personal bravery, led them in a charge up San
Juan Hill, and their reputation was made. Unfortunately for the
romantic image of the cowboy, the charge was on foot. Roosevelt
was a hero in the press, and was caricatured as Terrible Teddy
whooping it up on his bronco, firing his revolvers in the air. He
rode on to election as governor of New York State, and with little
delay, as McKinley's vice-president.

This was the frontier spirit exploited to inflame the voter, half
believed in, half sham. F.P. Dunne's realist Mr Dooley, comment-
ing on Roosevelt's colourful account of the Cuba campaign, said
'If I was him I'd call th' book "Alone in Cubia" or 'Th' Biography iv a Hero be Wan who Knows' or 'Th' Darin' Exploits iv a
Brave Man be an Actual Eye-Witness.'"[33] Very soon 'The Battle
of San Juan Hill' was a feature of Cody's 'Wild West,' and
'ROOSEVELT'S ROUGH RIDERS,' including 'Active participants in the
Charge led by Colonel – now President Roosevelt,' added to the
'perfect realism' of the scene.[34] Such inflation was not to everyone's taste. Old Africa hands despised Roosevelt's chest-thump-
ing, and mocked his comic-opera cowboys. When he turned his
hand to big-game hunting, the disgust among 'real frontiersmen' was general.[35]

The Spanish-American War confirmed the reputation of the
American frontiersman, in whatever theatrical character. The
Boer War (1899–1902) forced the public to imagine once more
the meaning of the imperial frontier. When the regiments from
around the Empire disembarked in Cape Town many of them
turned out to be mounted troops; they thought of themselves,
and often called themselves, 'Rough Riders.' The soldiers of
Canada, Australia, and New Zealand shocked the army of the
mother country with their virility and their size. Kipling, as
always, put it into words: 'You bloomin' Atlases,' his trooper said
after it was all over, remembering the colonials: 'My word! you
shook us up to rights.' These colonials were 'independent,
queer an' odd, but most amazin' new,' and they had their own
free and easy ways:

You 'ad no special call to come, and so you doubled out,
And learned us how to camp and cook an' steal a horse and
    scout:
Whatever game we fancied most, you joyful played it too,
And rather better on the whole. Good-bye – good luck to you![36]

But free and easy habits were dangerous, and many imperial officers, Baden-Powell among them, were to have trouble reconciling frontier democracy to their idea of military discipline.

At a time when fighting was expected to provide prestige and excitement, which the Boer War unaccountably was failing to do, the men from the old frontiers carried with them an air of raw adventure and enterprise. And if they did not have the prestige of the army regiments (and could be comfortably despised by regular officers, who were in the habit of despising any volunteer corps), they had their own rough glamour, and they attracted many admirers.

One of these was Winston Churchill, late of the 4th Hussars, already a veteran of several frontier adventures (Cuba, Malakand, the Sudan). When the war began he secured the plum job of principal war correspondent of the *Morning Post*, but he was quite ready to fight on his own account. On his first journey to the front he was captured and put in prison by the Boers; he escaped, and went looking for a new commission. To his joy he found himself attached to the South African Light Horse, who were mostly South African colonists, including 'a high proportion of hard-bitten adventurers from all quarters of the world.' 'I stitched my badges of rank to my khaki coat,' he wrote, 'and stuck the long plume of feathers from the tail of the *sakabulu* bird in my hat, and lived from day to day in a state of perfect happiness.' He found life with the irregulars was war as it should be:

Day after day we rode out in the early morning on one flank or another and played around with the Boers, galloped around or clambered up the rocky hills, caught glimpses of darting, fleeting horsemen in the distance, heard a few bullets whistle, had a few careful shots and came safe home to a good dinner and cheery, keenly-intelligent companions ... One lived entirely in the present with something happening all the time.[37]

Of all the cavalry units, the scouts were apt to provide the most excitement, for they played the game with the Boers with the most informality. One day Churchill rode with Montmorency's Scouts, forty or fifty of them, as they raced a group of Boers for possession of a kopje. The scouts dismounted near the summit to cut wire, were surprised by some hidden riflemen, and went to retreat. Shots crashed out, Churchill lost his horse, and found himself alone, on foot, under fire.

> Suddenly, as I ran, I saw a scout. He came from the left, across my front; a tall man, with skull and crossbones badge, and on a pale horse. Death in Revelation, but life to me!
>
> I shouted to him as he passed: 'Give me a stirrup.' To my surprise he stopped at once. 'Yes. Get up,' he said shortly. I ran to him, did not bungle in the business of mounting, and in a moment found myself behind him on the saddle.[38]

Churchill's admiration for these irregular troops extended to the Boers, who after all were frontiersmen too, who used the same tactics, and who trained in the same rough school. In his role as a war correspondent he reported to the *Morning Post* on the 'formidable and terrible adversary,' who could only be matched by men with the same fighting skills. 'The individual Boer, mounted in suitable country, is worth from three to five regular soldiers,' Churchill claimed. The answer, apart from overwhelming masses of troops, was more irregular corps. Only these would have the character and intelligence to equal the Boers. 'These unpalatable truths,' he added, 'were resented.'[39]

From Canada and Australia, from New Zealand and Rhodesia, came regiments of such troops, Mounted Rifles, Imperial Bushmen, Somebody's Horse, Someone's Scouts, each claiming to have the frontier experience that was needed. In an embarrassing gaffe the British government at first had requested unmounted troops from Canada and Australia, but what was to hand were men claiming to be frontiersmen, each keen to imitate the success of Teddy Roosevelt's boys. It was considered that the Canadian 'bronco busters' would be especially valuable in the new style of war: 'With nerves of steel and thews of wire, they could speak without boasting of their capacity for putting in thirty-six hours consecutively in the saddle, and for living "on the smell of an oiled rag".'[40] Once on the veld Strathcona's Horse put their stock saddles and lassos to use breaking fresh mounts, and discovered that other colonials were imitating the set of their cowboy hats.[41]

In each of their own countries these volunteers were symbols of national virility, and their exploits were reported on and celebrated back home. The 3rd, 4th, and 5th contingents of the New Zealand force in South Africa, for instance, though many of their number came from the towns, represented themselves as belonging to the hardy pioneering tradition of the back country. They too called themselves Rough Riders. To have fought in their ranks was a measure of manhood.[42]

The Rough Riders from every corps enjoyed a piratical reputation in the press: they were buccaneers, wearing the skull and crossbones of their trade. Only they would be a true match for the cunning Boers, whose ruthless use of such tactics as the white flag that meant ambush was well known. The Boers were a nation of scouts and spies who did not play the game like gentlemen. Fire had to be answered by fire. The Canadians of Strathcona's Horse became 'such adepts at leading Boers into ambush that the Imperial Officers christened them the "Scalp-Hunters".'[43] And other irregular corps, recruited on the spot, were equally free and easy. Roger Pocock, serving in Sutler's Scouts, called his fellow troopers 'a gang of robbers licensed to plunder the Boers,' and regretted that the 'shrieking prudes of England' and the nice morality of the professional soldiers had prevented his fellow frontiersmen from starving the Boers into subjection. The Lost Legion had answered the call of Empire, and theirs was a rough and ready code. The Legion had a new commandment to add to the Decalogue – 'Rob everybody in sight except Tommy.'[44]

Significantly, when the irregulars appeared in fiction, it was outsiders who joined their ranks: Scaife, the Harrow boy in *The Hill* who did not quite play the game (his grandfather's working-class blood coming out), or Raffles the gentleman cracksman, another failure from the public schools. Scaife raised 'Scaife's Horse' with his father's money; Raffles, who had lost caste by his life of crime, enrolled as a trooper to redeem his manhood. Dying his hair and lying about his age, but 'gaunt, grim and debonair,' he and his biographer Bunny found themselves in a very irregular squadron, a 'looting, cursing, swashbuckling lot' which got 'a bad name off the field,' but which did 'heroic work.' Suitably enough for a charming rogue, Raffles gave his life for his country.[45]

At home in England there were many who thought that the scout would win the war. Churchill himself had suggested that a corps of gentlemen fox-hunters might answer the need, but there were those who had even better ideas. Lord Lovat from his castle on the Beauly river in the Scottish Highlands began to recruit gillies and deerstalkers from his own and his neighbours' estates: they were skilled in the use of the telescope, they were hardened to rough weather, they would make grand scouts. The scheme proceeded in a feudal Highland way: the Frasers, Macdonalds, and Chisholms assembled at the castle, they were equipped with their new uniforms (including a jaunty slouch hat), and they were taught first to ride, for 'equitation is not the Highlander's strong point.' They ran up and down a mound in Beaufort park – the mound doing duty as a kopje – and practised the use of their telescopes. *Punch* mocked the 'gillie-collum' with its ponies, bags of oatmeal, and presentation whiskey (thirty cases from Fraser of Glen Burgie Distillery), but the Lovat Scouts did reach South Africa, and the regiment went on to serve in both world wars.[46]

Public awareness of scouting, and the scout's popular image during the Boer war, can be seen in the boys' magazines. The cheap juvenile papers used the scout as the hero of their stories; the middle-class boys' magazines (such as the *Boy's Own Paper, Chums,* and *The Captain*), treated scouting with reserve or enthusiasm, according to their attitude to things military. In May 1900 *Chums* ran a long article, 'Veldt-Scouring by Colonial Scouts,' which described what 'even the very dullest Chum' should know, that scouting was of the utmost importance in modern warfare. Of all scouts, the colonials were the best: 'hardy, tough, dangerous fellows they are; splendid horsemen, able to scent the presence of the enemy as if by instinct, and deadly shots.' *Boys of Our Empire* made Major Burnham 'Champion of the Week,' and told its readers that he was 'almost as famous as General Baden-Powell,' who had then just survived the siege of Mafeking. *Young England* praised Baden-Powell and Burnham as models of heroic behaviour, and recommended the 'little shilling red-cover book' (Baden-Powell's *Aids to Scouting*), pointing out what 'delightful exercise for eye and brain' it offered the active boy. The *Boys of the Empire* serialized *Aids to Scouting* and advertised a new and exciting game of scout based on its stories, while the *Public School Magazine* reviewed it with enthusiasm, under the headline of 'Sherlock Holmes in the flesh.' In its single mention of scouting the anti-militarist *Boy's Own Paper* revealed that though it kept silence on the war it expected its readers to be familiar with the heroes of the day. It printed a note on the Canadian scout Sam Steele, late of the Mounted Police and now with Strathcona's Horse, on his way to help Baden-Powell in his new posting to the South African Constabulary. Steele was 'a dead shot, a giant in strength, and the best horseman in the North-West.' The enthusiasm for the frontier spirit was to last throughout the decade, to be fed again with each new military crisis.[47]

Scouting at the turn of the century can be read both as history and as myth; both as what actually happened, and at the same time as the growth of popular legend. Each influenced the other: the legend was adjusted by day-to-day reality, reality itself was coloured and conditioned by the terms of the legend. Both elements can be seen in Baden-Powell, in his life, and in his writing. He was not content merely to describe his experiences: he made them dramatic. He was living an adventure, with himself as the chief actor; his writing, though it was presented as history or military theory, slid towards fiction. To reach an understanding of the impact of the frontier idea on Edwardian society we have to look for a moment at Baden-Powell's own myth-making.

In his own first account of the 'joyous adventure of my life' in Matabeleland he celebrated all parts of 'the game': the native warriors, the brave colonists, the craft itself, the masters of the craft. He published sketches of the Ndebele who shot at him, and the men he killed; he had himself photographed in his new frontier uniform. He drew pictures of the Deadwood coach, of Burnham, of himself skirt-dancing in retreat down a hillside, or creeping on all fours, or reading spoor at a gallop. He sketched a colonist's last stand, one man against eight blacks. He reprinted his own dispatches to the *Daily Chronicle*: here were the yarns, the cunning ruses, the careful deductions, the clever guesses, that were to be repeated again and again, in *Aids to Scouting*, in *Scouting for Boys*, and in the many other books he would write for Boy Scouts. He and Burnham might be one with Sherlock Holmes himself, or kin to Kipling's police officer Strickland, who, geniuses of disguise, speaking the language like the native, could sink into the dirty masses unchallenged, yet return to dress for dinner.

There is one particular item in his Matabeleland experience which both illustrates Baden-Powell's easy fictionalization of self, and at the same time reveals the nature of myth-making. Baden-Powell had in his accounts of his adventures taken care to note the names he had been given by natives, both friendly and hostile, perhaps thinking of Rider Haggard's Allan Quatermain, who earned from the Zulus the title *Macumazahn* – 'he who keeps a bright look out at night, or, in vulgar English, a sharp fellow who is not to be taken in.' It was the usual thing to return from the frontier with an honourable name: Burnham was 'He-Who-Sees-in-the-Dark,' the would-be Indian Grey Owl, 'He Who Walks by Night.' Baden-Powell claimed he was called by the Zulus *M'hlala panzi* – 'the man who lies down to shoot.'[48] On the

Ashanti expedition his stetson hat led to the natives speaking of him as *Kantankye* – 'he of the big hat.' In Matabeleland, in honour of his prowess as a scout, his enemies had awarded him a new name. They had called him 'Impeesa.' This name would play an important part in Baden-Powell's later history, both at Mafeking, and with the Boy Scouts.

There is a curiosity about the 'impeesa' story that demonstrates the process of myth-making, which so often seems to begin in a trivial detail, but then, by accretion and inflation, grows from the ordinary to the unusual till it reaches the legendary. The origin of the tale was in Baden-Powell's (published) diary, when he was describing scouting against native bands: 'My boy, who was with my horse, told me that they were calling to each other that "Impeesa" was there – i.e. "the Wolf," or, as he translated it, "the beast that does not sleep, but sneaks about at night".' Afterwards in his autobiography Baden-Powell amended this to 'the beast that creeps about at night,' but the popular version – as used later at Mafeking – was 'the Wolf that Never Sleeps,' a suitable honorific for the daring scout.[49]

Yet there is a difficulty: in whichever way *Impeesa*, or *impisi* (a Sindebele word from a Zulu root), is translated into English, 'wolf' can only be an approximation of 'the beast that ... sneaks about at night.' There are no wolves in Africa. The Boers knew the beast that sneaks about at night as the 'tijger-wolf' – but the tijger-wolf was the hyena. Experienced African frontiersmen made fun of Baden-Powell's blunder: there was, as one remarked, 'no more deadly insult' than to call a man a hyena.[50] Yet as we shall see in the next chapter, Baden-Powell would become for the world at large the 'Wolf That Never Slept,' the defender of Mafeking in the imperial cause.

After leaving Rhodesia Baden-Powell pursued his specialization in scouting. He was posted back to India in 1897, and given the command of the 5th Dragoon Guards; for the first time he had the freedom to train his own unit of regimental scouts. He wrote up his theories in *Aids to Scouting for N.C.O.s and Men* (1899).

Aids to Scouting it is not like the usual army pamphlet. In its style and personal anecdotes it has in it much more of the author himself than is usually the case, and it is decorated with familiar motifs of the forming legend (Burnham, Buffalo Bill, Sherlock Holmes, the bravery of the Zulus). More unusually, Baden-Powell treats the non-commissioned officer or the private as an individual, capable of thinking for himself, and so implicitly rejects the traditional army view of the soldier as a loutish automaton. He gives a straightforward outline of the science of military scouting, clear, readable, persuasive; he makes a strong argument for the need for accurate reconnaissance, and for scouting as the most practical way of obtaining information. He gives advice on how to scout, taking advantage of the weather, of camouflage, of local conditions. He explains how to take notes, and how to relay information accurately. He illustrates his points with stories of successful ruses and clever pieces of deduction, many of them repeated from *The Matabele Campaign.* He lists the principles which he formed in Matabeleland: the habit of noting detail, the need for intelligent inductive reasoning, the use of special knowledge, such as woodcraft. He repeats his theory that English soldiers, trained in the right methods, would be 'quite equal to many of the colonial scouts bred on the prairies.'[51] For the traditionalists in the army the idea that a soldier could or should think was heresy.

What is remarkable about *Aids to Scouting* is not so much its sensible advice about scouting, but rather that it is a book about character. Baden-Powell wanted to make scouting respectable, and to do this he had to convince his colleagues that the craft required abilities of a high order. The scout had to work alone, and he needed to be independent, resourceful, and intelligent. Above all, he needed to be courageous, with a type of courage quite different to the blind bravery of the cavalry charge. Baden-Powell thus begins *Aids to Scouting* with a new definition of that most important of public school virtues – pluck. A scout's pluck was 'grit,' born of confidence in himself, the courage of the hero who could be relied upon to go out alone against the enemy, to take calculated risks, and to endure. This gift was coupled to self- reliance, confidence, and discretion. Baden-Powell's ideas were an intelligent alternative to the military expectation of blind obedience, of standing the fire of the enemy, of going in with the bayonet, and they gained some acceptance in the years before the First World War.* As a popular book on the army explained in 1914, the soldier was no longer a 'mere cog in a machine. '"Obedience," was the watchword of yesterday. "Obedience and initiative" is the phrase of to-day.'[52]

In the history of the Boy Scouts, both the Rough Riders and the single scout have their place, not only for the impression they created of scouting as the most adventurous branch of war, but more particularly, in the way that they defined national virility. In Britain itself the problem of physical deterioration had been linked to the debilitating effects of urban life. Colonies that produced and would continue to produce tall, strong, hard men were a corrective to the effects of decadence at home. This Baden-Powell understood. In spite of his horror of undisciplined troops, he was strongly attracted to the idea of the frontier. Later he would call on the war scout in both his roles to inspire his message to boys.

By the time *Aids to Scouting* was published during the siege of Mafeking, amid news of the disastrous ambushes inflicted on army units by the Boers, and with no news of the heroic plight of the author, scouting was the most topical of military subjects. The papers took up scouting; they published letters on its virtues, they quoted from big-game hunters, self-appointed experts on the art. There was a debate on natural versus acquired scouting. Indians had a 'racial training that has lasted Heaven knows how many centuries' the author of an article in the weekly *Black and White* pointed out, but white scouts like Burnham were adaptable. The Empire had a ready supply of such men, for each and every member of the North-West Mounted Police was a competent scout.[53] The papers offered easy advice: if only Baden-Powell were in command of scouting for British com-

---

*One military writer argued that all officers should be good scouts, with a picked officer in every unit being a 'real expert at the art – a sort of happy combination of Baden-Powell, Burnham, Ghulam-Hussein, and Sherlock Holmes.' See Carter, *Training and Use of Scouts*, 24.

manders like General Gatacre or Sir George White, then no one would be trapped in 'Dutch ambuscades.'[54] B.-P. was 'a child of nature,' he had 'the keen senses of an Indian.' But B.-P. was trapped in Mafeking. The generals were advised to look for the next best scout, and the advice was finally followed. Lord Roberts sent for Major Burnham. B.-P., otherwise engaged, was about to become the hero of the British public.

CHAPTER THREE

The Wolf That Never Slept:
A Scout at Mafeking

He saw to everything, ordered everything, arranged everything. But at night, when the lone veldt was wrapt in darkness, he sallied forth to see what the besiegers were doing. His steps are as rapid as those of a man who has much to do and little time to do it in. Now he drops on his hands and knees and crawls along, then he shelters behind a rock, again he takes cover among some bushes; but his eyes are ever straining towards the Boer lines. Soon he is lost to sight in the darkness of the undulating veldt. Some hours later a dozing sentry ...

('*B.-P.*': *The Hero of Mafeking*, 75)

In 1903 Baden-Powell was visiting Wales, where he was made a freeman of the city of Cardiff. He had become a hero at Mafeking; he was still a popular public figure. Promoted to major-general just after the relief, the youngest general in the army, and now appointed inspector general of cavalry, he toured up and down the country on official and private business, speaking to the public, to mayors and aldermen, to boys' clubs, to regimental dinners. His message was the urgency of the dangers facing the nation, and the need to do something about them. Wherever he went, even if it was for a quiet week's fishing in Derbyshire, his activities were reported in the papers.

In Wales his visit inspired a local poet to write some verses, but the poet took the chance to express his personal disappointment. The Baden-Powell that stood on the platform and addressed the cheering crowds of Cardiff was not the Baden-Powell of Mafeking:

> The general came, the people cheered,
> To greet a warrior of renown:
> He seemed as coming to his own
> When he arrived at Cardiff town.
> But there was one thing all men missed –
> Our hero had forgot to bring
> The old slouched hat, the khaki suit
> He donned each day at Mafeking.

The poet expanded on this theme over several verses, telling his readers that the figure in the scarlet tunic, with the medals on his breast, was not the hero they remembered so well. 'When we think of you,' he concluded, 'we see you as you were,' in the old slouched hat 'as you paced the walls, the sleepless wolf of Mafeking.'[1]

The image of the hero is the meaning of its parts, and of those parts his clothing is the most obvious and visible sign. Davy Crockett is identified by his coon-skin cap, Lawrence of Arabia must wear a burnouse, Monty a beret. The uniform carries its own message. 'The old slouched hat' meant Baden-Powell, and it meant the frontier. It appeared on all the mementos of Mafeking, the commemoration plates, the buttons, the medals, on the beer mugs, the song sheets, the match boxes, the biscuit tins, on all the hundred and one souvenirs of the hero. It represented many things, but most of all, it stood for defiance, energy, and Englishness. To be precise, Baden-Powell wore not the soft-brimmed slouch hat of the irregulars, but the hard-brimmed stetson, a 'Boss of the Plains.' To the public, however, one cowboy hat was much the same as another.

The creation of the Hero of Mafeking took place over some seven months, mainly in the British press. Detail was added to detail, fact was elaborated, fiction was invented. Baden-Powell grew into his image, and accepted his story. He became much more than an individual; he was a symbol of the nation. At the centre of this symbol was his reputation as a scout.

The story of Mafeking has been told many times. Contemporary biographers treated it as salutary heroism, while modern historians, such as Brian Gardner, Thomas Pakenham, and Michael Rosenthal, have played down the importance of the event and its central figure, accusing Baden-Powell of a variety of sins, from military incompetence to racial prejudice and genocide. More recently Tim Jeal, re-examining the evidence in detail, has tried to rehabilitate Baden-Powell, pointing out the difficulties Baden-Powell faced with untrained troops, and the resourcefulness with which he led the garrison through the very real horrors of a long siege.[2]

The following pages are intended neither to debunk nor to defend Baden-Powell's reputation. They are concerned not so much with the facts of history as with the making of a myth, and with the response of the media and the public to Mafeking. They describe the process that turned a small military event into a symbol of patriotism, and the commanding officer of a relatively unimportant unit into a British hero. They also prepare the way for the story of the Boy Scouts: without Mafeking, its hero, and the image of the frontier, it is hard to see how the Scout movement would have got off the ground.

The Boer War of 1899–1902 marked a critical point in the history of the Empire, for it seemed to indicate a sharp interruption to the smooth course of colonial expansion and British success. It is not too much to say that what happened in the first year of the war was a shock to the national psyche: it led to a questioning of imperialist values, and it provoked extreme defences of those values. Disaster followed disaster; English generals made mistakes; English soldiers were slaughtered; Magersfontein, Colenso, Spion Kop, Modder, Tugela – the list of defeats seemed endless. The Boers had better weapons, they kept their heads down, they knew the country, and they were mobile. The language of the dispatches told of British forces regrouping or consolidating or reforming; it seemed all too certain, in spite of circumlocutions, that the army was in confusion and retreat. Week by week the troopships set sail for South Africa, week by week the imperial Army grew in size. Canada, Australia, New Zealand sent their contingents; the Indian army was depleted to add to the force. It was probable that the Boers would be overwhelmed by weight of numbers, yet still the victory seemed uncertain. Generals were replaced and sent home; Lord Roberts, field marshal of the army, hero of the Afghan wars, his own son among the war dead, went to take charge. And still the news of Boer successes had to be reported, and the public in England was puzzled that the conflict lingered on.

For the press one event alone had the simple glory of a boy's story, and one soldier showed all the pluck, resourcefulness, and style that could be expected from soldiers of the Queen. The siege of Mafeking began in October 1899, almost with the opening of hostilities; when the relief came finally in May 1900, the town had resisted for 217 days. The celebrations of the relief in Britain were unprecedented in their excess, and Baden-Powell, the commander of the garrison, was idolized. 'Plucky little Mafeking' was proof that the rot had not really set in, that England was not decadent.

Mafeking was a small town on the border of the Cape Colony and Bechuanaland, a station on the railway that ran between the Cape and Rhodesia. Though it lay far from the scene of the main fighting in the Transvaal, as a railway depot it had a certain strategic importance. More crucially, it was of symbolic importance. For the British, Mafeking marked the edge of the South African frontier, the line between Boer and British territory, the jumping off spot for the Chartered Company and Rhodesia. To the Boers, Mafeking was the town from which the abortive Jameson raid had set out for Johannesburg in 1895.*

*Dr Jameson hoped to provoke the (mainly British) 'uitlanders' to rebel against the government of the Transvaal. The affair was bungled, there were questions of complicity on the part of the Foreign Office and more certainly the Cape government – Jameson was Cecil Rhodes's chief lieutenant – and some feeling that Jameson, handed over to the British for punishment, had escaped with only token punishment.

When the war began the town was defended by a regiment raised on the spot from volunteers in Bechuanaland and the Cape Colony. Baden-Powell had been put in charge of the whole frontier area of Rhodesia, Transvaal, and the Bechuanaland Protectorate; he had split his force in two, one regiment under his subordinate, Colonel Plumer, to patrol the country to the north, the other regiment, under his own command, to defend Mafeking.

Mafeking lay on the dry African veld, a collection of mud brick buildings with corrugated iron roofs, a railway yard, a convent hospital, a bank, an hotel, police barracks, some shops, a public library. It had a population of about 1,700 whites, and west of the white town was the native settlement, where 5,500 Barolong had their huts. Some two thousand native refugees were to add to Baden-Powell's problems. The place had no natural defences. When the Boer siege began on 13 October 1899, Baden-Powell had with him the Protectorate Regiment and a few detachments of police and volunteers. To these he added three hundred armed townsmen, for a total of 1,183 white men under arms. In addition, he was able to arm at least 750 mixed-race and black Africans, and to use another 300 natives to help dig trenches.[3] He had few guns, and those he had were small, and old. He had at the beginning of the siege plenty of food, for the local merchant had filled his warehouses before war was declared.

The siege itself was odd as sieges go. Baden-Powell had neither the men nor the arms to resist a determined assault, but the Boers were reluctant to attack in strength. They surrounded Mafeking with several thousand men, perhaps as many as 7,700 at one stage, and they brought up several powerful guns. They shelled the town six days of the week, resting on Sundays. The British dug trenches around the perimeter to resist Boer advances, and constructed dug-out shelters in the town which offered protection from shrapnel and bullets. When the large Boer siege-gun began firing, most of Mafeking retreated to the dug-outs. The shells knocked holes in the buildings, but luckily did not often explode on first contact. Casualties however were a steady drain on the defenders, and the constant presence of sudden and violent death affected morale. Over the course of the siege, Baden-Powell had little opportunity to take the offensive, but to keep up the garrison's spirits as much as anything else he did send out some parties to reconnoitre and to counter-attack; these sorties, for the most part, were discouraging failures, with a loss of life he could hardly afford. Just before the town was relieved, the Boers attempted an assault, which, had it been supported, would have ended the siege. Long before the relief came food was running out. By the last weeks, the defenders were suffering much from a greatly reduced, monotonous diet.[4]

For the first five months of the siege Mafeking took up little space in the daily newspaper accounts of the war, though it was mentioned regularly; as public interest grew, more and more background stories on the town and its commander appeared in print. There was little hard news, but what there was about Mafeking was good, and in contrast to the dreary succession of disasters that was the story of the main campaign, the cheerful dispatches took on a crucial importance. As early as November 1899, in the second month of the war, Baden-Powell was written up in the popular press; he had led a varied and colourful life, he was good copy. By February of the next year, in the absence of any better news, the newspapers were discussing the possible relief of Mafeking; by the spring, Baden-Powell and his defenders were the centre of public attention. He had corrected the proofs of *Aids to Scouting* in the first few leisure moments of his command, and as his sister reported to him, it was now selling like a house on fire.[5]

Five war correspondents were shut up in the town at the beginning of the siege; they were able to send their stories by native runners through the Boer lines, for transmission to London. Though their copy took five or six or more weeks to see print, these journalists helped heighten the drama of the siege: they wrote about the inventiveness and the courage of Baden-Powell and his men, they described the hardships they shared with him, they spoke with condescension of the pusillanimous enemy. Incidentally, they also alerted the public to the social importance of some of Baden-Powell's fellow prisoners: Lord Edward Cecil, the Prime Minister's son; Lady Sarah Wilson, a daughter of the Duke of Marlborough; several officers from aristocratic families. In a journalistic coup which added to the excitement, the *Daily Mail* accredited Lady Sarah as its correspondent.

Long before the extraordinary scenes of public joy which marked the raising of the siege, the British press discovered that the defense was exemplary. Boer and Briton were compared as black to white. The defenders of Mafeking were indomitable; they conducted themselves with a kind of light-hearted humour that contrasted most favorably with the stodgy psalm-singing habits of their opponents. Baden-Powell himself typified this *esprit* whenafter what came to be represented as a particularly ineffectual shelling of the town, he sent off a message to Colonel Plumer which, shortened by a telegraph clerk, sounded suitably dramatic and defiant: 'All well. Four hours bombardment. One dog killed. BADEN-POWELL.'

In time, the public were shown more examples of Baden-Powell's impudence and ingenuity. He invented imaginary minefields and imaginary barbed wire; he used a megaphone to broadcast orders that would confuse the Boers. He had grenades made from tin cans; his men discovered an old naval gun, which fired cannon balls, and they fabricated another gun in the railway workshop. They invented a searchlight and used it to illuminate the Boer lines.

The press soon learned of the routines of life in Mafeking, of the entertainments and sports, of polo, pony-racing, football and cricket matches, of concert parties and gymkhanas. These things kept up morale, and were almost an insult to the enemy. From the military point of view, nothing much happened, though the few skirmishes in the trenches showed English 'coolness.' The style of the combatants, it was reported, was the difference between English spirit and Boer dullness. The English were inventive; the Boers shelled the town with predictable regularity.

Baden-Powell himself seemed to embody all that was best in the character of the defenders. He was resourceful, and ever cheerful. His behaviour was exemplary, his uniform was always immaculate. No detail was beneath his notice. He gave orders that, in their directness, said all that was needed: 'sit tight,' he told his men, 'and shoot straight.' *The Times* summed it up, writing the day after the news that the siege had been lifted:

> Perhaps no person whose name has become more prominent in this war is more admired and trusted than Colonel Baden-Powell. No man has done so much with such slender means. None has shown a more unquenchable cheerfulness in the presence of crushing dangers and cruel trials. None has displayed a greater fertility of resource in devising expedients and in turning to the best account the gradually dwindling powers of a half-starved population.[6]

These were temperate words, almost peculiar in what was then an atmosphere of national hysteria. When they were printed the relief had been expected for weeks, and preparations to celebrate had been made. Days had passed, and still the happy rumours were unconfirmed; when the telegram with the good news finally reached London on the evening of May 18, the public was more than ready. The streets were mobbed, Union Jacks and pictures of Baden-Powell were everywhere.* The crowds treated themselves to an orgy of rejoicing, their 'uproarious behaviour' suggesting to the press the new verb 'to maffick.' Baden-Powell's name was cheered repeatedly; his mother's house was mobbed. The lord mayor, who had been waiting for days to make his speech, told the crowds outside the Mansion House that 'British pluck and valour' had triumphed. Queen Victoria telegraphed her hearty congratulations. In the theatres patriotic fervour ran high. At the Palace, for instance, as the *Morning Leader* reported,

Arthur Playfair recited Bernard Ramsey's 'Mafeking,' and a

---

*The *Daily Express* had told its readers to pick up free flags, souvenir sellers had their buttons and mementos on the street, patriotic songs and verses were written and printed.

breathless crowd intently listened. As the tableau curtain was raised, when the reciter reached the last lines:

How it suffered – ay, and triumphed

For the pride of Britain's names

and disclosed a portrait bust of Baden-Powell, draped with the Union Jack, the house rose and fairly howled with delight. They sang 'For he's a jolly good fellow,' they cheered, they sang 'Rule Britannia'.

Baden-Powell reaffirmed English manhood, at a time when the regular army had failed; he was surrounded and outnumbered and he had resisted. He was the lone scout, the guardian of the frontier, the sleepless wolf, defiant on the barren veld. Only his vigilance had kept the enemy at bay.

How did this heroic image take shape? The journalists who were trapped in Mafeking had been slow to see the possibilities of the siege. Their relationship with Baden-Powell was a difficult one, full of mistrust on both sides. Vere Stent, Reuters' correspondent, was matter-of-fact and unambitious; Major F.D. Baillie, representing *The Morning Post*, scorned sensationalism and turned in brief factual reports. The man from the *Daily Chronicle* was shot in a drunken quarrel, the *Cape Times* reporter was captured by the Boers. Lady Sarah Wilson was something of a thorn in Baden-Powell's flesh, and he had ordered her out of Mafeking at the beginning of the siege, ostensibly for her own safety. She was not easily defeated. She spent two months as a sometime prisoner of the Boers, but contrived to return on 7 December, exchanged for a horse thief, and by January was able to continue dispatches to the *Daily Mail*. The story that the public discovered it wanted had to be supplied by Angus Hamilton, whose status with *The Times* was somewhat questionable, and by Emerson Neilly of the *Pall Mall Gazette*, whose press permit Baden-Powell removed for a time as punishment for trying to smuggle uncensored copy out of the town. Apart from Lady Sarah, who thrived on danger and confrontation, none of the journalists had much reason to enjoy their assignment.[7]

In the middle of November 1899, some six weeks into the

siege, Hamilton reported to *The Times* that there was nothing to report: 'the picture is not unlike those presented by farcical melodrama ... distress is wholly absent, danger is purely incidental.' He attempted to assess Baden-Powell's character, noting that Baden-Powell was 'swayed by ambition,' with a 'keen sense of the possibilities of his career.' He was, Hamilton thought, 'eminently a man of determination, of great physical endurance and capacity, and of extraordinary reticence.' By the New Year Hamilton had begun to see that the real story lay not with the inaction and boredom of siege routine, but with the personality of the commander. There was now something extraordinary about Baden-Powell: 'Every passing townsman regards him with curiosity not unmixed with awe. Every servant in the hotel watches him, and he, as a consequence, seldom speaks without a preternatural deliberation and an air of decisive finality.'[8]

The story of the brave colonel began to develop a life of its own. Here was a man of action in control of a thousand details, a man who knew everything and saw everything, who was taking up the burden of the hero, alone, unaided. As Hamilton put it, this hero had two characters: in the daytime he was the perfect administrator, when darkness fell, he became the daring scout:

> He loves the night, and after his return from the hollows of the veldt, where he has kept so many anxious vigils, he lies awake hour after hour upon his camp mattress in the verandah, tracing out, in his mind, the various means and agencies by which he can forestall the Boer move, which, unknown to them, he had personally watched. He is a silent man, and it would seem that silence has become in his heart a curious religion. In the noisy day he yearns for the noiseless night, in which he can slip into the vistas of the veldt, an unobtrusive spectator of the mystic communion of tree with tree, of twilight with darkness, of land with water, of early morn with fading night, with the music of the journeying winds to speak to him and to lull his thoughts.[9]

And so on. Baden-Powell was the watcher of the night, the scout so mysteriously in touch with nature and the instincts.[10]

Though the other correspondents grumbled that there was still nothing to write about from Mafeking, and that they were busy making 'bricks without straw,'[11] Emerson Neilly also began to pad reports of siege life with dramatic accounts of the commander's nightly reconnaissance. The sentries, he said, spoke of 'one who silently steals out of the blackness of the night, and is on them before they have the time to challenge.' This mysterious scout even appeared in disguise, and the sentries told 'of a bearded stranger, dressed in grey tweed, who has the stature of B.-P., and strolls around the works, and makes such remarks as "Keep a keen eye in that direction, you never know what may be stirring or where they are".'[12] Here in embryo were the main themes of the heroic image: the hero's watchfulness, his coolness, his common sense, and, most important, the hint that in some way he brought to the dangers of the siege the superior skills of the frontiersman. Baden-Powell, who prowled the ramparts of Mafeking disguised as a civilian – and who knew what else? – was Natty Bumppo reincarnated in the khaki uniform of a British officer.

'Br'er Baden-Powell is too cute a fox for Br'er Boer,' Neilly had announced in February. The 'commander' he now found was a 'wonderfully tireless man, ever on the alert, ever with one eye on the enemy and the other divided between the town and that nightmare, the native stadt. Some say he never sleeps.' He was everywhere, in the canteen, in the hospital, at the graveside; Neilly noted he had a hundred and one duties. He was the model of strength and good sense: he even wrote his diary with his lefthand, for practice, since as a soldier he knew that some day he might lose his right hand. His midnight scouting was becoming extraordinary: 'Napoleon himself never kept keener vigil.'[13]

It was Neilly who made Baden-Powell the heroic Wolf. Although the 'impeesa' story (from *The Matabele Campaign*) had been circulating from as early as October in the British papers, Neilly reported to the *Pall Mall Gazette* in February 1900 that 'all the African natives who encountered him' still called Baden-Powell 'the Wolf That Never Sleeps.' The phrase caught on: it appeared in cartoons and drawings, it gave Harold Begbie the title for his popular biography, and by the time Neilly collected his Mafeking pieces and published them as *Besieged with B.-P.,* the words had such currency and power that his dedication ran 'To THE WOLF THAT NEVER SLEEPS, who watched afar from his housetop by day, and by night prowled on the veldt to guard his whelps.'

This name is at the centre of Baden-Powell's legend. It had been awarded in romantic circumstances by a warrior tribe to their worthy conqueror and was recorded by the hero himself; it joined him to the pattern of the 'real' African heroes, like Allan Quatermain. That it was a fraud,* and that those Ndebele warriors had actually called Baden-Powell a hyena is only ironic to us now. What mattered at Mafeking was the heroic idea. Baden-Powell was the noble wolf: like the wolf he prowled in the night, like the wolf he seemed to go without sleep, like the wolf he could silently appear and disappear. And so he should be known as Wolf to all the world.

Wolves are associated with darkness and the supernatural; it seemed but a step to attribute unusual powers to the hero himself. *The Times* reported that Baden-Powell struck awful fear into the hearts of his enemy. General Snyman, the Boer commander, was said to have a superstitious belief that Baden-Powell visited his laager every night and had some supernatural power of making himself invisible.[14] Baden-Powell's biographers extemporized on the theme. In their eyes, the Ndebele, being so much closer to the secret sources of magic, had first divined the hero's true nature:

Silent in his movements, with eyes that can detect and distinguish suspicious objects where the ordinary man sees nothing at all, with ears as quick as a hare's to catch the swish of grass or the crackling of a twig, he goes alone in and out of the mountains

---

*Baden-Powell may have been misled by Rider Haggard. Allan the white hunter, who should know, calls the Zulu warrior Umslopogaas, 'Old Wolf' (*Allan Quatermain*, 586).

where the savages who have marked him down are asleep by the side of their assegais, or repeating stories of the dreadful Wolf over their bivouac fires.[15]

The images might be Rider Haggard's – in a bad moment.

It is impossible now to recover the impact of a popular hero, for we would need to live through the contemporary tension and excitement, we would need to be committed to belief, to the heightened atmosphere of wartime, to the simplicities of 'us' against 'them.' The story of the siege was reported first by the journalists in Mafeking; the sparse facts in their dispatches were picked up by the press at large.[16] What began as an exercise to sell newsprint, and was supported with huge enthusiasm by the jingo papers, spread outwards beyond the media, until it seemed to become at last an expression of national identity. By this time the myth was in full flower, its bloom marked by an accretion of ephemerae. Here *Tit-Bits* may be as important as *The Times*, a face on a shaving mug more significant than the portrait in *Vanity Fair*. It is necessary now to go to the details, for here we can see a dramatization of the ideology of empire.

At first sight jingoism and little else seems the dominant note of the Mafeking excitement: a loud noise of breast-beating, patriotic fervour; a sentimental and indulgent chauvinism; a crude, competitive xenophobia. If we look more closely, these extremes adjust a little, for much of jingoism was a popular debasement of upper middle-class beliefs in patriotism, in imperial duty (of spreading white rule and ending barbarism), and in the public school code. In a peculiar way Mafeking explains what the establishment wanted its dependants to believe and to imitate: if the servants of the Empire could only be like Baden-Powell, then all would be well with England.

He was the subject first of complimentary stories in gossip papers like *Tit-Bits* and *M.A.P.* (Mainly About People). As news from Mafeking came in, and as the stories of the Mafeking journalists were printed in the papers they were contracted to, other papers were forced to look for their own sources, or content themselves with reprinting.* Reporters searched Baden-Powell's past, they read his books and articles, they interviewed his mother and sister, they went to see his old school and his ex-headmaster. It seemed that Baden-Powell could do everything. The colonel, the *Star* said with some accuracy, was a 'flamboyant figure of a thousand legends. A whole literature of anecdote has grown up around a man who was practically unknown a few months ago.'[17]

The gossip papers ran stories on his many talents, on his skill in kite-flying, on his experiments with his brother in ballooning, on his remarkable invention of a military bicycle. His poster for the military tournament of a few years back was dug up by the *Sphere*. His tales of adventure were reprinted and paraphrased, his sketches reproduced, his jokes repeated. There seemed no end to it. He had been a spy. He could play the comic roles in Gilbert and Sullivan. At Mafeking he took a hand in everything: on siege Sundays he was the ringmaster for the parades and gymkhanas; at the concert parties he gave comic turns, impressions of 'Signor' Paderewski the pianist and 'Gentleman Joe' Chamberlain the politician. He drew the design for the Mafeking siege notes, he posed for his own portrait on the Mafeking stamps. Even before the siege was lifted the biographies were ready; in one of the most popular, Begbie's *The Story of Baden-Powell: The Wolf That Never Sleeps*, the author tried to sort out the actual from the apocryphal, but his uncritical adulation merely strengthened the legend. By June 1900 Begbie's book was a best-seller.

When it came to the siege itself, nothing seemed so exemplary as Baden-Powell's words of defiance to the Boers. 'All well. Four hours bombardment. One dog killed' was referred to again and again, and the public reminded of it in subsequent telegrams, which often merely stated 'All well here.' The *Pall Gazette* took to headlining its reports with 'ALL WELL HERE,' till the

---

*No attempt has been made in this chapter to report on all the coverage of Mafeking, though the newspapers quoted represent a sample from both the serious and the popular press.

three words became an incantation that might itself ensure the success of the defence. On one occasion, General Cronje demanded that the garrison surrender to avoid further bloodshed. 'When is the bloodshed going to begin?' was Baden-Powell's reply. On a further demand for surrender, he instructed the messenger to 'tell General Cronje that I will let him know when we have had enough.'[18]

Other colourful sayings were discovered in Baden-Powell's past. Dr Haig-Brown, his ex-headmaster at Charterhouse, remembered Baden-Powell's last words to him before he set sail for South Africa. They were memorable enough. 'I hope,' B.-P. had said, 'they'll give me a warm corner.'[19] They did, and Mafeking became the 'Warm Corner.' Journalists searched Baden-Powell's published work, and there they found mottoes that characterized the man. With the Ashanti he had found caution a useful tactic – 'softly, softly, catchee monkey' was the way he put it. His own advice to his Mafeking garrison had made the same point: 'sit tight and shoot straight.' By the end of the siege these phrases had been repeated so often in the press that they were part of the legend itself. 'All well here,' 'enough,' 'a warm corner,' 'softly, softly,' 'sit tight and shoot straight' – each was a succinct expression of English defiance.

What are we to make of all this? Are such details at the heart of the myth, or are they merely journalistic hype? Baden-Powell was wonderful copy for the press, and the variety of his talents and skills really did seem astonishing. But the hyperbole is surely evidence of a widespread desire to believe in the superlative. We want our heroes to be supermen, to be larger than life. We want them to have magical powers. We want them to bring us luck. 'If we can credit all the stories of B.-P.'s marvellous cleverness,' the Star said the day after the relief, 'he is a supernatural being. The ordinary is no part of his equipment. He is a man of marvels and miracles.' Baden-Powell could have been a much more ordinary officer and still have been the man of the hour; what elevated him to the heroic level and gave him *mana* was that he incarnated the spirit his class and caste most admired. He belonged to them, but he had gone to the frontier and faced its danger.

He was a modern adventurer, but he was one of their own; he was the heroic scout, and at the same time an English officer, a man whose virtues and character were prototypically English.

Baden-Powell was essentially a middle-class hero. His credentials were impeccable; he had been born to a suitably upper-middle-class family and had gone to a fine public school. He had made a good career in the army. His practice of writing up his adventures and selling his writing to the press might not be 'quite done' (though it had been done by the Victorian hero Colonel Fred Burnaby, and was being done by Winston Churchill), but on the face of it, his self-publicity was suitably mock- ironic. The notes struck by one of his own, the correspondent for a military journal, are sure and true: he was 'this versatile sabreur ... commonly known as, tout court, "B-P" ... prince of scouts ... prince of good fellows.'[20] The nickname of this paragon was affectionate, for B.-P. was a soldier of soldiers.

The hero is only a hero when he exhibits those virtues that are already approved of by the public, and his celebration is in essence public self-admiration. This truth was announced again and again in 1900: 'We are proud of the British spirit today,' a popular weekly wrote, 'proud with the pride of nationhood ... In the proud roll of great deeds performed by our country's noblest sons, the name of Mafeking will hold high place. It will be a witness to the world for a long, long time of British pluck, British endurance, British resolve, British devotedness to duty in the face of all danger, and British triumph over all obstacles.'[21] The emphasis is clear enough. 'We English are what we are,' one of Baden-Powell's biographers claimed, 'because we love, admire, and in our own small way strive to emulate the example of our heroes, and in the man who held Mafeking for seven weary months ... we see a hero the importance of whose personality we do not think it possible to exaggerate.' The Englishness of Baden-Powell's character was important.* The *Graphic*

---

*Though the terms 'English' and 'British' were synonymous at the popular level, 'British' was considered a vulgarism by the upper classes: Scots, Welsh, and even Irish were confidently subsumed in the word 'English.'

reminded readers that there was 'a dash of Nelson's blood in his veins,' and *Vanity Fair*, still ringing the patriotic note eleven years after the event, would recall his 'bull-dog persistence.'[22] Even his nickname 'B.-P.' identified him with the nation, for in the slang of the day B.P. stood for British Public.

He represented the spirit of young England; he was a Peter Pan just before Peter's time, cocking a snook at the Boers. The *Manchester Guardian*, reminding its readers of the value to the nation of the public school system, commented that Baden-Powell at Charterhouse was 'the pattern of the clean, active, spirited and generous schoolboy.' One of his biographers noted that there were few enough anecdotes to record about his schooldays because he was so normal – 'by way of contrast to the type of "Stalky & Co."' There were 'no stories of naughtiness or stupid dare-devilry' in his schoolboy career, another writer said, adding that he was a model child, whose 'ruling passion was the acquisition of knowledge.'[23] It was important that his schooldays were mentioned, for 'the boy was father to the man': Baden-Powell was 'the ideal English schoolboy, and the ideal British officer.' The two went hand in hand. 'Happy is the man who carries with him into middle-age the zest and aims of a clean boyhood.'[24] It was obvious that his impudent challenges to the enemy, his ingenious ploys and counter-ploys, his cheery whistling as he went about his duty, spoke of the spirit of boyhood. As several papers said, the whole siege was a jolly lark to Baden-Powell. Although forty-three years old, Baden-Powell was 'youthful': he was still a bachelor, and all the girls were in love with him. Mafeking might have been the 'cock house' match, and Baden-Powell the captain of his side.

Three notes were struck by the press again and again: the hero was gallant, the hero was plucky, and the hero had a sense of humour. All three virtues were thought to be characteristically English, all three were admired in the public schools. The word 'gallant' was applied early on in the siege, both to Baden-Powell and to the town. It was 'gallant little Mafeking,' and the 'Colonel and his gallant defence,' and after the siege was lifted, 'the gallant Colonel' and his 'gallant conduct.' What did gallantry consist of under these circumstances? By the conventions of the time, an officer was expected to be gallant, that is, he had to apply the code of the gentleman to war; he had to sacrifice himself to save the weaker, to protect women and children and the defenceless. What made Baden-Powell's position at Mafeking by definition gallant was that he was outnumbered. It was 'gallant *little* Mafeking,' and the Boers had become the bullies. 'The surly, slim, guttural giant has fallen and the little boy of Mafeking is once more free.'[25] It is significant that there were few occasions for such gallantry in the Boer War, and often it had to be acknowledged that the Boer was the one who deserved the honour.

Baden-Powell was the personification of pluck. His defence was plucky, his defiance of the Boers was plucky, his determination against the odds was plucky. B.P. also stood for British Pluck. 'Bravo Sir!' the boys of Bishop's College, Claremont, telegraphed to Baden-Powell on news of the relief. 'We admire and congratulate you. British Pluck for ever.' And one of the songs that was written to celebrate his triumph and his promotion was titled 'Major-General British Pluck.' Pluck was a favourite word of the time. It meant rather more than simple courage, since it carried a connotation of spirited behaviour in adverse circumstances: the long, weary ride of the last survivor from Kabul, the courage of the piper who kept on playing though shot in both legs, the fruitless attempt to save the colours in the Zulu massacre at Isandhlwana. In general usage, the word meant refusing to give in, as we can tell from the context in which it was so often placed: Baden-Powell, *Vanity Fair* said, defended Mafeking 'with a dogged, plucky, humourous pertinacity.' As with gallantry, pluck seemed to demand adverse circumstances, 'sporting' conditions, courage against the odds. The young schoolboy who fell on the ball at the feet of the charging forwards was the image that came most readily to mind. Baden-Powell, it can be remembered, had thought it necessary to give his own definition of pluck when he came to define the meaning of scouting.[26]

A third English virtue was a sense of humour. Harold Begbie struck a typical note when he described Baden-Powell as a 'hero

– and a humorist.' He was 'the funniest beggar on earth,' 'full of pranks,' but 'straight,' a loyal friend and an enthusiastic soldier. 'But it is ever his fun first.'[27] Baden-Powell's fun was delighted in by the newspapers, and it became a crucial part of his legend. He loved impersonations and hoaxes; he squashed silly women. This essentially English attitude to the serious things of life was a measure of racial superiority – superiority to dour Scots, to dull Germans, to barbaric Boers. Life was a game, and the most serious parts of it, like war, were the best sport of all. *Vanity Fair*, celebrating the eponymous 'Mafeking,' demonstrated to its readers that they all belonged to that self-mocking, superior club, as it described the hero's career in a series of witticisms: 'His father being a parson and his mother an Admiral's daughter, he was naturally born a fighting man: three and forty years ago. He fought with his nurse; he fought at Charterhouse, and then he joined the 13th Hussars. He treats life as a joke; yet is so keen on soldiering that he presently became Adjutant ...'[28] The gallant colonel, joining in spirit with *Vanity Fair*, could show his pluck by insouciant, self-mocking irony, by an attitude which denied that things were serious, that backs were against the wall, that men were starving and dying. It was all a jolly good game – but everyone knew what pluck it took to say so!

In newspapers and magazines cartoons and pictures of the hero are the most accurate representations of his image: they must make their point with economy; they must evoke instant recognition. Two themes were dominant in the first months of 1900: Baden-Powell as the sportsman, and Baden-Powell as the imperial officer, dressed in his frontiersman's kit. The two were not self-contained – in fact often Baden-Powell was the heroic sportsman – but whatever he was doing, he had on his cowboy hat. Both sport and the frontier were important metaphors in Edwardian life, and both expressed in not altogether dissimilar terms the meaning of war.

The length of the siege and its nature lent itself to the conceit that Baden-Powell was playing cricket with the Boers, defending his wicket in a long innings. (This was given confirmation when one of the Boer leaders asked Baden-Powell if he and his men could join in the Sunday games and entertainments, and was told that as soon as hostilities were over Baden-Powell would be delighted: 'Just now we are having our innings and have so far scored 200 days, not out, against the bowling of Cronje, Snijman [*sic*], Botha, and Eloff: and we are having a very enjoyable game.'[29] And so the newspapers ran cartoons showing Snyman bowling to B.-P., and B.-P. defending the wicket 'Mafeking.' In one such, the hero's bat was labelled 'British Pluck,' and the ball was a bomb.

In another sporting metaphor, the game at Mafeking was football. The *Daily Graphic* had shown Baden-Powell standing guard over the veld, and titled the picture 'the intrepid Goalkeeper.' This was from a Charterhouse source that was much quoted, until it became a happy prophecy: the school journal of 1876 had said 'R.S.S.B.-P. is a good goalkeeper, keeping cool, and always to be depended upon.'[30] *Athletic and Sporting Chat* showed B.-P. on the field of Mafeking, saving Boer footballs from all angles. 'Goodold Baden! Stick at 'em. You can easily keep out all the shots the Krugerites send in.' The *Navy and Army Illustrated*, a week after the relief, chose to title its portrait of Baden-Powell (in dress uniform) 'The Gallant "Goal-Keeper of Mafeking."' 'Well Played, "B.-P.!"' the *Sketch* declared, on another full-page photograph.

As the siege wore on, the cartoons and drawings and photographs showed Baden-Powell in a variety of heroic poses. He was pictured by the *Illustrated London News* as 'the Defender,' and more dramatically, with his dog, 'his wish realized,' in 'a warm corner.' 'I'll let you know when we have had enough' was the caption for another drawing in the same journal, which showed him taking Cronje's surrender. Two weeks before the relief *Punch* drew him at 'The Eleventh Hour,' telling Mafeking to cheer up, for 'Bobs' (Lord Roberts), sending relief, was a man of his word. The *Illustrated London News* tried him again standing tall against the sky (Baden-Powell was on the short side), binoculars in hand, his dog Beetle faithful at his feet, and behind him an old gun, carefully marked 'B.-P.'s Baby.' *The Irish Daily Inde-*

pendent pictured 'Baden-Powell's Diversions,' the hero amusing himself in a wonderful ambidextrous way, drawing Kruger with his right hand and signing telegrams 'All Well' with his left. After the relief the *Sunday Times* presented him as Atlas, carrying the burden of Mafeking – 'For this "Relief," Much Thanks.'

It is difficult to estimate the impact of an image on the public, but it is possible to see in the repetition of the various poses an evolution towards the heroic. The cartoons and the pictures emphasize the hero's heroism, of course, but more significantly they demonstrate his isolation. He is not just a good man doing his duty; he is a superman performing miracles. The *Sketch* showed him leading a mounted charge at the head of his men, and *Under the Union Jack* pictured him as a perfect gentle knight inviting the captured Commandant Eloff to dinner – both images in the tradition of the hero performing an emblematic action at the centre of a group – but a more striking set of images had the hero alone, carrying the burdens of all. 'B.-P.'s vigil: a last look round at night in Mafeking' was the caption to the *Graphic*'s vision of the solitary hero defending the lonely outpost of Empire; again he was 'the Wolf who never sleeps,' on one of his nocturnal prowls around the Boer laagers.

A nickname or title does something in itself to give the hero a human side. Baden-Powell became 'Our B.-P.' to many newspapers and, by extension, to their readers. The possessive is significant. Many leaders are given nicknames by their men; some of these are affectionate, such as Lord Roberts's 'Bobs'; some express dislike; some are mere puns on proper names (Major-General Sir William Gatacre was known as 'General Backacher,' which matched his obsession for physical fitness).* The nickname of a hero should say something; it should join the hero to

*Baden-Powell had begun life in school nicknamed 'Bowel,' 'Guts,' and 'Bathing-Towel.' This last was his preferred nickname. In the army he had gathered others, more or less harmless, such as 'Baking-Powder,' and 'the Bloater.' Bathing-Towel was still current during the siege, and after the relief a few of his military friends in England sent him a card of congratulation addressed to 'Bathing Towel, Mafeking.' The card was delivered. While he owned to this, it had no meaning; it was just a play on words. At Mafeking the men of the Protectorate Regiment called him 'Backdoor Powell,' and some of the newspapers thought this was a compliment.

his public. 'B.-P.' was just right. B.-P. went with everything. *M.A.P.* summed up what the man in the street thought:

British Public,
British Pluck,
British Peerage,
Baden-Powell.[31]

The initials turned out to be lucky, for all sorts of peculiar coincidences seemed to connect them to Mafeking. The old naval gun discovered and used in the siege had B.P. stamped on it – B.P. had been the mark of the founders. (Baden-Powell called the gun the 'Lord Nelson'; another gun, fabricated in the railway workshop, was named 'The Wolf' in his honour.) 'The old slouched hat' was a B.P., a 'Boss of the Plains.' It made a man think: William Luff, writing in *The Christian,* discovered a sermon in Baden-Powell's initials, for the hero reminded him of his Beloved Prince, who came Bringing Pardon.

In 1900 verse had a currency that it has now lost: it was still used as a formal speech to advise, record, and celebrate. The serious journals had a place for political poems, the daily newspapers liked a verse on some event of the day, the music halls needed topical songs. Much verse was patriotic, much jingoistic. The poet laureate Alfred Austin made a ballad of the bungled Jameson Raid: the poet could attempt to transform the questionable and indifferent into simple glory. Kipling, single-handedly, created a vernacular style, and gave the man in the street his voice. Early in the Boer War the newspapers printed his 'The Absent-Minded Beggar,' a reminder to the nation of its responsibility to the common soldier. The poem was recited in the music halls within a month; it was made into a melodrama; it was set to music by Sullivan; it raised £250,000 for war charities. It was widely imitated.

As early as 2 December 1899 the *Daily Chronicle* had a Kiplingesque piece on 'The Man That's Sitting Tight.' Here was the 'Man in the Street' taking a look at the gallant colonel, and celebrating his bulldog spirit:

we likes 'im fur the sly
Sorter twinkle in 'is eye –
The man thet's settin' tight.

The Man in the Street appeared in print again to characterize
B.-P. as 'The Obstinate Man,' – 'you never did see such an obsti-
nate man.' But perhaps the most popular of his efforts, to judge
by the reprints, was addressed to Baden-Powell's subordinate
Colonel Plumer, who was thought to be heading for the relief of
Mafeking. Here the Man in the Street confessed that '... for the
likes o' me, there's a kind of fancy feeling, for the chap they call
B.P.,' and he went on to elaborate (telling Colonel Plumer):

> For the man you've got to get at is a man as mustn't fall,
> He's a man what's fighting desperate with his back against the
>   wall;
> He's a man what keeps his heart up, sends a joke by telegraph
> But it ain't the joke that makes a man feel bursting full of larf;
> There's a something in his spirit which is different from the rest,
> And it's no use my explainin', but we likes ole Baden best.
> So hustle, Mister Plumer, stir your stumps, sir, make a move ...[32]

Whether the Man in the Street was the voice of the people, or
just the journalist's dummy, he seemed to know what lay at the
heart of popular patriotism.[33]

When the relief of Mafeking came, the poets had a field day.
There were comic verses on Baden-Powell's horse – eaten by a
trooper – and 'appreciations' from the Man in the Street: 'And
there's not a man can match him at his own particular biz. –/
He's the genuine sort of Sparklet that can make an Empire fizz!'
There were verses on 'Sit Tight,' and verses on 'That Heroic Lie'
[i.e., 'All Well'], and on cricketer 'Captain' Baden-Powell ('218,
not out'). There were tributes to the Empire's hope and pride,
to 'The Immortal Handful,' to 'Plucky Mafeking.' Highland
dancers danced 'the Baden-Powell Schottische,' entertainers
sang 'Major-General British Pluck.' In the Theatre Royal, Ply-
mouth, Miss Bessie Rignold was the leading attraction at a 'Patri-

otic Naval and Military Night,' at which she delivered the patriotic recitation 'B.-P., Who Kept the Old Flag Flying.' The mails to South Africa were heavy with congratulations, and the postcard sellers offered this ready-made message to the public:

> Dear ———,
> We have shouted 'Rule Britannia,' we have sung 'God Save the Queen,' we have toasted 'Gallant Baden' half a score. We have sent our very best respects to plucky Mafeking, and have hoisted flags and bunting in galore. With a wild and frenzied madness – born of joy – the Empire cheers; while we Britishers rejoice throughout the land. In this hour of jubilation I am sending you a line, with the wish that I could warmly shake your hand.
> Yours exultantly ———,[34]

The myth had produced its own debris, a thousand and one instances of its life and progress.

Mafeking fever had begun in journalistic and commercial excess,[35] but the event was genuinely popular. Some historians have argued that the working class was hostile to imperialism, and while this may have been the case among some union leaders and intellectuals, many working-class people on occasion were happy to wave flags and sing the choruses of music hall songs.[36] Welsh miners, years later, could still cheer the general: on Baden-Powell's visit to Wales in 1907, 'the Rhondda boys were fairly taken up with the distinguished visitor ... as the procession marched through Pentre in the evening to the Workmen's Hall, they closed round his carriage, and with caps aloft they yelled: "Good old B.-P."'[37] Long after Mafeking, stories about Baden-Powell showed up in popular literature.

The celebration itself was a curious phenomenon, and though the few Liberal or Radical newspapers were alarmed at the excess (the *Westminster Gazette* printed a hostile cartoon of a Jingo mafficking, and *Reynold's Newspaper* reprinted it), most voices agreed that the jubilation was harmless, and indeed, justified. Mafeking was the moral centre of the war, said the *Pall Mall*

Gazette, it was a 'sportsmanlike' triumph, because Britons were outnumbered, and thus the defence deserved celebrating. *Under the Union Jack* claimed a moral victory, and added, 'the enthusiasm to which the relief has given rise is a healthy sign in the life of the Empire.' London was moved to ecstasy, the *Morning Post* said, by 'a deed that was only possible because at the secret call of Empire an entire community, little, but of exquisite quality, became as one man. Mafeking was another Lucknow, another Rorke's Drift. The latest chapter in the proud history of the Empire had been written.

Looking now at the defence, it is possible to give both a specific and a general explanation of the transformation of fact into legend. Baden-Powell was a colourful figure, and the 'official' judgment of his character, 'that he had a certain unquenchable and almost exotic attraction towards the unusual in warfare,' that he was a professional soldier by training, but 'a soldier of fortune by predilection,' does not seem too far fetched.[38] The defence *was* stubborn; Baden-Powell *was* efficient, ingenious, and determined. The siege went on a long time. The rest of the war news was bad, and there were journalists trapped in Mafeking. The newspapers pumped up the excitement, but there was more to it than that.

Heroes do not create themselves, nor can anyone be a hero. Psychologists, from Jungians to developmentalists, have argued that we need heroes, whether as projections of the collective psyche, or as models in our emotional growth. Such theories must be speculative. As historians we are safer on more limited ground. The hero is a hero because he expresses a particular social truth; his myth is the dramatization of collective belief, a story which both vitalizes and justifies an ideology. Here the evidence lies in historic fact, and not buried in the unconscious. Baden-Powell in 1900 represented the essential values of the dominant caste in English society, embodied in the military officer. The beliefs of that caste were by and large acceptable to the middle class at this time of crisis, and could be represented as belonging, in the interests of the nation, to the working class. As ex-public schoolboy, as gentleman, as officer, Baden-Powell began with the appropriate makings of a hero; circumstances, the media, and the public's need to see what it believed in, transformed and glorified, created his myth. His novel identity as frontiersman and scout was proof that the English soldier was a still a man.

After Mafeking, as the youngest general in the imperial army, Baden-Powell had a brief, difficult command in the Transvaal, and was then ordered by Lord Roberts in June 1901 to organize the force that would police and administer justice in the conquered Boer states. He was given as one of his divisional commanders the Canadian Mounted Policeman Colonel Sam Steele, who had just completed his duty as officer commanding Strathcona's Horse.*

Baden-Powell's idea of what was needed to restore civil order in South Africa was straightforward. He wanted a police force with a military training and high ideals of fairness and probity. The country was still in the middle of a guerrilla war, with a Boer population made yet more hostile by such repressive policies as the concentration camps, with irregular troops looking to loot everyone in sight, and with hundreds of 'loafers' and 'wasters' freed from uniform. The South African Constabulary (SAC) was formed from men seconded from the army, with many recruits from the colonies, particularly from Canada. As Tim Jeal makes clear, Baden-Powell's problems, both with his superiors and with his recruits, were considerable.[39]† The SAC was used first as an auxiliary to the army, manning blockhouses and patrolling the barbed wire. Later it took on more pacific duties, policing the country, carrying the mails, tracing stolen animals. By 1902 the force numbered over ten thousand men.

---

*Steele had a high opinion of Baden-Powell; he had issued each man of Strathcona's Horse with a copy of *Aids to Scouting.* According to Steele, he and Baden-Powell became friends. In 1906, for his last tour of duty as inspector general of cavalry, Baden-Powell made Steele his adjutant general, delaying the latter's return to Canada.

†The Canadians, in particular, were often drunk and undisciplined, and Steele, according to one of his officers in what is probably a prejudicial account, was a foul-mouthed bully (Gwyn, *The Private Capital,* 361–3). Steele's version is of course different: he claimed that with his help, Baden-Powell based the organization of the SAC on the character and methods of the North-West Mounted Police (Steele, *Forty Years in Canada,* 379).

What is of interest here is the image that was to emerge of the SAC, and the use Baden-Powell would put this to in later history. When he designed the trappings of the SAC with his usual self-mythologizing inventions, he emphasized all that he thought best in the tradition of the frontiersman, and he added to that the essence of the public school code. He wrote in his manual *Notes and Instructions for the South African Constabulary* that each man must 'play the game,' not only when he was under the eye of authority, but also when he was alone, 'simply because it is "the game" and is expected of you as a man of honour.'[40] The corps was gathered from every portion of the Empire, and once filled with this spirit, would be the finest corps in the world. Its uniform, which Baden-Powell designed himself, was a frontiersman's outfit: short-sleeve flannel shirt with a soft collar, neckerchief, bandoleer, stetson hat, breeches for mounted duty, short trousers for unmounted, khaki tunic for parade dress.[41] As in the North-West Mounted Police, the working unit was kept small, with men in patrols of six, each patrol having its own leader. Baden-Powell gave his force a motto based on his own philosophy, and on his own initials: 'Be Prepared.' In all these things – in its code, its uniform, its organization, and its motto – the SAC became a model for the Boy Scouts.

It was no accident that the Hero of Mafeking should in a few years inspire the most successful youth organization ever. Baden-Powell believed in his own legend, just as he believed in the values it embodied. When he came to write *Scouting for Boys* he began with his frontier experiences. Every boy, in effect, had to become a scout, and each in some way had to recapture part of that magic that was Matabeleland and Mafeking, which exemplified so well the true nature of manhood.

PART TWO
Scouting for Boys

Zulu Warriors or 'Red Indian' Braves? The Frontier Spirit in *Scouting for Boys*

It may be that he is not a great soldier of the sort of which Napoleons or Moltkes or Kitcheners are made. *Suum cuique.* He is the Frontiersman, the born leader of Irregulars, and the Empire has need of such. Furthermore, he has the knack of seizing the imagination of boys, and a deep sympathy with them. He is doing his day's work for the Empire by training a number of manly little fellows to keep their wits about them and their eyes skinned. We shall profit thereby another day, in a much greater affair than Mafeking.

(Newspaper cutting, *c.* 1909)

It was frequently said by his contemporaries that Baden-Powell had discovered the one thing which alone would make a youth movement successful: he remembered that boys loved adventure, and he had found a way to let them have fun in a world of their own. He brought the excitement of the frontier within their reach; he would let them join in the adult games of war. That Scouting was a means to an end was also recognized: the ultimate aim of Baden-Powell's movement was to turn out good citizens, future soldiers who would stand by Britain in the coming crisis. This chapter will describe how Baden-Powell brought

the spirit of adventure to his first recruits, and how he used the
trappings of the frontier as a powerful form of indoctrination.

In the summer of 1907, the year before the formation of the
Boy Scouts, Baden-Powell had held an experimental boys' camp
on an island off the Dorset coast. His idea was to try out his
Scouting material, then in a fairly advanced stage of planning.
He collected a group of thirteen- to sixteen-year-olds: some were
public school boys, sons of his friends; others were Boys' Brigade
boys, or sons of farmers, shopkeepers, and clerks.[1] All twenty-
one boys, plus his nine-year-old nephew Donald, were to camp
for a week on the island, to practise campaigning, woodcraft,
observation, scouting, and saving life. Mixing boys from different classes was part of the experiment.

The Brownsea camp has gone down in Scouting lore as the
creation story of Scouting, the moment when the well-known
patrol system was first attempted. (The boys were divided into
four patrols: Ravens, Wolves, Curlews, and Bulls.) It has also
been cited as the first and most typical instance of Baden-Powell's ability to catch the spirit of adventure that was to characterize the contemporary impression of Scouting. That spirit was to
be part of the later camps and jamborees, and was perhaps most
typically represented in the serial covers of his new handbook,
with drawings of Boy Scouts spying, tracking, and exploring
unknown country. Although on Brownsea Island he lectured the
boys on patriotism, chivalry, and the Empire, and treated them
to something of a military regime, Baden-Powell knew what was
exciting and interesting. He woke them up in the mornings with
his kudu horn, a trophy from the Matabele campaign. He flew
the Mafeking Union Jack, riddled with Boer bullets. He told the
boys yarns from his adventurous past, and taught them new
games; he let them cook for themselves. He led them out on
night 'patrols,' and let them 'arrest' the visiting gentry. He conducted them in a Zulu marching chant, and had a local black-
smith make them harpoons so that they could play 'whale hunt'
from rowboats. In the words of his American biographer, this
was 'the island adventure.'[2]

What Baden-Powell did in the first months of the Boy Scout

movement was to take out a patent on adventure. To its recruits Scouting offered freedom, and a chance to break out from the restricted and often stifling atmosphere of the Edwardian home, where the feminine atmosphere would be all too likely to make a boy soft. It allowed any boy (and a few girls) to take part in a simulation of the frontier world. A boy could wear the uniform of the frontiersman, he could make camp and sit around the campfire, he could take to the countryside to follow spoor. The appeal of Scouting was in its novelty. The woods became a place of risk; the old game of hide-and-seek was made up-to-date in the new game of 'man-hunting.' These things in themselves were not innocent of ideological intent; they were most seductive precisely because they fitted in so well with the larger – and familiar – context of adventure and the masculine ethic. Baden-Powell's Boy Scout movement was nothing if not a creative invention; to understand it in its pristine state we need to detour for a moment towards its imaginative background.

As a literary idea, adventure has its own conventions, rooted in human culture. Its stories tell about leaving home and the experience of male initiation, the rite of passage that conducts the immature youth into the new world of the adult. Adventure is a journey into the unknown: the young hero will see strange things and fight for his life, he will return home at long last, older and wiser. These are the themes of adventure; to its stories a culture will add its own particular values, its hopes and anxieties. In the period that produced Scouting, the narratives of adventure matched nicely with the 'plot' of imperialism: the frontier was the unknown land, the hero was the frontiersman, his conquest of territory or native the heroic deed. The Empire itself was the scene of adventure, and its proof.

An example will define the nature of adventure as it was understood in a popular sense during the late-Victorian and Edwardian years. Under the heading 'Adventures' in the index of volume 12 (1889–90), the *Boy's Own Paper* lists stories on African lions, alligators, snakes, a dust storm, ballooning, a day in the jungles of South-Eastern Africa, a yacht race, and a West Indian hurricane. In addition, it gives a 'cannibal tale of the sea,' a story of pirates in the China seas, an account of a young lad's night in a Tunisian graveyard, 'travels in Africa,' and the report of the embarkation of a troopship ('Eastward Ho!'). This is a typical and informative mix of subjects. Adventures are dangerous or exciting encounters with alligators or pirates, life-threatening moments in a dust storm or a hurricane, thrills on a yacht or a balloon. They take place out there in the jungle or among the Moslem tombs; they belong to the bold, to the hunters, the explorers, the inventors, and the sailors. Even the presence of a troopship, about to leave Portsmouth harbour for Suez and India, gives the promise of a new beginning, and, with its caption 'Eastward Ho!' echoing Kingsley's Elizabethan romance, points to the horizon of Empire.

What the *Boy's Own Paper* called adventures were factual, but even in their reporting the conventions of the code are observed. Heroes, if they are young, are 'high-spirited, headlong English boys to whom every kind of adventure or misadventure, from heading a storming party to getting lost in a tiger-haunted jungle, is simply a "jolly lark".'[3] Such boys are naturally plucky, and in their insouciant courage announce their claim to manhood. Other tales are told by eye-witnesses, 'salted' hunters, 'old India hands,' the naval officers and returned colonels who have lived the life adventurous. There is a formula for their tales: 'the strangest thing I ever saw,' 'the bravest man I ever met,' 'the tightest fix I was ever in.' This succession of superlatives becomes part of the discourse of adventure, defining its social meaning. The hunter who shot the great white hippopotamus, survived the charge of the black rhinoceros, fought off the crocodiles, outstared the lioness, and crawled wounded back to camp ('A Day in the Jungle of South-Eastern Africa') exhibited not only *sang froid*, as he himself admitted, but presented to his young reader a dramatic proof of national virility.

Baden-Powell, a veteran of this frontier scene, offered to boys a personal testimony of the adventurous life. In his many books he reminded his young readers of Mafeking, of the Ashantis, of the Northwest Frontier of India, and of Matabeleland, the places where he had had his own good times. He suggested that

Scouting, and in particular the outdoor life, gave boys a chance to join in spirit with 'the heroes of the wild, the frontiersmen and explorers, the rovers of the seas, the airmen of the clouds.'[4] In his first handbook, *Scouting for Boys*, he endorsed the fiction of adventure, suggesting that Boy Scouts read Scott and Stevenson, Kipling, Conan Doyle, Dr Gordon Stables, Herbert Strang, and Frank Bullen. He approved of adventures; he liked the ethic of the adventure story, with its messages of honour, chivalry, glory, daring, and, perhaps most important, its account of becoming a man.

It was into this context that Scouting was born, responding to a code of adventure now coloured by a purposeful imperialism. Baden-Powell was highly conscious of the code and its discourses. He himself had always enjoyed campaigning, especially when it meant the 'the flannel-shirt life,' living rough, sleeping under the stars. To his biographer Harold Begbie, he was gripped by 'vagabonding,' that contemporary craze for roaming far from home,[5] 'that desire which every son of Adam feels at times – the longing for wild, unartificial life.' Those who answered the call, in an image which pitted an enfeebled civilization against a challenging barbarism in the service of the Empire, became wanderers over the surface of the earth, soldiers of fortune in 'the vast, drear, and inhuman world, where men of our blood wage a ceaseless war with savage nature.' It was wonderfully far away from, in Baden-Powell's own words, '"dear, drowsy, after-lunch Old England".'[6]

Adventurers returned from this frontier of the spirit with their tales. 'We've told yarns by the camp-fire in the prairies; and dressed one another's wounds after trying a landing at the Marquesas; and drunk healths on the shore off Titicaca,' wrote the young hero Quincey Morris to his friends in Bram Stoker's *Dracula*, reminding us of the glamour of the idea. Kipling's particular phrase, 'but that is another story ...' would characterize the mood, and suggest a thousand and one nights of imperial romance. Echoing this discourse, Baden-Powell told his life in yarns; he divided *Scouting for Boys* into a succession of 'Campfire Yarns,' and he would spin yarns for generations of Boy Scouts.

The yarn, with its small mock-modest disclaimer of absolute truth, spoke of initiation into the bonds of a virile fraternity; it belonged to the men who tested themselves on the frontier, who brought the dreams of Empire home.

From the start, Scouting claimed proprietary rights to adventure. When Arthur Pearson launched *The Scout*, adventure articles and stories were given a prominent place, and although Baden-Powell and his officers feared for the paper's sensational tone, in his own commercial way, Pearson got it right. One of the first numbers introduced 'The Men Who Write for *The Scout*' to the readers: ex-cowboys, explorers, big-game hunters, sailors.* In a series called 'The Work of To-day's Scouts' they told about their adventurous lives as trappers or railway builders; in another series they described 'The Tightest Corner I Was Ever In.' Here boys could learn about the world they might enter, in which boldness and pluck were the first virtues, and in which somehow, the excitements of the active life were a splendid kind of patriotism. The sensational fiction of *The Scout* repeated the message, making the point that there was little difference between the yarn and life itself: both showed the way to adventure on the borders of the Empire. The Scout movement, with its invitation to boys to enter a new world, and its implicit promise to initiate them into manhood, was to replicate this fiction's basic themes.

When a boy became a Boy Scout, Baden-Powell was able to make an elaborate game out of almost everything. Play-acting was encouraged, 'let's pretend' flourished. Scouting had its own rites and rituals; it appeared with all the attractions of a secret society, from dressing up to knowing the password. (As the phenomenon of fraternal clubs testify, the delight in these things can continue on into adult life.) Scouts had their own salute and

---

*John Mackie was introduced as an explorer, pioneer, gold-digger, a man who had served in the North-West Mounted Police and in the Boer War. Alexander Macdonald, who 'started his roving life early,' was an explorer. Captain Gambier, RN, who went into the navy when he was thirteen, had fought savages in the Pacific. The Australian Louis Becke was 'another famous "adventure man."' *The Scout* 2 (May 1908): 63.

secret sign, they had their own (left-hand) handshake. In the spirit of his time, Baden-Powell plundered native cultures and appropriated their symbols, and soon his Scouts were singing their own 'war songs':

Een gonyama – gonyama.

Invooboo.

Yah bobo! Yah bo!

Invooboo.

And

Be Prepared!

Zing-a-Zing!

Bom! Bom!

Chanting their new songs, the boys became Zulu warriors boasting of their bravery – 'He is a lion!' 'Yes! he is better than that; he is a hippopotamus!' – their cries echoing the chorus of the savage *impi*. Baden-Powell, borrowing now from the 'Red' Indian, watched his Scouts sing and stamp round in a circle, while one of their number, dancing in the middle, showed how he had killed his enemy, or how he had stalked and slain a buffalo. The boy in search of romance could hardly do better, all his wild games honoured and given formal recognition. These moments were among Baden-Powell's most powerful creations. They were not altogether innocent, particularly in the way in which they reinforced racial stereotypes, but the social meanings were disguised: Scout ceremonies seemed to be merely juvenile imitations of Baden-Powell's adventures. This was what scouts did. The messages of virility, of loyalty to the group, of resourcefulness, were masked and made 'natural.' A simple theme ran through Baden-Powell's instructions, as the joys of the frontier were compared over and over again to the snares of civilization. The values of men and of women were antithetical. 'Manliness,' he said, 'can only be taught by men, and not by those who are half men, half old women.'

Baden-Powell from his youth was a great improver on the fact. His talent for story-telling and his ambition at every turn to further his career were forces that drove him to romanticize his past. This habit ran in the family: his mother, who did everything she could to push her sons' prospects, invented an aristocratic pedigree for the Powells (besides hyphenating their family name), and traced her own descent from Admiral Lord Nelson.[7] Baden-Powell himself kept warm another family legend, repeating and publicizing the story that he was descended from Captain John Smith, the founder of Virginia. He sculpted a bust of Smith and presented it to Louth Grammar School in 1906. Much was made of this fact in the press, and the imperial connection between the two heroes was emphasized.[8] But Baden-Powell went beyond commonplace inflation into full-blown mythologizing: he had an enormous talent for making a legend out of his own life.

In inventing the Boy Scout movement, Baden-Powell put the heroic past within reach of every boy:

Item – the *scout uniform*. Consisting of flannel shirt, short trousers, stockings, and kerchief, it was a copy of frontier clothes, as tried out by Baden-Powell in Matabeleland in 1896 and perfected in Kashmir in 1897. In many parts it resembled the uniform Baden-Powell had designed for the South African Constabulary in 1900.

Item – the *hat*. A copy of the SAC hat, which itself was modeled on the 'B.P.' ('Boss of the Plains') stetsons long favoured by Baden-Powell, suggesting cowboys, the Mounties, and the frontier. In yarns about his scouting days, Baden-Powell liked to reminisce about his 'dingy old cowboy hat,' which of course sported a 'ragged bullet hole.'

Item – the *bootlace* around the hat. Inspired by a thong of good fortune given to Baden-Powell by an old native of Mafeking, to make him smile and whistle when he was sad. It reminded the Scout that 'the darkest hour is before the dawn.'

Item – the *staff*. Copied from one used on the Ashanti campaign, 1896, either from one used to test the depths of the swamps, or from one used to hang telegraph wire from the branches of the jungle;[9] recommended for feeling the way at night in *Aids to Scouting*.

Item – the *badge*. Modelled on the badge Baden-Powell awarded to the scouts of the 5th Dragoon Guards under his command in India, 1897–9. Described in *Scouting for Boys* as an arrowhead, the sign which showed the north on a map or a compass, but elsewhere and afterwards more pacifically called a fleur-de-lis.

Item – the *motto*. 'Be Prepared,' 'B.P., my initials' (explained thus in the periodical parts of the handbook, an explanation suppressed in the first complete edition).

Item – the *Scout's chorus*. The *Eengonyama*, 'He is a lion,' etc. Heard by Baden-Powell in Zululand in 1888.

Item – *Dinuzulu's beads*. Spoils of the Zulu war of 1888, and supposed to have belonged to the Zulu chief, whose photograph Baden-Powell kept, showing Dinuzulu wearing such a necklace. Used by Baden-Powell (after 1918) to reward scoutmasters who passed woodcraft training courses, a bead at a time (until replaced by replicas).

Item – the *special badge and title of 'Wolf'*. To both Scouts and Wolf Cubs, B.-P. would become the 'Old Wolf.'

Item – the *kudu horn*. Used at the Brownsea camp, and blown by Baden-Powell at Scout gatherings such as the jamborees. Spoils of the Matabele campaign, supposedly used by Ndebele chiefs to call their men together, or to give the alarm.

To these can be added a number of other details. The famous lesson on knots probably had its origin in Baden-Powell's Ashanti experience, when the bridges his native scouts constructed were secured with creepers. From the Zulu connection came the 'horn' formation of the *impi* used in 'charges' at Scout rallies. The Scout code for death, 'Gone Home,' may have been inspired by the Zulu expression 'Gone beyond,' which Rider Haggard had made known in *Nada the Lily*. All these things came with a sense of belonging; they were part of a life, and they had their meaning in that life.They were not so much invented, as turned into legend, becoming, as one of Baden-Powell's biographers said, the talismans of Scouting.[10]

It is difficult now to appreciate the impact *Scouting for Boys* made on its first publication. There had been nothing quite like it before. It had, to begin with, the appearance of an authoritative text. As the demand for it grew, and as each of the early years saw a new edition, some modifications were made, but the handbook hardly changed. In the second edition a few appropriate acknowledgments were made (notably to Ernest Seton Thompson, from whose woodcraft books Baden-Powell had borrowed extensively); in the fourth edition (1911) the 'Scout Law' was completed with a tenth article – 'a scout is pure in thought, word and deed.' Some rearrangement of the parts was put in place, the material on Scouting organization was expanded, and the section on games was cropped. In the main, however, *Scouting for Boys* appeared to have sprang full-grown into life. It described a reality, not a proposal; it showed an organization already in existence, not evolving. It offered the clothes, ranks, laws, and even prehistory of a special society into which the chosen might be initiated. It came decorated with the aura of a hero, and it was presented as the imitation of that hero's life.

Scouting for Boys was encyclopedic. It gave to the new recruit not only the most detailed and thorough information on the society he had joined, but it instructed him in adult, and often military, skills, especially the professional business of 'scoutcraft.' It told him how to track, and what signs to notice round a dead body. It taught him campaigning and camp life, even instructing him in the proper way to slaughter animals – 'cattle are generally poleaxed' – and gave him the basic rules of hygiene, how to make a wooden tooth-brush, how to dig a latrine. Like any encyclopedia, it provided a store of useful information: on trees and how to recognize them by their leaves, on animals and how to know them by their tracks, on the stars, on the signals tramps gave to each other, on the insignia of military and naval officers. It taught a Scout how to save a drowning man, and how to stop a runaway horse. Nor was his instructor neglected: addressed in passages placed in italics, the scoutmaster was told that when he conducted his meetings, he was not to preach to the boys or bore them, but to let them have fun, to let them be rowdy now and again, to work off their energies in games, and songs, and dances. The whole handbook was a mixture of instruction and entertainment, of exhortation and history. Laws were presented as yarns, and all was made personal and intimate.

Baden-Powell had the ability to treat boys as grown-ups; he asked them to take his enthusiasms as their own, and he invited them to read and study adult texts. When it came to the theory of scouting – and to its brother discipline, detective work – he cited the latest authorities, refusing to patronize his readers. For scouting he referred them to Captain Stigand's *Scouting and Reconnaissance in Savage Countries*, for bridge-building he sent them to the War Office's *Manual of Military Engineering*, for police work he told them to read Dr Gross's *Criminal Investigation*. One more of his 'authorities' must be added: Conan Doyle's Sherlock Holmes. If the frontiersman is the dominant symbol in the imaginative life of Scouting, Holmes, surprisingly enough, seems to be its founder's guardian spirit.

Conan Doyle in a popular sense was the spokesman for the new scientific method, his invention an incarnation of rationalism. Criminal investigation was now a 'positive' science, a force for justice and order against whatever might threaten society – anarchism, or the immorality of the decadents. The clue, correctly interpreted, offered a solution to the most perplexing puzzle; reason conquered all. Scouting was the new detective work used outdoors, and the instinctive sleuthing of a Chingachgook was exposed as no more than intelligence applied. Ironically, readers of Conan Doyle often feel they are in the world of magic, and Holmes's amazing deductions are a sleight of hand.

In *Scouting for Boys*, besides his several mentions of Holmes, his reconstruction of a murder case as a play for Scouts, and his references to police work, Baden-Powell was to recommend to Scouts the standard textbook on police detection, the first English translation of Dr Hans Gross's *System der Kriminalistik*. Gross presented a thorough analysis of the scientific method, stressing the importance to any investigation of medical, chemical, ballistic, or microscopic expertise. He had chapters on footprints, on blood, on poisoning, and lengthy discussions of the everyday business of the working police officer in cases of theft, fraud, or arson. What strikes the modern reader as interesting about *Criminal Investigation* is the nature of its subjective opinion, which contrasts so strangely with the scientific method. For Gross, women are at the bottom of most crimes – 'cherchez la femme' he says (p. 9); young boys make good witnesses whereas young girls do not (pp. 62–64); 'tattooing is almost exclusively met with among people of an energetic disposition' (p. 113); gypsies without exception are cowards and thieves (pp. 242–55), and so on. Considering the gamey nature of many of Gross's details – his discussion of violent injuries, of postmortem dissection, of rape, prostitution, and brothels – this seems an odd text for an Edwardian moralist to recommend to young readers. Yet in its own way *Criminal Investigation* was another imaginative and adult invitation to the serious game of scouting.

In its composition, the handbook was born of a happy marriage between Baden-Powell's own distinctive style and the anecdotal, rag-bag technique of Pearson's popular magazine *Tit-Bits*.[11] Though in an obvious way the scrambled-together apparatus of parts, chapters, yarns, and sections made journalistic sense, it also allowed Baden-Powell to vary his rhetoric, to target different audiences – in short, to send out a number of related but different signals to the reader. The main divisions of the text, the 'Camp Fire Yarns,' with all their suggestion of frontier romance, of stories told by old scouts, tall tales round the smoking embers, turn out to be almost anything at all: stories of

Mafeking, the doctrine of Scout Law, how to stalk, instructions on self-improvement, accidents and how to deal with them, whatever, in fact, comes next.

The first portion of the text addressed to boys was the 'Camp Fire Yarn No. 1.' This included three sections: on the Mafeking Boy Scouts, on scouts' work, and on Kipling's *Kim*. None of these pieces referred to the new organization. The first said that 'Boy Scouts' were useful in Mafeking; the second stated that adult scouts were clever and brave, and that they existed in peace time as in war; the third gave an example of 'what a Boy Scout can do.' The Mafeking story was an introduction to Baden-Powell's heroic life; it joined the boys of Britain to the boys of Mafeking, it invited the boy reader to share in the excitement of the heroic deed, adding a line on the meaning of virility. In Mafeking during the siege there was a cadet corps of boys, 'and a jolly smart and useful lot they were.' They did men's work, and served their country.

The second section began with an appeal to patriotism: 'I suppose every British boy wants to help his country in some way or other.' He can do that, Baden-Powell said, by becoming a Scout. A scout 'is generally a soldier who is chosen for his cleverness and pluck to go out in front of an army and find out where the enemy are ...'; besides war scouts there were other scouts, 'peace scouts.' These were the frontiersmen and explorers, the adventurers and sailors, all the men and women who made the Empire. These were motivated by duty, ready to lay down their lives for their country. All were prepared. The third section was a synopsis of *Kim*, whose adventures, Baden-Powell said, 'are well worth reading, because they show what valuable work a boy scout could do for his country if he were sufficiently trained and sufficiently intelligent.'

In this introduction, then, the would-be Boy Scout is taken directly into the adult world of action, into war, towards the heroic imperial task, into a world in which the Empire must be vigilant against its enemies. The information for the most part is presented on the boy's level. This is what boys did, this is what a boy can do: boys rode through the shells (and they were scouts);

brave men built the Empire (and they were scouts); a boy could train to be a spy, could wear a secret sign, could disguise a secret agent (and he was a scout). Already the scout has been defined as heroic, patriotic, adventurous, resourceful, manly.

For the reader willing to examine *Scouting for Boys* with fresh eyes, and anxious to establish its several meanings in the original historical context, one difficulty is knowing where to begin, especially since the handbook itself had several beginnings, and yet immediately assumed a legitimacy which dispensed with introduction or apology. The simple assertion of the title – 'Scouting for Boys by B.-P.' – linked to the formality of the sub-title – 'A Handbook in Good Citizenship' – announces a paradox that will be consistent throughout the text, a contradiction in style between the dramatic and the educative, between sensation and the normative, between hot and cool. The drawings on the cover and the frontispiece suggest excitement (the Boy Scout spying, the Boy Scout in action); the full weight of the author's name – 'Lieut.- General R.S.S. Baden-Powell, C.B., F.R.G.S. – ' reminds at least the adult reader of established and sanctioned authority. The list of the handbook's contents begins with another hint of this juxtaposition, as it shifts from the civic obligations of Scouts (their duties) to their promised life as a gang (their secret signs, laws, etc.). The foreword for instructors and the notes to scoutmasters that open each chapter strike a didactic note, but the text itself, addressed to the boy, is an invitation to adventure. These two quite distinct voices are characteristic both of the handbook and of the movement itself, for they carry the twin ideological messages of Scouting, the contradictory impulse to inspire both initiative (virility) *and* discipline (good order).

At no point in the handbook does Baden-Powell tell his young reader what a Boy Scout *is*. *Scouting for Boys* is a title on the lines of *Gardening for Boys*, or *Marksmanship for Boys*. Scouting is already practised by adults; now it is to be introduced to boys. Scouting is an activity of war, a military skill. *Boy* scouts exist; they do not need to be invented. They have been 'useful' in recent history; they have already engaged in 'active service,' that is, in war. *Scouting for Boys* will apparently tell the boy reader how to join the ranks of these Boy Scouts – that is, how to be a *boy* scout. Then comes the complication; something serious is added. There will be more to the game than wearing a uniform and lighting a fire with two sticks: the Scout will have to learn the Law.

One voice in the handbook is rhetorical, the other symbolic. The first carries the social injunctions, the instruction in Scout Law, in good citizenship. It refers to the social codes; it is explicit, and announces itself in imperative voice, as orders to the reader: 'every boy ought to learn how to shoot and to obey orders. The other discourse works in a different way, through pictures, by association. It is essentially iconic, its meanings carried by implication: the weight of the word 'scout,' the meaning of the campfire, the significance of a war dance. This discourse refers to the code of adventure and to its associations with the imperial frontier. The two discourses support each other, the meanings of one reinforcing the values of the other, although logically, they are often in contradiction. Together, they carry the ideology of Scouting.

There is one message for the boy reader, and another for the adult. The yarn of the Mafeking Boy Scouts tells the boy a story about other boys in a war who were dressed in uniform and became soldiers, not actually shooting the enemy, but carrying orders and keeping a lookout and earning their medals. They risked their lives, B.-P. said: 'I said to one of these boys on one occasion, when he came in through rather a heavy fire: "You will get hit one of these days riding about like that when shells are flying." And he replied: "I pedal so quick, sir, they'd never catch me." These boys didn't seem to mind the bullets one bit.' The conventions of adventure apply: shells and bullets cannot hurt the hero. Then the voice switches: the Mafeking boys 'were always ready to carry out orders,' they were always ready to 'risk their life every time.' The conventions give place to the demands of the sermon: 'Would any of you do that?'[12]

To explore a little further the code of adventure: the covers of

132 Sons of the Empire

the six fortnightly parts tell the boy reader what it is that *boy* scouts do. Actions mean more than words. In the first cover a boy is spying. Concealed behind a rock, he watches a ship, his Scout's hat and staff beside him. He seems rather a small boy,* unlike the figure on the second cover, who, dressed in full kit like a soldier, with haversack and blanket roll, is tracking, studying the signs of a trail on the ground. The Scout on the third cover is also in full kit, but wears a badge. From a mountain-top or the crest of a hill, he is keeping a lookout. The fourth Scout is poling a small boat, apparently using his staff. The fifth stands on a rock with the sea behind him, holding the flag. Has he claimed a new-found-land for Britain? The Scout on the sixth cover is running, stretched out at full speed. He must be carrying a message, perhaps under fire. In all these illustrations meaning is in the doing – in tracking, observing, rowing, claiming a territory, running – and meaning refers to the adult context. These figures are scouts; it is secondary that they are also boys. Boy Scouting in its outward forms was an imitation of its adult model.

These then were the most significant parts of the code of adventure in the handbook: the use of the war scout, a glamorous military figure; the use of the scout's uniform and its associations; the hint of a secret society and its ritual; the promise of freedom in a separate world of boyhood; the sharing of adult knowledge. That the signs of the code were mixed together did not matter, for Scouting provided the context.

The frontier was the inspiration of Scouting, and in a peculiar way it also corroborated the most popular contemporary theory of male adolescent development, which stated that if only civilized boys could be trained to duplicate the savage life, then they might have everything that the savage had not yet lost – virility, hardiness, martial spirit. This seemed to justify Scouting itself. Baden-Powell liked the idea; Ernest Thompson Seton, with his own qualifications, was a whole-hearted enthusiast; and John

*This drawing was not Baden-Powell's own. The others were.

Hargrave, one of Baden-Powell's most controversial Scout officers, was a complete disciple.

The 'recapitulation' theory was the invention of G. Stanley
Hall, the distinguished American psychologist. In what was a
male-centred argument, Hall applied the the concept of evolution of species to the development of the adolescent, arguing
that each child repeated the cultural epochs of human history.
As mammals had evolved from fish, so the infant seemed to
swim; as evolution advanced to the apes, so the young child
crawled and climbed; and as our Stone Age ancestors hunted in
packs, so the pre-adolescent roamed and played in gangs. A
child, to develop and mature, should be led through the stages
of evolution. Proper habit-making was the method, the outdoors
was the scene of operations, and the crucial years were ten and
upward. This was where Scouting came in, for recapitulation
explained the movement's educational value, showing its appeal
to boys, justifying its rituals and secret codes, making sense of
the whole business of gangs of boys following spoor, rubbing two
sticks together, squatting round a campfire. Boy Scouts were little cavemen joining the brotherhood of the gang, being initiated, as one enthusiastic social worker put it, into the company
of frontiersmen 'and other romantic adventurers who also com-
prehend these magic signs.'[13] With the help of a hero-leader
they would evolve correctly towards adult ethics and morality.

William Forbush (whose layman's version of Hall's theory
Baden-Powell recommended to scoutmasters in *Scouting for Boys*)
called the process 'Reproducing the Race Life':

The psychologist, who believes that each child reproduces the
Race Life, regards the years of infancy as rehearsals of prehistoric
and feral ages, and the years of early childhood as reproductions
of the protracted and relatively stationary periods of the barbarian
days ... [it is since these ages were] so long and deep, because man
has been a savage so much longer than he has been a Christian,
that this subconscious heritage needs to be recognized, and the
work of habit-making, which is the analogue of that past, must,
during childhood, be made the central endeavour of all nurture.

In infancy the instincts had full play, in late adolescence idealism could be cultivated, but in the middle years of childhood
habit was all-important. The eleven-to-thirteen-year-old boy was
a kind of small barbarian, full of savage superstitions; the contents of his pocket and his mind revealed 'a recourse to charms,
incantations, and anthropomorphisms.' He was at an Old Testament level of development, before the dawning of conscience,
and the key to his training, naturally enough, was obedience.
'The law must come before the gospel, the era of nature before
the era of grace.'[14]

In keeping with the evolutionary origins of this theory, 'gang-
spirit' was at the centre of savage society; adapted for young
boys, 'gang-ethics' had both the advantages and drawbacks of
tribal behaviour. It was up to a youth leader to direct the natural
energy of the gang to the best goals: to work with the gang and
not against it. The gang could be like the mob, blind and con-
scienceless, packed together as a herd, following the worst. Such
were the hooligans. With a little direction from a leader, the
gang could be a band of brothers, working not for self but for
all, and united in the bonds of friendship.

The leader played a crucial role. The power of the gang, Forbush claimed, was almost always represented in one person: 'If
he be within the gang, as is usually the case, it is that virile lad
who has constituted himself the chieftain. He is the key-boy of
the group. If it be a person outside the gang, it is the adult
whom the gang has agreed to make its hero.' The gang was thus
drawn to its hero for the same reasons that a tribe of savages
honoured their chief: he was a man of power. This leader was a
fighting man, not a saint; an adventurer, not a respectable citizen. Boys liked boxers, soldiers, Teddy Roosevelt. 'It may partly
be the fascination of meeting men who are still in the feral state
that helps account for the strange associates [the boy] craves.'[15]

Here was the justification for the frontiersman – the white savage, the buccaneer, the very type of modern man in the feral
state. Here, too, was the justification for the role of youth leaders, for Seton as the Chief Indian, for Dan Beard as the Head
Man, for Baden-Powell as the Old Wolf. All were heroes for their

gangs to worship. As the boy became adolescent, so his romantic, constructive, and imaginative instincts developed. Without losing his love of his hero, he moved from the gang-stage into the 'chivalric period,' becoming a moral and responsible citizen. Scouting was, it seemed, designed to make use of this theory.

While there is no reason to believe that the recapitulation theory had much influence on Baden-Powell's thinking about Scout training, it did provide an after-the-fact justification for the movement. More crucially, it connected with his own opinions on the hardiness of the native races he had encountered on the frontier. If boys were to be encouraged to imitate feral man, then the most obvious models for Boy Scouts were those natives who had not been softened by modern society, who were disciplined, and fought well. It was 'axiomatic in the youth movements,' one early Boy Scout later reported, 'that the life of savages was far superior to that of civilized man.'[16]

It was an imperial habit of mind to divide non-Europeans into martial and non-martial races: the martial races kept their virtues sharp by war, the non-martial races were soft and 'over-civilized.' Within the Empire itself the Indian army relied on the Sikhs, and made a cult of the Gurkhas. English officers argued the merits of their opponents: the Pathan tribesmen of the Northwest Frontier were brave, the fuzzy-wuzzies of the Sudan fanatical. The Maoris, briefly, had put up a good show. The Maasai and the Swazis looked well; the Zulus, in particular, knew no fear. Among the 'civilized' nations, the Japanese, with their recent victory over the Russian fleet and their siege of Port Arthur (1904–5), were highly rated; Baden-Powell praised their courage and acts of self-sacrifice in *Scouting for Boys*. He compared their warrior code of bushido to western chivalry, and recommended books on their martial arts, such as ju-jitsu. But it was the savage races who had the most to teach the soft and degenerate Englishman.

At Isandhlwana in 1879 a British army was slaughtered by Cetshwayo's Zulus; according to the official returns, 52 officers, 806 soldiers, and over 500 native troops were killed; few at the camp escaped. The British public was shocked, and the successful defence of Rorke's Drift just afterwards hardly compensated for the surprise. Here was a native race capable of taking on trained white soldiers, and even without modern weaponry, defeating them. The Zulus were immediately romanticized: in *King Solomon's Mines* (1885) Rider Haggard brought them to life for the British public. His storyteller Allan Quatermain described the 'Kukuana' regiment as

> the most magnificent set of warriors that I have ever seen. They were all men of mature age, mostly veterans of about forty, and not one of them was under six feet in height, whilst many stood six feet three or four. They wore upon their heads heavy black plumes of Sakaboola feathers ... About their waists and beneath the right knees were bound circlets of white ox tails, while in their left hands they carried round shields measuring about twenty inches across.[17]

Under the command of his uncle General Henry Smyth, Baden-Powell had fought a Zulu army in 1888, helping defeat the rebellion of Cetshwayo's son, Dinuzulu. The sight of Zulus in action made a deep impression on him. He told soldiers who doubted their own courage to think of the Zulu saying 'if we go forward we die; if we go backward we die; better go forward and die.'* In his autobiography he was to remember the amazing sight of a friendly Zulu *impi* or regiment, their 'brown bodies polished with oil,' their splendid uniforms of feathers, furs, and cow tails, and most impressive of all, their unison singing, the few notes of a solo, the 'immense roar' of the chorus, the shields struck with assegais in accompaniment, the stamping of warriors' feet – the whole 'a glorious sound.'[18] This moment, of course, was translated into the first of the 'Scout's War Songs,' the 'Een gonyama' chorus.

In *Scouting for Boys* the Zulus make a dramatic but unexplained appearance with their war song; later in the handbook

---

*He liked this saying well enough to add it to his autograph. See Aitken, *Baden-Powell* (1901), verso of title page.

their virtues are made explicit. Becoming a Scout is a step towards manhood; the Zulus, it turns out, are scouts, and their tough initiation ceremonies are designed to cull weaklings from the tribe. When a boy is old enough he is stripped of his clothing, painted white, given a shield and an assegai, and turned out alone into the bush. He has to survive for a month, until the paint wears off. If he is seen before, he is hunted and killed. 'Unfortunately,' Baden-Powell added later, 'for the ordinary boy in civilized countries, there is nothing of this kind.'[19] He told this story to his Wolf Cubs, and made the point that Zulu society was hierarchical, with veteran warriors respected and feared by the younger men. The Zulus believed in discipline; the young boys were apprenticed to the warriors, and had to 'learn how to behave when it came to their turn.'[20] For Baden-Powell the Zulu stood quite simply as a superior fighting man, understanding the principles of good order, obeying the best of military habits. Here he was reflecting the consensus of military opinion.

The other 'savage' who enters the story of the Scout movement is the 'Red' Indian. Again, his character owed as much to popular imagination as to life: had not Cooper shown him as the one original scout, and had he not taught the North American frontiersman the secrets of the forest? As with the Zulu, the Indian too would be reinvented, revealing after all not so much his own reality as the character of his white appropriator. The imagined Indian made a very definite impact on the Scout movement, but he was never fully accepted as a suitable model of manhood. The reason for this was pragmatic: the Indian had the wrong sponsors.

It was not for want of trying. The Indian's champions pictured him as a stoical warrior superior even to the white frontiersman, a pagan more religious than a Christian, a child of nature more manly than the Anglo-Saxon, a Spartan more self-denying than the sternest Puritan. This invention was formed in the shadow of the destruction of the native nations in the American West; it had to compete against white stereotypes of the cruel or degenerate Indian, against the image of the Indian as stock villain in thousands of popular fictions. Yet the heroic brave, the real scout of scouting, had enormous appeal.

The man who carried the campaign for the Indian to its furthest point was Ernest Thompson Seton, whose nature stories (such as *Wild Animals I Have Known*) were highly popular from 1898 on and into the new century. Seton was born in England in 1860; he grew up in Canada in Toronto. He romanticized the disappearing aboriginal nations, and took an early dislike to General George Custer and all other Indian-haters. He gave his own account of his childhood in the autobiographical novel *Two Little Savages*, a story of a boy's escape from puritanical parents to a farm, where after chores were done he and the farmer's son learned to play Indian in the swamp. Seton's boyish interest in Indians began, typically enough, with James Fenimore Cooper's Leatherstocking Tales, but to these he added all the lore of the dime novels. 'He tried to do everything as an Indian would do it,' he said of Yan (himself), 'striking Indian poses, walking carefully with his toes turned in, breaking off twigs to mark a place, guessing at the time by the sun, and grunting "Ugh" or "Wagh" when anything surprised him.'[21] Yan and his friend Sam, the two little savages of the title, were taught native ways and native lore by an old man who had been a scout on the frontier: they learned how to light a fire with two sticks, how to build a teepee, shoot a bow and arrow, stalk an animal, and live at peace with each other.

If there was nothing unusual about Seton's boyhood craze, which was the adventure of many boyhoods at least since Cooper's romances were published in the 1820s, it was odd that it remained for him a lifelong ideal, and one that he promoted with an enthusiasm that only intensified the older he became. His early career as an artist and an amateur naturalist, with his years on the Manitoban prairie and his visits to the American West, together with his fascination for wild animals, were the foundation for his series of nature books. By the end of the 1890s, and now living in the United States, Seton was making a good living from these when he turned his attention back to the

Indian. He gives an account in his autobiography of the beginning of his own youth movement, the Seton Woodcraft Indians, which started when he thought of teaching a gang of boys who had been vandalizing his property the ways of Indian life and lore.[22]

His first program of woodcraft was sold in instalments to *Ladies Home Journal* (and the charter and by-laws of the Seton Woodcraft Indians was published by the magazine in 1902);[23] then followed publication of *How to Play Indian, The Birch Bark Roll*, and *The Book of Woodcraft*. He met Kipling, who told him that his Woodcraft Movement was a good thing, and just what boys needed, but that he should write some fictions to make it all more interesting. And so he published *Two Little Savages* and *Rolf in the Woods*, and went to England to see if he could start the Woodcraft Movement there. He spoke to C.B. Fry, who was working with the new boys' magazine *The Captain*, and Fry told him that the Seton Indians would hardly do for English boys: there was no discipline in the Woodcraft life.[24] In 1906, again in England, he spoke to Lord Roberts, and Roberts promised to bring the Woodcraft Movement to the attention of Baden-Powell, who was beginning to think that the youth of Britain needed training for the struggle that lay ahead. Seton gave Baden-Powell *The Birch Bark Roll*, Baden-Powell gave him *Aids to Scouting*, and both were enthusiastic with what they saw. The trouble began afterwards, for when Baden-Powell published *Scouting for Boys* in 1908, Seton claimed that his games had been copied, and the aims of his Woodcraft Movement ignored.[25] Seton, who throughout his life was apt to feel the world was against him, then entered into his long quarrel with the establishment of Scouting.

Seton's ideal had its source far from the real woods and plains, as he afterwards confessed. He looked to his own European heritage for a hero, he said, and could think of none who matched his needs. He wanted a hero who would suit North America: 'I would gladly have taken a man of our own race, but I could find none. Rollo the Sea-King, King Arthur, Leif Ericsson, Robin Hood, Leatherstocking, all suggested themselves, but none seemed to meet the requirements, and most were mere shadows, utterly unknown ... There was but one figure that seemed to answer all these needs: that was the *Ideal Indian* of Fenimore Cooper and Longfellow.'[26] This is the surprise of Seton's imagined world: his Indian model of manhood was based on fiction, and not on the living fact.

By the beginning of the twentieth century, the Indian had become a stereotypical figure in popular culture. He had been quite tamed, and had played all the parts from cruel barbarian to picturesque native. Now he might be rehabilitated and made hero. The Indian had always been the 'other' to the white man, always defined as different, or abnormal. When self or white clearly stood for civilization, and other as clearly for savagery, the racial dispositions were simple. When, as in Seton's case, the Indian represented civilization, and 'civilization' in turn was sick, then, too, the oppositions were straightforward, but their meaning was reverse and sometimes contradictory.

To Seton and his disciples in the youth movements, the Indian meant, to use his own words, nature, picturesqueness, and a Spartan character. The first linked his ideal with the cult of the outdoors, and the second with the charm of difference: with an interesting appearance, with the game of scouting, and savage warfare. As hard athlete, the 'Spartan of the West' answered the deterioration of the east, and, ironically enough, in his toughness and masculinity he echoed the self-denying ethic of Seton's own Presbyterian upbringing. Yet the Indian was not just an ideal; he represented to Seton a stage in social and psychological development. He was, in fact, the key to boy nature.

In both his fiction and his handbooks Seton had argued that boys in their Indian play would discover a primitive side of themselves: the heroes of *Two Little Savages* dance to an Indian warchant, 'till their savage instincts seemed to revive.' Seton took a theory of the instincts from the psychologist William James, who thought that the instincts were rooted in human history: to Seton the boyish taste for hunting and playing in the woods was obviously instinctual. He admitted that some Indian traits, such as love of glory, were a weakness; boys shared these, but a good youth leader could make the best of them. Later he came to see that Hall's theory of recapitulation was an obvious explanation of a young person's social development. The Jamesian instincts – fear, love, curiosity, ambition and so on – were now tailored in Seton's scheme to recapitulation: boys had the caveman instinct, the hunter instinct, the initiation instinct, the hero-worship instinct. 'Boys are nearly primitive man: they associate to hunt, fish, roam, fight and to contest physical superiority with each other,' William Forbush, Hall's popularizer, had said. Forbush approved of Seton's Woodcraft Indians: it was 'an orderly endeavour to systematize and direct that fever for "playing Indian".'[27] Through imitating the perfect savage each boy would be able to direct his instincts towards maturity. Yet the contradiction remained, for if the Indian was but a stage in the process of recapitulation, he could not at the same time be the highest type of manhood.

Seton was not a logical thinker, and he usually found it possible to ignore the difficulties of his position. His heart ruled his head. Romanticism came first. His Indian was a man who lived at one with nature, who reverenced life and the body, who denied materialism, who was a simple socialist of the woods and the prairies. He had known several North American natives, but he preferred his own ideal Indian to their more problematic and sometimes disturbing reality. In the months before he published his program of woodcraft in the *Ladies Home Journal*, he met the Sioux Charles Eastman, or Ohiyesa, a doctor and author, whose autobiography and nature stories were soon to compete with his own work. He claimed to have learned from him about Indian life. Yet Seton's Indian was not Ohiyesa's Sioux, as a reading of Ohiyesa's *Indian Boyhood* reveals. There were limits to the social harmony of the Sioux; their culture was much more complex and much less idyllic than Seton would later suggest. Sioux society depended on the strength of the individual (grandmother, uncle, medicine man); it was fiercely competitive; though the Sioux practised mutual aid within the clan, they lived in a state of tension or war with other native nations. The Sioux themselves did not place much trust in instinct, but relied on systematic training. 'It seems to be a popular idea that all the characteristic skill of the Indian is instinctive and hereditary. This is a mistake. All the stoicism and patience of the Indian are acquired traits, and continual practice alone makes him master of the art of wood-craft.' Seton's Indian, in contrast, was an expression of Seton's own dream of the uncomplicated life, his protest against his own over-sophisticated culture. 'The civilization of the Whiteman is a failure; it is visibly crumbling around us,' he said.[28]

Though Seton became Chief Scout of the Boy Scouts of America, his characteristic awkwardness, combined with his anti-militarist convictions and his devotion to the Indian, made a quarrel with the bureaucracy of Scouting inevitable, and in 1915 he was forced to resign his position. Scout officials in both Britain and the United States resisted his ideal (Dan Beard thought it was unpatriotic), and were content to fall back on the old negative stereotypes. The Indian was lazy, drunk, too much of the native; a quite unsuitable model for civilized boys. As his editor at Doubleday Page told Seton in 1908, 'there are too many Americans who think of Indians as dirty and loafing degenerates or as savages.'[29]

In England the recapitulation theory was pursued by John Hargrave, one of Baden-Powell's more charismatic scoutmasters, who, under the pseudonym of White Fox, gained for a few years considerable power in the Scout movement. He was much influenced by Seton. In *Lonecraft* (1913), *The Wigwam Papers* (1916), and *Tribal Training* (1919) Hargrave pushed the Indian as the model for the Scouts to imitate, and developed his system of 'tribal training,' on the understanding that 'the boy is a primitive man.' Hargrave's model Scout troop became an Indian tribe, with Indian names, Indian chants, and an Indian powwow. Boys took tests of initiation: the Test of the Supple Limb, the Test of the Keen Eye, the Test of the Sharp Nose, the Test of the Fleet Foot, and so on. The Indian was a non-smoker (except on formal occasions), was supple and strong (compared to the English 'loafer'), and apparently did not masturbate. He seemed in fact to resemble nothing more than a hearty lover of the outdoors, even to taking a cold dip every morning.

Baden-Powell had little time for this. Although he had at first encouraged Hargrave, and put him in charge of his camping and woodcraft centre at Gilwell Park, when it became clear that Hargrave was organizing his own movement within Scouting, his dismissal in 1921 was inevitable.[30] Baden-Powell had at first tolerated Hargrave's additions of buckskins and moccasins to Scout kit, but finally reached a point when he felt Hargrave's Indian enthusiasms had to be resisted. Baden-Powell was a pragmatist; the Indian might be occasionally useful, but he was Seton's property, and not in his own experience. In 1914 the Boy Scout Association decorated several of its publications with a striking picture of an Indian brave: he is kneeling protectively behind a Boy Scout on a hillside, and together they are looking into a rosy future (a rising sun marked by the date 1914 and a question mark). At the end of the war that followed, Baden-Powell drew a sketch of 'The Genesis of Scouting,' which showed a brave hunting down a buffalo. These pictures were as close as the movement came to accepting the Indian as an ideal of manhood. Hargrave's own interest in the Indian was as short-lived. Even before he was expelled from the Scout movement, he had set up his own rival group, abandoning tribal training in favour of a native English invention called the Kibbo Kift. This movement was based on an idea of medievalism – green jerkins and the forest – but it was not much of a success.

In summary, Scouting's advocacy of the frontier and the martial races formed a substantial element in its successful myth-making. When Ernest Thompson Seton rhapsodized about 'the magic of the campfire,' and claimed that 'no unkind feeling long withstands its glow' or when Baden-Powell quoted an old scout who believed that 'there was a charm in the open-air life [from which] one cannot free himself after he has come under its spell,' they were both giving expression to the contemporary idea that civilization itself was debilitating, and that in the fresh air lay health and the best kind of manhood, for nature, as Baden-Powell added, not only made strong men, she made 'gentle men.' Life in the open was an initiation, a test of strength: Scouts could tramp, explore, take to the water, or climb mountains.[31]

If the program offered would be defended again and again as a training in good citizenship, it had, for the first generation of Scouts, the appeal of a grand adventure, and it possessed in the campfire a romantic symbol of fellowship. As Tim Jeal says, reminding us of the often stifling confinement of middle-class Edwardian life, the idea of going off with friends on an expedition was 'intoxicating.'[32] Troops of Scouts, pulling their trek-carts, tramped out of the towns to the countryside, to camp in a farmer's field. The scene became an idyll in Scout literature: 'happy voices, joyous laughter ... [a] hike across the fields to a neighbouring village, a tracking game back to the camp, tea, games, and then a singsong round the camp fire.'[33] As Baden-Powell put it in the title of one of his later books, boys were now 'Adventuring to Manhood.'

CHAPTER FIVE

The Laws of the Jungle:
Teaching Boy Scouts the Lessons
of Good Citizenship

What life more healthy for boys, combining as it does the judicious training of brain and body, the whole ulterior object being to raise the poorest classes and prevent them from possibly drifting into hooliganism, improving their health, character, and aims, whilst it teaches the wealthier classes to extend a sympathetic comradeship to Scouts who are less socially favoured and to make them all good and useful boys – able men and patriotic citizens?

(Alfred Pearse, *Boy's Own Paper,* 1908)

In the light of what was to become Baden-Powell's most enduring creation – the well-mannered, helpful, and above all, obedient Boy Scout – there is considerable irony in his choice of the frontiersman as an ideal model of manhood. The frontiersman's virtues, whatever they were, seemed to lie at the other end of the scale from the dutiful Scout: he was his own man; if he had an attitude to authority, it was one of distrust; and he did not take kindly to military discipline. Many who had met the frontiersman, and who had worked with him, were doubtful, and reported that individualism was at best a mixed blessing.

Baden-Powell had had his own unsettling experiences. He had started as an enthusiast of the cult of the frontier, but the further his own active frontier life retreated in memory the more he came to fear what he had seen of its ugly side. In his thinking about Scouting he was torn in two. When he toured North America in 1910 he told his audiences that Canada and the United States had what he needed, the energy of the new countries and the resourcefulness of the pioneers. But he was quick to add a reservation: 'It doesn't do to make boys too self-reliant.' English boys, he said, were degenerate; what he wanted was 'to put some of the wild man back into them,' though if they 'get too wild they lack courtesy and deference to the weak and helpless.'[1] The frontier spirit was certainly the inspiration of Scouting, but it was also a danger. It needed containing; it could be inflammatory; colonial masculinity might well get out of hand.

As a rule, imperial officers were not comfortable with the idea of an independent soldier, nor were they at ease with that other colonial infection, democracy. The frontier, however, was no place for class distinction or rigid separation between officers and men. The self-declared Lost Legionary Hamilton Browne, serving as an irregular in the Maori Wars in New Zealand in the 1870s, found it was share and share alike in the Forest Rangers, and, luckily for his own peace of mind, was soon on easy terms with all his fellow troopers. The frontiersman might come from any background – there were navvies, soldiers, gold-diggers, ex-sailors, farmers' sons, public school men, defrocked parsons, drinkers of every description. It did not do to be too fussy about social origins.[2] When Baden-Powell met Browne in 1896 Rhodesia, he was entertained by his yarns of life on the edge of Empire, seeing in him the novelty of a man who could win loyalty from, and be friends with, the hard men of the ranks, who thought for himself, but who had learned to judge the formalities and stupidities of army protocol as somewhat less than appropriate in the face of a Zulu *impi*.[3] Yet Browne at least was 'Home-born,' bred to a 'fine old Irish family,' and understood the manners of the officer caste. Colonials were another matter, and they were not usually inclined to be obedient and deferential to their superiors.

The Australians were a case in point, and their bloody-mind-

edness was becoming well known. The bush balladeers, Banjo
Paterson and Henry Lawson, set down in their stories and their
verse their notion of the bushman, who, hard as nails, as good or
better than anyone else, was loyal before all else to his mates:

> They tramp in mateship side by side –
> The Protestant and 'Roman' –
> They call no biped lord or 'sir,'
> And touch their hats to no man![4]

Between them, Lawson and Paterson went a long way to describe
and create a popular Australian identity. When the Australians
reached South Africa for the Boer War their reputation had preceded them: they were rough and ready, they were horse-thieves,
and they had a casual way with discipline. To hold his own with
the English aristocrats he met, Paterson, working as a journalist,
found himself playing the part of the 'Wild Colonial Boy.'[5]

Both by training and by personal inclination, Baden-Powell
had a horror of disobedience, and in his lessons of citizenship
for Boy Scouts he came close to making a fetish of discipline.
Significantly enough, he illustrated his teaching with a tale
about the frontier. He told Scouts the story of an officer under
his command in South Africa, who though 'a brave man and an
active scout,' was 'not good at obeying orders, and in the end
this cost him his life and did harm to our plans ... if my scout had
only learnt, when a boy, how to obey orders, it might have made
a great difference that day to him, to us – and to the enemy.'[6]
Boys had to learn to obey their superiors; obedience, both for
boys and soldiers, was the first lesson of life. There is nothing
particularly striking about this story – it is one of many Baden-
Powell told on the same theme – but what appears to count is
that the disobedient scout seems to have been a Canadian.

Baden-Powell had Canadians under his command in the
South African Constabulary, and found too many of them undisciplined. He considered them wasters and loafers. 'So very few,'
he complained, 'are sufficiently sober.'[7] These memories must
have come to mind when he came to write the preface to the

Canadian Scout handbook in 1911, for he qualified a reference to the frontier tradition of Canada by a warning to every Canadian boy of the dangers of insubordination. He repeated his favourite story of the disobedient officer: 'I have no use for a fellow who cannot obey orders,' he wrote. Canadian boys are 'already good Scouts in the woods, but to be perfectly reliable you must also be sure that you are disciplined and can obey orders, however distasteful they may be, without any hesitation – and cheerily. Canada can be a very big nation in a few years if each one of you determines to do his bit in making it so. A nation is not made merely by its territory or wealth, it is made by its men.'[8] Considering the context of this advice, the criticism seems both extreme and prejudicial.

Baden-Powell's difficulty with the supposed character of the Canadian boy dramatizes the inevitable conflict between the ideal and the real, between the myth and actual experience. (Baden-Powell had no first-hand knowledge of Canada until his visit there in 1910.) The idea of the frontier did not exist of and for itself: it was strength and freedom imagined, and its expression depended equally on its sponsors' fears and dreams. Baden-Powell's criticism points to the chief puzzle – and the main strength – of the Boy Scout scheme, to the tension between its invitation to adventure, and its insistent demands for obedience and good order. The 'romance of Scouting,' to use the term Baden-Powell's admirers used, had its necessary complement in the instruction in good citizenship; which, as we shall see, was a training in the familiar and comfortable middle-class codes of behaviour, and in a simple expression of imperialism.

A preoccupation with obedience as the first virtue for young people was not peculiar to Baden-Powell, but was shared by many of his contemporaries, who remembered it as an article of Victorian faith, and saw it now as the first step in restoring national efficiency. The Boys' Brigade, formed to promote 'reverence, discipline, self-respect, and all that tends towards a true Christian manliness,' had reviewed these virtues in 1893, had added obedience, and had put it at the top of the list. Seton, in spite of his anti-authoritarian inclinations, made 'don't rebel' the first law of his Woodcraft Indians, and the theme of listening to mother ran through his animal stories. Baden-Powell reiterated this idea, quoting from the nature books by the American William Long, who, as Baden-Powell told Scouts, 'shows that animals largely owe their cleverness to their mothers who teach them while yet young.' The Chief Scout stood *in loco parentis*, and believed in an ordered hierarchy of command, for in Scouting, as in other tribes, the wisdom of the elders passed on down the line to the youngest boy, and the most junior scout was expected to look up to his patrol leader, just as the patrol leader looked up to the scoutmaster. At the top of the pyramid was the 'Old Scout.' And obedience was an important part of the theory of recapitulation. When it came time to set down the rules for the Wolf Cubs, Baden-Powell's first law, improved from the ritual of Kipling's wolf pack, was 'the Cub gives in to the Old Wolf.' The appeal of the *Jungle Book*, we can guess, was not only in its neat fit to his own persona of 'Old Wolf,' but also in the strong figures of adult authority it described.

In his subtle, resonant story Kipling had dramatized the problem of discipline and the child. Mowgli had spirit enough to break the rules, but in the end, he had to learn his lessons from Baloo the bear and Bagheera the panther. Respect your elders: there are no excuses even for a dearly loved man-cub. Obedience was the first law of the social contract: every cub of the wolf pack had to learn it; it was the man-cub's first lesson. Mowgli's safety depended on obedience, and, as it became clear, so too did the safety of the whole jungle.

> Now these are the Laws of the Jungle, and many and mighty are they;
> But the head and the hoof of the Law and the haunch and the hump is – Obey![9]

The *Jungle Book* can be read as many things – a parable on the fall from Eden, a lesson in imperialism – but here Kipling was responding to his generation's hunger for good order. The early history of the Scout movement should be read with this anxiety in mind.

Baden-Powell's concern with obedience is most obvious in the opening pages of *Scouting for Boys*, where it seems to sit awkwardly with the invitation to join up and have fun. The handbook in fact poses a question: who is the *real* Boy Scout? Its several answers suggest a paradox: a dare-devil, independent boy, full of spirit and initiative, and at the same time a boy who is clean, who does what he is told, and who is respectful to his elders and betters.

Two recent interpretations of Scouting emphasize the opposing sides of this paragon. Stressing the importance of citizenship training, Michael Rosenthal argues that Baden-Powell's intention was to produce dutiful and conforming boys who, obeying their middle-class leaders, would help arrest the decline of the nation and the Empire. Tim Jeal expresses reservations about Rosenthal's emphasis, reminding us that Baden-Powell's intentions were not so simple, and that in his prescription for the perfect boy, intelligence and individuality typically preceded loyalty and self-discipline. Jeal suggests that in fact the essence of Scouting lay in its promise of escape and in its elements of fantasy. Both positions provide part of the answer, but both tend to simplify a complex and tangled reality.[10]

Scouting was of course not one single truth, and it was directed to several different audiences. Its program depended in part on ambiguity, on the statements it made both as imaginative game and as propaganda, in its quite different appeals to the boys themselves, and to the scoutmaster or parent. For the boy it might be a wonderful adventure; for the adult it was more certainly an activity based on sensible moral precepts. For the boy, it might be a chance to join a gang; for the adult, it gave instruction in good behaviour. The lessons on good citizenship – often disguised as one more 'Camp-Fire Yarn' – were both insistent and pervasive: they were given as dogma in the Scout Law and the Scout Oath, they were explained at length under the headings of endurance, chivalry, and patriotism, they invaded every other part of the handbook's teaching, whether on woodcraft, camping, or the saving of life.

In the most familiar and obvious parts of *Scouting for Boys* – the Scout motto, the Scout Oath, and the Scout Law – Baden-Powell preached that Scouts were first of all to obey adults, particularly those in authority. Obedience was a soldierly virtue. It was not an end in itself; discipline prepared the boy, like the soldier, to serve his country. The Scout's motto was 'Be Prepared ... which means that a scout must be prepared at any moment to do his duty, and to face danger in order to help his fellow-men.' The catalogue of moral precepts, such as duty, honour, loyalty, brotherhood, courtesy, humaneness, obedience, cheerfulness, and thrift, were but a means to this end. Without preparedness the nation might be defenceless, at the mercy of its enemies. The Scout Oath (later changed to the Scout Promise) made this clear. The Scout had to promise on his honour

1. I will do my duty to God and the King.
2. I will do my best to help others, whatever it costs me.
3. I know the scout law, and will obey it.

Duty was national service, with God and the King representing the nation. The injunction to help others was expanded in the Scout Law. Linked with the duty of being useful, it was explained as self-sacrifice, and shifted from the moral to the social obligation. Knowing the Scout Law, and obeying it, became another part of a boy's duty; the emphasis in the oath itself was on obedience.

The Scout Law rested on those qualities which made the best soldier. As Michael Rosenthal points out, six of the original nine laws 'have as their essential thrust the Scout's unquestioning loyalty and his absolute willingness to carry out any orders given him.'[11] Only laws 5, 6, and 9, on courtesy, kindness to animals, and thrift, were concerned with other parts of good behaviour:*

---

*The nine laws were expressed as 'Thou shalt' rather than 'Thou shalt not,' for Baden-Powell and Scouting took pride in emphasizing the positive. The recruit would be 'born again' as a Scout; he would become all that Scout Law said he was.

1. A SCOUT'S HONOUR IS TO BE TRUSTED.
2. A SCOUT IS LOYAL to the king, and to his officers, and to his country, and to his employers.
3. A SCOUT'S DUTY IS TO BE USEFUL AND TO HELP OTHERS.
4. A SCOUT IS A FRIEND TO ALL, AND A BROTHER TO EVERY OTHER SCOUT, NO MATTER TO WHAT SOCIAL CLASS THE OTHER BELONGS.
5. A SCOUT IS COURTEOUS.
6. A SCOUT IS A FRIEND TO ANIMALS.
7. A SCOUT OBEYS ORDERS of his patrol leader or scout master without question.
8. A SCOUT SMILES AND WHISTLES under all circumstances.
9. A SCOUT IS THRIFTY.[12]

The explanation accompaning each of these laws suggested that what was important was a cheerful readiness to obey orders, and all the other virtues were secondary to discipline. The ideal Scout could be trusted (Law 1), and was faithful to his superiors, even his employers (Law 2). This last point is a particular reminder of middle-class concern about working-class behaviour, and, in its significant initial omission of the category of parent from those to whom the Scout owed obedience, again confirms Baden-Powell's fears of working-class irresponsibility.[13] The Scout was asked to obey an order because it is his duty, just like a soldier or a sailor (Law 7); he obeyed cheerily and readily (Law 8). The law on friendliness (Law 4) suggested compliance as much as egalitarianism, but proved adaptable (especially after the First World War) in the movement's shift towards international brotherhood.

Though Baden-Powell's motive was to produce a tractable, dutiful boy, some parts of the Scout Law had another emphasis, or were read as having another emphasis. The phrase 'a Scout's honour is to be trusted' soon became the touchstone of Scouting, and 'Scout's honour' passed into the language as the guarantee of truth. The handbook was taken at its word: Scouting *was* the road to good citizenship, and the Scout, for all his military pedigree, became the epitome of civilian virtue. He was kind and polite to all (Law 5); he was useful and helped others (Law 3). He did a good turn every day (Law 3). He was a friend

to animals (Law 6). He saved his pennies (Law 9). These precepts became important in broadening the adult appeal of
Scouting; they became part of the squeaky-clean image of the
movement, the young Boy Scout helping old Mrs Britannia
across the road. Here was the conundrum of Scouting: the Boy
Scout turned out to be the antithesis of the real-life frontiersman, but the frontier spirit, in its appeal to boys, made the
movement possible.

The formal instruction of Scouting represented the imposition
of middle-class ideology on young boys at large. It cannot be
understood without reference to the Edwardian class system, to
middle-class codes of behaviour, and to popular imperialism.
First, the class system. As the epigraph to the chapter suggests,
the 'poorest classes' were most in need of instruction, while the
'wealthier classes' wanted only to be taught forbearance and fellowship. Public school boys were assumed to have 'character,'
while board school boys had to be trained to conform. For all its
very real inclinations toward egalitarianism, in its first years the
Scout movement did see itself bringing the gifts of the rich to
the deserving poor.

Because there is a lack of substantial statistical evidence, the
question of the class composition of the movement is a difficult
one, but some generalizations may be made. The movement was
run by middle-class volunteers; ex-military officers and parsons,
both in Britain and in the Empire, seem to have provided most
of the scoutmasters. The difficulty in the early years of recruiting
enough of these men may have limited the growth of Scouting;
certainly this was the contemporary impression. 'Perhaps the
greatest impediment to the development of the movement,' said
one official, describing Scouting to the teaching profession in
1912, 'is the difficulty of securing as Scoutmasters gentlemen of
education, position, and experience.'[14] The last words of this
statement are revealing: the administration of the movement
took for granted that its instructors had to come from the gentlemanly, moneyed classes. The majority of the boys themselves
belonged to the middle or lower middle class, with a larger pro-

portion of recruits, relative to the general population, in the more prosperous Home Counties.[15] There were some working-class recruits, but it is fair to say that most of these were from the upper working class – that is, from that section of society which shared, sometimes to an extreme, middle-class ideas of respect-ability, thrift, and the work ethic. It is important to look at Scout-ing's main constituency, and to consider the ways in which boys themselves might, or might not, be receptive to the lessons of Scouting.

By the Edwardian years lower middle-class and upper work-ing-class children, particularly boys, were becoming more aware of themselves as a group. The consciousness of upper middle-class boys had been formed by the public schools; the conscious-ness of the lower working class was already quite distinct, and peculiarly resistant to outside influence. Scouting, to a large in-between section of British youth, was revolutionary. As one early enthusiast afterwards testified, young people of the lower mid-dle class were 'electrified' by the opportunity to break bounds and behave as they secretly wanted to. The new movement allowed this group to assert its own identity, and to react against its social oppressors.

> With an astonishing perception they leapt at Scouting as at some-thing for which they had long been waiting, divining that this was a movement which took the side of the natural, inquisitive, adven-turing boy against the repressive schoolmaster, the moralizing par-son and the coddling parent. Before the leaders knew what was happening groups were springing up spontaneously and every-where bands of boys, with bare knees, and armed with broom-sticks, began foraging through the countryside.[16]

The 'natural' boy was itself a social construct; Scouting, in invit-ing boys to behave naturally, was in effect taking an upper mid-dle-class view of childhood and making it available to a wider audience. The appeal of the movement was thus greatest to those boys from families in that uncertain territory between the middle and the working classes, in families that had the strictest ideas about upbringing, and paid most attention to the officers of respectability – to, in Leslie Paul's words, the repressive schoolmaster, the moralizing parson, and the coddling parent. Boys from this social group could now imitate their social betters and have their own imaginary adventures in the countryside, and, like Richard Jefferies' rather precious hero Bevis, turn the woods into African jungles, and an island in a pond into an exotic Formosa. Scouting now gave form and legitimacy to freedom. It made possible what previously had been reprehensible to adult authority – namely, boys in gangs wandering about the countryside. As one of the first recruits testified:

> In imagination I was a pioneer pushing my way through impenetrable jungle with the stars as my compass; then a backwoodsman of the great forests with my shelter of brushwood and my cooking fire and the smell of woodsmoke and the aroma of sizzling bacon in my nostrils. That was what Baden-Powell was offering to us – the outdoor life away from the towns, the right to do the things people told us not to do.[17]

Yet ironically, Scouting succeeded in cultivating an image of good behaviour. As one recruit from the twenties recalled, 'the Scouts were respectable in every way.'[18]

It is clear from the early history of Scouting that the main ideological battle, was fought at both edges of the movement's primary constituency. At the upper end of the social scale, Scouting was soon regarded as *declassé*, and the public schools devoted themselves to their cadet corps. Public school boys had comparatively more freedom to begin with; to them Scouting might be less revolutionary. Anything that was generally popular was suspect: public school boys could indicate class superiority only by removing themselves from the horde.

The conflict was most bitter at the other end of the social scale. The families of poor working-class children could not afford the Scout uniform, and they had an almost immediate distrust for what Scouting was offering, sensing that it was yet another organization pushing middle-class values of order and patriotism. Scouting represented to them not freedom or release from discipline at home, but one more symbol of authority. Stephen Humphries, in his analysis of working-class children's attitudes, has identified one typical form of resistance to authority as 'larking about,' a calculated and hostile behaviour in the presence of teachers, policemen, or other outsiders. Larking about was 'rooted in the aggressive, insulting and coarse traditions of working-class humour.' This behaviour was used against the youth movements, successfully frustrating most of their attempts to 'instil order, regularity and patriotic duty into the working-class younger generation.'[19] In some parts of industrial Britain, such as South Wales, Yorkshire, and the East Midlands, the working class had long disliked military recruitment, and identified Scouting with militarism.

The Scout movement thus recruited mainly from the large constituency between these two extremes. Scout troops were taught to recognize their 'natural' class enemy. They were told to hold their heads high when street-corner louts called them names; they were told not to fight with working-class gangs.* The world was divided simply in two, the regenerate and the degenerate, as a verse in an early number of *The Scout* made quite clear:

> Gathered at the corner are the Slouchers,
> Huddled limply up against the wall;
> Their cigarettes a-smoulder,
> Dirty-fingered, round of shoulder,
>   Frowsy-looking wasters, one and all.
> Which is one to take for an example?
>   Fellows like these good-for-nothing louts,
> Or the lads who come along
> With their bugles going strong,

---

*Scout propaganda tried to prove that class hostility could be redeemed. An early Boy Scout film showed a Scout troop being set upon by a crowd of hooligans; they defend themselves with their staves, one lout trips and falls into the river, he is rescued by a Scout, the troop provides artificial respiration, and so makes a convert.

Ramping past,
Tramping past,
Merrily as a song?
Choose between the Slouchers and the Scouts![20]

These lines contain most of the prejudices of this particular side-show of class warfare: the Slouchers are limp, dirty, and smelly, the Scouts strong and straight-backed.

For its first recruits, then, Scouting provided an identity. It allowed boys to assert those feelings which, as members of their class and age group, they already possessed: adventurousness, within limits; loyalty to each other; a need for achievement; a desire for some freedom from adult control. At the same time, Scouting's program of social training was not often inhibiting to the majority of boys who joined. Scouting preached little that was outside the boundaries of dominant middle-class belief; since most recruits were already conditioned to accept this teaching, moral instruction did not often seriously interfere with Scouting fun. Baden-Powell was aware of the danger of boring his audience; his intention was always to make moral and patriotic instruction interesting.

Baden-Powell's lessons in good citizenship reflected middle-of-the-road opinion. The success of *Scouting for Boys* as a popular text was based on his extraordinary ability to set down in a straightforward way the basic tenets of conservative morality and popular imperialism; the success of the movement itself rested on his ability to weld these articles of faith onto the movement's innovative frontier image. Both symbol and dogma were necessary to the success of Scouting; the one captured the imagination, the other 'normalized' the new. The Boy Scout, his bare knees at first almost an indecency, was transformed by the familiarity of sensible advice into the good citizen, till he became for the middle class a symbol of cleanliness, courtesy, and honour. Our own familiarity with this lingering image of the Boy Scout may prevent us from seeing where the ideal came from.

It is the business of ideology to indoctrinate its audience in the values of their class, gender, and race. Boys are not only told how to behave; they are given an identity. The moral and social codes are necessarily concerned with the essential interests of their sponsors, with questions of power, with who belongs, and who does not. Middle-class boys will be instructed in each of these parts of knowledge: they will be told why they are superior to others, and who is different from them. Working-class boys may be expected to accept the same values, while their own, illegitimate, beliefs are discounted. The silences of the codes – what they do not say – are a part of the discourse. The conventions of the public school code, for instance, in which women appear as either mothers or sisters and are thus something between a sacred object or an embarrassment, are evidence of a definite and pronounced ideological statement on gender. The public school code was concerned in the first place with making men; both here, and in the Scout movement itself, a feminine presence was notably and crucially absent.

In *The Lanchester Tradition* (1913), G.F. Bradby's novel of English public school life, a new headmaster, an outsider to the system, is appalled at the conservatism, self-interest, and philistinism that he finds in his new school. 'He had always taken on trust,' the reader is told, 'the virtues that are considered inherent in the public school system – loyalty, discipline, gentlemanly behaviour, and a subordination of the individual will to the interests of the community.'[21] Leaving aside Bradby's critical tone, this list of the public school virtues, which may be taken as typical for the slightly earlier Edwardian years, could be applied equally to the social morality of *Scouting for Boys*. For 'instruction in good citizenship,' the sub-title of Baden-Powell's handbook, the 'subordination of the individual will to the interests of the community' becomes of prime importance. Loyalty, duty, and gentlemanly behaviour follow closely behind. Boy Scouts were taught that good behaviour and a sense of responsibility were not limited to the privileged few. They were shown that, in the performance of their cheerful service to the community and to the nation, they belonged to the same sort of superior club as the public schools.

Though we should not forget that Baden-Powell was a soldier, with a soldier's outlook on life, an important element of the ethic of Scouting draws strength from Baden-Powell's public school experience. Baden-Powell had been to Charterhouse; the values of his school, and the brotherhood of his fellow old boys, were to remain with him for life. There is a revealing passage in one of his early books, when he describes an encounter with a fellow Carthusian in a West African jungle.

> Surely we have seen that eye and brow before, although the beard and solar topee do much to disguise the man. His necktie of 'Old Carthusian' colours makes suspicion a certainty, and once again old school fellows are flung together for an hour to talk in an African swamp of old times on English playing fields.[22]

This image of two Englishmen meeting each other by chance in some part of the Empire and discovering that they shared their school days is a classic Victorian motif, a sign of fraternity, of the superiority of the chosen, and the burden of duty. The old school tie is a symbol of a masculine world of shared experience, its wearing an image of belonging.

The officer caste shared public school values: it cherished conformity, it insisted upon discipline, it relied upon a hierarchy of command. In 1900 the biographers of the nation's newest military hero picked out Baden-Powell's public school career as the pivotal ingredient in his triumph, the foundation of his character. Every successful regimental officer owed his success to his public school, it seemed; his school and its ideals were the essence of Englishness. When Harold Begbie's *The Wolf That Never Sleeps* was reviewed in the *Public School Magazine* in July 1900, the reviewer noted that the author had seen fit to dedicate his work to public schoolboys in particular; Begbie's biography of Baden-Powell was 'the very best sermon upon how a boy, and afterwards a man, should live.' He thought it 'a delightful and instructive life-story of a brilliant soldier and an honest English gentleman,' and declared that it would appeal to 'all who love a breezy tale of adventure, and admire a clean, straightforward, manly life.'[23]

It is difficult to isolate Baden-Powell's use of the public school code in *Scouting for Boys*, for the ethic permeates the handbook. In general, Scouting broadened the base of the code, while retaining its basic features; Scouting was a less exclusive club, but Scouts were still expected to 'play the game.' For Baden-Powell the morality of the Scout was centred in personal conduct, in behaving honourably, in being loyal to friends, and in obeying exactly the rules of the movement. The Scout was, if not an absolute conformist, an obedient follower; above all, he was expected to be a gentleman.

In his yarns in the handbook on how to behave, Baden-Powell advised unselfishness, self-sacrifice, kindness, and generosity – all virtues which demanded that the Scout put others before himself. He spoke of the right kind of friendliness (but warned Scouts about the foolishness of wasting their money 'standing treat'), of politeness to all, including social inferiors, and of courtesy to women. The sexes, of course, would remain separate. These thoughts are all quite orthodox for the time, referring to the upper middle-class code of the gentleman, and incorporating the Victorian idea of chivalry. No part of this morality would have jarred with ideals spoken of within the public schools, although Kipling's Stalky & Co. – the realists of public school fiction – would have criticized its tone as pious.

Again, Baden-Powell's attitude to religion matched the accepted attitude of the public schools: it was sensible, and generous; it was not doctrinaire, and, in keeping with the contemporary mood, it was far from evangelical. Every Scout should believe in God, he said, and do good to other people. Religion was a very simple thing; it did not matter that there were different sects. He told Scouts the favourite Victorian story – taken from Bede's *Ecclesiastical History* – of the pagan noble's response to Bishop Paulinus, who had been sent by Gregory to convert King Edwin's Northumbrian court. Life was like the flight of a sparrow 'through the great hall, when one is sitting at meals with the log-fire blazing on the hearth, and all is storm and darkness outside.' The sparrow hovers for a short time in the warmth and the light, and then flies out again into the darkness.* So it is with the life of man – until the coming of Christ, who 'has opened a door for us to enter a brighter room.' Scouts should remember the sparrow, and try to do good on their short flight through life. Baden-Powell's refusal to go further than this was an important factor in making Scouting accessible to a wide constituency. Though he was accused of not paying enough attention to religion, he resisted attaching the movement to the established church.

In his advice on self-discipline, Baden-Powell's thoughts were again in line with public school ideals, and his language was the diction of the public schools, though his specific advice belongs to a somewhat old-fashioned standard. He spoke of the value of honour: 'a captain sticks to his ship to the last.' He talked of fair play, noting that it was in the British tradition – 'other nations are not all so good.' He demanded honesty, and said that cheating at any time was a sneaking, underhand thing to do (a more realistic public school judgment made a distinction between cheating to avoid work – permissible – and cheating for personal gain – criminal.[24] He insisted that true Scouts were good losers: 'you will at once cheer the winning team or shake hands with and congratulate the fellow who has beaten you.' The language of the public schools permeates almost all his writing: referring specifically to the advantages of a public school education in *Rovering to Success* (1922), he says that the best things there are 'learnt on the playing field,' such as 'clean play and true sportsmanship,' 'straight dealing and sense of honour.' Every public schoolboy can expect to be 'licked into shape' by his comrades.[25]

To summarize Baden-Powell's relationship to the public school code, it should be reiterated that he and his movement cannot be understood outside of its context. His attitudes in all things were not quite orthodox. Though his advocacy of cold baths and physical fitness was in tune with the cult of athleticism, he did not push team games within the Scout movement. Nor

---

*Rider Haggard puts this much of the story into the mouth of his Zulu hero Umbopa in *King Solomon's Mines.*

did he advocate a class-conscious sense of superiority; any boy
could be a Scout. He spoke about, and paraded in public, those
feelings which Kipling considered a public schoolboy guarded
in his heart, which should remain sacred and apart, unmentioned but understood by all: patriotism, duty, loyalty, the flag –
the holy subjects which Raymond Martin, MP, Stalky's 'Jelly-bellied Flag-flapper,' cheapened before the boys of the United Services College. He was a popularizer, and if he had any qualms, if
he felt in any way that he was profaning the public school temple, he gave no sign, and indeed, his attendance at high and
holy days at his old school, Charterhouse, was exemplary.[26]

Although the public school code might appear to be the dominant influence in the moral fabric of Scouting, there is an
equally important middle-class ethic which, though easy enough
to identify, is not so readily labelled. We know, or suppose we
know, what Victorian values were: a set of beliefs centred around
the responsibility of the individual, a trust in hard work, thrift,
sobriety, and family life. This ethic is summed up in the idea of
self-help, in the need to work hard and make a success of oneself
in life. Self-denial was part of its nature, cleanliness one of its
chief virtues. It was connected to evangelical morality, and
closely linked to the cult of respectability. It may be described as
the most thoroughgoing expression of the ideology of work. It
could include a considerable distrust of governmental interference or social legislation: deserving cases among the sick and
unemployed might be given charity, but if the mass of the poor
would not help themselves they were probably lazy, improvident,
without ambition, and certainly dirty. The prophet of self-help
was Samuel Smiles, author of *Self-Help* (1859), *Lives of the Engineers* (1861–2), *Character* (1871), *Thrift* (1875), *Duty* (1880), and
Life and Labour (1887). These popular works were all written to
the same pattern, in which Smiles illustrated the moral precept,
again and again, with stories from the lives of successful men.

Self-help is a powerful presence in *Scouting for Boys*; one of
Baden-Powell's stories will do for illustration. Two frogs fall into
a bowl of cream. One gives up and drowns; the other, 'a more

manly' frog, keeps on struggling to swim, and just as even he is ready to abandon hope he finds himself standing 'all safe' on a pat of butter. His fable demonstrates Smiles's crucial virtue of perseverance, for, as Baden-Powell says, 'a man who cannot face hard work or trouble is not worth calling a man.' The idea of work is linked to masculinity: the virility of a man is defined by his ability to churn through life for the material reward of his labour. Why was this ethic thought necessary for young boys? Baden-Powell was a strong believer in Victorian values. His precepts in *Scouting for Boys* were not, of course, exactly the same set of values which had so influenced middle-class society fifty years before – social conditions had changed, perceived social needs were different, a shift of emphasis was inevitable – yet it is remarkable how persistent the old moralities were. For his own reasons, Baden-Powell preferred to trust a code that placed the onus for change on the individual, and sought the resolution of social problems such as poverty, drink, bad health, and the wasted lives of young people in the good habits of hard work and thrift.

His social animus was directed against the bogy of the hooligan, against working-class loafers and shirkers, and against the possibility of lower middle-class boys joining the degenerate in their idleness. He had read studies of the problem of deprived or criminal adolescent boys in such texts as Charles Stelzle's *Boys of the Street and How to Win Them*, Robert Sherard's *The Child Slaves of Britain*, and Bramwell Booth's *The Abandoned Child*, all of which he recommended to scoutmasters. His attitude to the problem was straightforward: Scouting (that is, useful and profitable work), accompanied by lessons in good citizenship, was a sufficient cure for the social disease. The work of Scouting was presented to boys as fun, but fun with a purpose in mind.

The surveys of Charles Booth in London (1889–1903), and Seebohm Rowntree in York (1901) had gone far to discredit the common Victorian assumption that poverty was the fault of the poor themselves: both Booth and Rowntree showed that poverty was endemic, and that upwards of a third of the people were poor. Unemployment, disease, drinking, the behaviour of boys on the streets, were not the curable habits of an ignorant and wilful population, but rather the results of being underpaid and hungry. Ideas of social responsibility gained ground during the Edwardian years: Lloyd George, leading the radical wing of the Liberal party, advocated social reforms, and succeeded, between 1908 and 1911, in moving the Old Age Pensions Act and National Health Insurance Act through Parliament. Baden-Powell, however, held fast to conservative opinion, and believed that even the poorest boy might pull himself out of the gutter. 'Some of you are certain to become rich men, and some of you may die in poverty and misery. And it just depends on your own selves.'

Baden-Powell considered that the moral training of a boy was at the heart of good citizenship, and gave in *Scouting for Boys* explicit advice on self-improvement. Prefacing a long Camp-Fire Yarn with a word to potential scoutmasters, he said that the subject 'opens ... a wide field for the most important work of all in this scheme of Boy Scouts, and gives you the opportunity for doing really valuable work for the nation.' He focused on the problem of boys' spare time, on the absolute necessity for boys to be usefully active or employed in work that had a future. 'A great amount of poverty and unemployedness,' he told scoutmasters, 'results from boys being allowed to run riot outside the school walls as loafers, or from being used early in life as small wage-earners, such as errand boys, etc. and then finding themselves at the commencement of manhood without any knowledge of a trade to go on with, and unable to turn their hand to any work out of their one immediate line.'* His emphasis was thus on work. Addressing the boys, he divided his self-improvement Yarn into six loosely defined sections: duty to God, thrift, how to make money, how to get on, sobriety, and fortitude (these are interrupted by hints and practical suggestions).

His chief concerns can be gauged by listing what he was against: loafers and slackers, the selfish, the improvident, the

---

* *Scouting for Boys*, 259. He seems here to be referring to a problem discussed in one of the social texts he recommended to scoutmasters, Leslie Cornford's *The Canker at the Heart.*

self-indulgent, the cowardly, and the disobedient. His yarns on self-improvement, thrift, getting on, and sobriety are explicit advice to such potential sinners, but as important a remedy to backsliding is the doctrine of work. His practical advice is constructed around information and activity; boys must be given knowledge, and they must be taught how to employ themselves usefully and profitably. Thus they are told all sorts of useful knowledge, from how to dig latrines to how to fell trees, and they are expected, as Scouts, to learn useful skills, proving their competence by adding one badge after another to their sleeves.

The work of these hobbies very quickly became an essential part of Scouting, and its extent was demonstrated to the public during the first Scout exhibitions. At the Birmingham display of 1913, for instance, an event attended by five thousand Scouts, Scouts were showing their skills as carpenters and farmers, printers and basket-workers. 'In the arena and in surrounding booths, Scouts who had earned the Pioneer's badge were building bridges and signal towers; Cooks were cooking; Signallers signalled; Cyclists cycled; Firemen put out fires; Ambulance-men gave first aid while still other Scouts demonstrated the physical fitness side of scouting through wrestling and boxing, gymnastics and Swedish drill.'[27] Not surprisingly, Baden-Powell recommended in *Scouting for Boys* a considerable number of guides to crafts and hobbies, from carpentry to raffia work. He also listed many handbooks on physical fitness.

If Baden-Powell's repeated emphasis on work was characteristic of the self-help ethic, so too were his attitudes to cleanliness and to sex. Smiles had regarded cleanliness as 'more than wholesomeness'; it was the essence of self-respect, it was part of the moral condition. It was, moreover, 'the best exponent of the spirit of Thrift.'[28] Baden-Powell's insistent advice on washing and the cold bath, and beating one's underwear in the morning with a stick (to shake out lice or fleas), echoed not just his contemporaries' search for good health, but at the same time showed a practical knowledge of the habits of the poor, coloured of course by distaste. The middle class was clean, the working class dirty and verminous: 30 per cent of all school children in

London were found to be flea bitten in 1907.[29] To be clean was to be morally superior: in Smiles's words, 'the dirty classes of the great towns are invariably the "dangerous classes" of those towns.'[30] Baden-Powell's advice on sex was again characteristic of his caste, though perhaps it was more outspoken than would be typical. He told his Scouts to be chaste, for in line with most of his contemporaries he believed that masturbation led to degeneracy. Baden-Powell's blunt advice on masturbation has been mocked by several recent writers, though his beliefs were quite in line with contemporary medical theory: G. Stanley Hall, for instance, stated that there was 'a close bond between this habit and degeneracy.'[31] Tim Jeal, as part of his psycho-sexual approach to his subject, attributes Baden-Powell's tone to latent homosexuality, claiming that he was intensely fearful of sex, and fought a 'ferocious lifelong battle against masturbation.'[32] This is as may be. Saving semen, like saving pennies, was another good habit to be practised on the road to manhood.

Baden-Powell recommended Samuel Smiles to his young readers. Much of his moral advice was expressed in Smiles's tones, and his illustrations often seem to be taken from *Self-Help*, *Character*, *Thrift*, or *Duty*. He wanted his readers to take responsibility for their own moral development. He had Smiles's sense of the importance of living for the good of others, and for performing one's duty to the country. He shared Smiles's fondness for penny savings (a Scout had to have at least sixpence in the savings bank), and he shared Smiles's hatred of idleness and drink. He reused many of Smiles's maxims, such as 'save your pence and you'll get pounds.' He was, like Smiles, something of an egalitarian. Curiously, he also reiterated Smiles's objections to bearing reins, and to the cruelty they inflicted on horses. There was however another, and louder, voice of self-help.

When Baden-Powell was busy writing *Scouting for Boys* in 1907, and during the first, chaotic months of the movement, he had the assistance of the journalist Peter Keary, who was working for the newspaper owner Arthur Pearson. Keary was also the author of Pearson's Success Library, a collection of self-improvement books such as *The Secrets of Success*, *Get On or Get Out*, *Do It Now!*,

and *Success after Failure*. These, in a spirit of unrelenting cheerfulness and a flood of jokey catch-phrases, told readers that all it
took to succeed in life was energy, hard work, and self-interest.
Though at first sight it might seem that a man of Keary's commercial type would be anathema to Baden-Powell's gentlemanly
breeding, the two had something in common. Both had a sense
of what the public wanted to hear. Willingly or unwillingly,
Baden-Powell recommended Keary to his readers, and Keary's
voice echoed through the pages of *Scouting for Boys*.[33] The book
which made Keary a household word was *Do It Now!* Here he dispensed 'Sure-Cure Pills' for 'despondent young men,' a collection of slogans set out in headlines: 'don't monkey with your
character.' 'Man, know thyself.' 'Don't spend all you earn.'
'Manage your time.' He introduced, as though he was reporting
a horse race, the 'success stakes result:

1. HARD WORK.
2. INTELLIGENT STUDY.
3. KEEP AT IT.

Also ran: wish it was pay day, can't stop, born tired, going court-
ing, don't care, not my job.'[34] Keary's slogans were common currency in 1908, as that reliable guide, P.G. Wodehouse's Psmith,
did not fail to note. 'That,' said Psmith approvingly, 'is right.'
'Speed is the keynote of the present age. Promptitude. Despatch. This is no time for loitering. We must be strenuous. We
must hustle. We must Do It Now.'[35]

The connection between Keary and Baden-Powell was more
than their original business together: they each shared the same
liking for a catch-phrase, making self-help a matter of uplift and
hearty fun. At the Birmingham exhibition of 1913 a publicist for
the Scouts noticed the mottoes that decorated the walls of the
exhibition pavilions, which were

exhortations which laugh in the face of sorrow, and are eloquent
of the spirit that is behind these bare-armed, bare-kneed boys,
who turn London suburbs into prairie land with their swift imagination, and replant the streets of Birmingham with the oak, the
ash, and the thorn of old England. The mottoes ... are all put

before the boys by their versatile Chief Scout. They read: 'Be a brick.' 'Pass it on.' 'Try whistling.' 'The oak was once an acorn.' 'Smile all the time.' 'Stick to it, stick to it.' 'Don't stand with your back to the sun.' 'Don't shoot the musician, he's doing his best.' 'Softly, softly catchee monkey.' 'When the cat's away, the mice will play (the little rotters!).'[36]

The last section of Baden-Powell's program of education in *Scouting for Boys* was called 'Patriotism; or, Our Duties as Citizens.' It began with a lesson on the Empire. The Empire, Baden-Powell said, needed the help of boys. Rome fell because of bad citizenship, bad citizenship was apparent in England today, football and other spectator sports were a symptom of decay, Scouting was a scheme to make good citizens. To begin with, Scouts must learn about the Empire, 'how it grew,' and 'how it must be held.'[37] They must be taught the meaning of the imperial symbols.

For many of his fellow Victorians, Sir John Millais's painting *The Boyhood of Raleigh* had a particular importance, for it seemed to dramatize the imperial destiny of the nation. Raleigh is seen as a young boy on the seashore, sitting with his knees drawn up, listening intently to an old sailor. The sailor is telling a yarn, and pointing out across the ocean. From this imagined moment of history, this image of adventure stirring in young Raleigh's mind, come reminders of a glorious past, and whispers of a triumphant future. As the Elizabethan seamen sailed forth to conquer the New World, so too the present generation of Englishmen might follow the pointing finger out across the seas toward the ends of the Empire. Baden-Powell redrew *The Boyhood of Raleigh* for *Scouting for Boys*, adding as caption 'Instruction of Boy Scouts.' Scouting was carrying on the heroic imperial dream.

Drawing on a familiar patriotic vocabulary, Baden-Powell told his Scouts that the history of the Empire was a history of exploration and expansion: the Crusaders had carried chivalry into distant parts of the earth, Raleigh and Drake had faced the dangers of unknown seas and powerful enemies to take and

9 'The Uncles' – Ernest Thompson Seton, Baden-Powell, Daniel Beard, 1910

10 *Above*: 'The Boyhood of Raleigh,' painted by Sir John Millais, 1870

11 *Right*: Ernest Thompson Seton in Indian costume, 1917

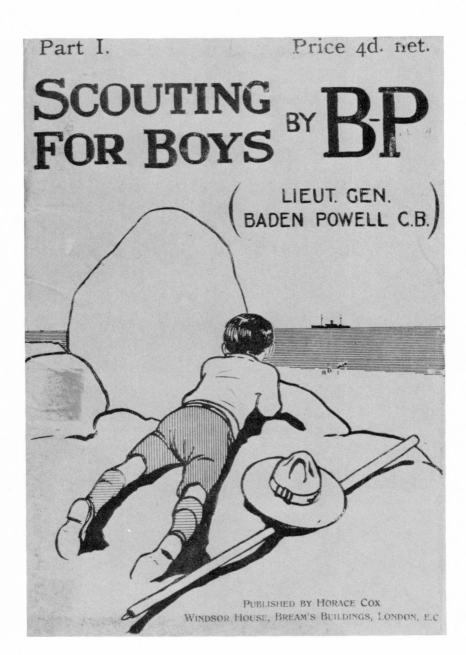

12 Cover of Part 1 of *Scouting for Boys*, 1908

13 *Punch*'s cartoon of 1911 reproduced on the cover of a report for
Canadian Boy Scouts, 1912

ABOUT TORONTO'S LACROSSE TEAM—ILLUSTRATED.

CHUMS

No. 509.—Vol. X.] JUNE 11, 1902.

14 *Above*: The spirit of adventure: a young frontiersman in a tight spot.
Chums, 11 June 1902

15 *Right*: 'Our Youngest Line of Defence': Boy Scout to Mrs Britannia:
'Fear not, Gran'ma, No danger can befall you now, remember
I am with you.' *Punch*, Sept. 1909

16 'The Scouts on a doomed ship demand to be treated as men.'
Arthur Mee's Hero Book

hold new lands, Cook and Clive had opened up new countries, Livingstone had pushed his way through the deserts and forests of Africa, and Franklin had braved the ice and snow of the Arctic. And there were women heroes too who had been courageous, and who had shown that girls as well as boys could do useful work in the world as they grew older.[38] The names of the heroes marked the record of the past; their deeds verified the cause of Empire. They were all frontiersmen, and peace scouts. Boys had to be taught the meaning of their story.

It was to his favourite hero, Captain John Smith, the Elizabethan colonizer of Virginia, that Baden-Powell gave the lines which epitomize his version of imperialism. 'Our mission,' Smith said, in a play on the story of Pocahontas that comes early in *Scouting for Boys*, 'is to *clean* the world.' This vision of a dirty world waiting for the good order, common sense, and decency of English rule is a striking fusion of the ideologies of puritanism and imperialism, but it is by no means untypical of contemporary opinion, saying obviously what is often less clearly expressed by more tactful writers. Baden-Powell's Smith was a splendid character who always did his duty, 'a tremendous worker, very keen, and very brave.' He had, in fact, all the qualities a Boy Scout should admire, and most of all, he put his soldiers – and his country – before himself. As he proclaims to the wondering Indians in Baden-Powell's play, 'I am ... an Englishman, which is something more than a mere man.'[39]

To understand this statement, which probably now seems extreme in its jingoism, we have to place it in the context of 1908. *Scouting for Boys* had as one of its chief aims the making of good citizens, and good citizens were above all patriots. Baden-Powell believed in the lessons of history. Throughout his handbook he cited example after example of the heroes who had created what was clearly a magnificent and valuable thing, the British Empire. He gave their names and their deeds, he drew their pictures. He dramatized their actions in plays and tableaux. He lectured on their patriotic sacrifice. Scouts should follow the path they had marked out.

In the whole of this considerable educative exercise, Baden-

Powell was drawing on a well-formed myth of an heroic and triumphal history. The popular version of this myth can be found in the stories that were used to teach Victorian and Edwardian children patriotism, in which a number of historical incidents demonstrate a more or less uninterrupted progress towards the sane and satisfactory present. During the years 1880 to 1914 there was a noticeable shift, as part of an emerging imperial consciousness, from a utilitarian or Christian social morality to a more obviously patriotic program. At a popular level, the strengthening of the Empire was also proposed as the cure for a decadent society; this meant not only painting the map red, but training a generation to think imperially, to prepare itself to serve the nation. The young had to be given 'character' to make them fit and willing to work in the imperial cause.[40]

The educative role of this myth of an heroic history was central. Boys and girls could be taught imperial values; they could learn the meaning of duty and sacrifice through the drama of the past, which, now and again, threw up perfect types guaranteed to appeal to their youthful idealism. Nelson, said Dr Gordon Stables, in his preface to an historical novel Baden-Powell advised his Scouts to read, was 'notably a boy's hero; so good, so gentle, and yet withal so brave.[41] Alfred Miles, introducing a series of imperial reciters, distinguished between true and false imperial sentiment, the first belonging to 'the man of thought, who believes in the destiny of his race,' the second 'born of avarice and vanity, and sustained by brute force.' He claimed that the right kind of verse would encourage 'a healthy National spirit.'[42] In this kind of imperial program the exemplary life of the hero testified to England's glorious past, to her proud present, and to her dream of the future. The heroic life – Drake's, Nelson's, or Gordon's – was referred to in every patriotic lesson.

It makes little sense to separate here the myth as it appears in history or fiction; what is of account is its imaginative rendering. Charles Kingsley in *Westward Ho!* (1855) had told the story of the Devonshire lad Amyas Leigh, who sailed with Drake around the world, lost his sweetheart to the Jesuits, plundered gold on the

Spanish main, and fought the galleons of the Armada. No reader could mistake the message. Introducing that great sea-fight of 1588, Kingsley proclaimed the common belief that the Armada was a turning point in history, determining 'whether Popery and despotism, or Protestantism and freedom, were the law that God had appointed for the half of Europe, and the whole of future America.'[43] The blood of the bold Elizabethans beat in the veins of the men of the modern age; England's glory was that she had been chosen to dominate the world in an Anglo-Saxon Protestant hegemony.

As Thomas Hughes reminded his readers, opening *Tom Brown's Schooldays* (1857), 'much has yet to be written and said before the British nation will be properly sensible of how much of its greatness it owes to the Browns,' who had for centuries 'been subduing the earth in most English counties, and leaving their mark in American forests and Australian uplands.' These Browns, 'getting hard knocks and hard work in plenty,' were the men who fought at Crecy and Agincourt, who fought the Span-iards and the Dutch, who served with Wolfe, Nelson, and Well-ington, and who now 'are scattered over the whole empire on which the sun never sets.'[44] And as Tom's own story set out to show, as long as England produced Browns in abundance, England's place in the sun was sure. Popular history, little differ-ent in its romantic nature from fiction, became a parade of Tom Browns, a recitation of their brave deeds that showed the nature of English manhood. The virtues of courage, self-sacrifice, stead-fastness under fire, and endurance were repeated in example after example.

Racial theory, so large a part of this myth, is significantly ambiguous. The English were either a mongrel race, and hence stronger, and better; or a pure race, and hence stronger, and bet-ter. Charles Kingsley's Devon men in *Westward Ho!* were a mix-ture of 'trusty Saxon serfs,' 'free Norse rovers with their golden curls,' and 'dark Silurian Britons'; their mingled blood the source of their strength and intellect, and their 'peculiar beauty of face and form.' But the English at the same time were Anglo-Saxons, a distillation of the best of the northern races, Saxons,

Danes, and Vikings. This accounted for their vigour, for their love of fighting, and their need for adventuring. As Ernest Protheroe pointed out, in a history Baden-Powell told his Boy Scouts to read, the Norman conquest was not a calamity, because the Normans were originally Norsemen; they were of the same blood as Harold and his Saxons. When Saxon met Celt, it was the Saxon who overcame: in Dr Gordon Stables's *Hearts of Oak* the Englishman typically enough boxes the Welshman into submission, and thus wins his loyalty. 'I want to be with a brave man,' the Welshman confesses to his English conqueror.[45]

This then is part of the contemporary context for *Scouting for Boys*. Baden-Powell told Scouts that other nations were pressing forward in the race for empire; he added that England could not afford to sit still or let things slide. 'If every citizen of the Empire,' he said, 'were to make himself a really good useful man, our nation would be such a blessing to the civilized world, as it has been in the past, that nobody would wish to see it broken up by any other nation.' Scouts were to be prepared: the true patriot was the man or boy who would be useful to his country when the time came, and who knew that 'UNITED WE STAND. DIVIDED WE FALL.' What could boys do? They could help the police, they could learn to shoot. They could begin by understanding the meaning of the navy and the army, the history of the flag, the organization of the government, and the role of 'our king,' whose title of Emperor meant 'be prepared.'[46] Baden-Powell directed scoutmasters to the usual authorities on imperialism, to H.O. Arnold-Forster's *History of the British Empire*, to Sir C.E. Howard Vincent's *Through the British Empire in Ten Minutes* (Vincent was a Conservative MP who designed an imperial map for schools), to books on the nation's heroes buried in Westminster Abbey and St Paul's, to Fitchett's *Deeds that Won the Empire*, and to Sanderson's *Heroes of Pioneering*.

Like many of his contemporaries who wrote for children, Baden-Powell considered heroic history important in the education of recruits. Addressing himself to potential scoutmasters, he told them to fly the flag on every appropriate occasion; to get up small pageants to illustrate scenes from history, to take Scouts to the service museum and show them models of Waterloo and Trafalgar. He went further, and mentioned episodes he thought most suitable for staging, such as Major Wilson's last stand in Matabeleland, the wreck of the *Birkenhead,* or the sentry at Pompeii.* He thought that the storming of Badajoz, an incident from the Peninsular War against Napoleon, could be made into a game between sides, French and English. He provided a script for the storming of Delhi (the assault on the Cashmere gate during the Indian Mutiny), which made a point of English audacity and martial sacrifice, and he adopted Sir Henry Newbolt's poem describing a confrontation between the hero of the Mutiny, John Nicolson, and a rebellious native leader, Mehtab Singh. In Baden-Powell's rendering, Nicolson lectures Mehtab Singh on the meaning of the Empire, and on the secrets of imperial rule: 'You forget that you are dealing with a Briton – one of that band who never brooks an insult even from an equal, much less from a native of this land.' Britons must be respected – 'that's how we hold the world.'[47] These tableaux, clumsy as they may be as theatre, are sufficient lessons of imperial power and racial superiority. Not untypically, considering the contemporary change towards a more secular patriotism, Baden-Powell had little room in his propaganda for Victorian models of Christian virtue such as General Sir Henry Havelock, the hero of the Indian Mutiny, or General 'Chinese' Gordon, the martyr of Khartoum. He preferred Sir Henry Newbolt's more straightforward images of heroism.

In one tableau we can see Baden-Powell's quite orthodox linking of the public school code and the Empire, when he made use of the favorite Edwardian patriotic poem, Newbolt's 'Vitaō Lampada,' with its contrasting scenes of the school cricket match and the regiment's last stand in the desert, and its simple

---

*The last two were both familiar examples of discipline and self-sacrifice for duty's sake: soldiers on the troopship *Birkenhead* had stood to attention when the ship went down; the sentry at Pompeii had stood faithful at his post to death. These stories were cited by Smiles, and were also in Charlotte Yonge's *Book of Golden Deeds,* which Baden-Powell recommended to Scouts.

story of duty and good form. He renamed the poem 'Play the Game.' Taking the sequence of the verses, Baden-Powell's version fell into three scenes. In the first tableau boys are playing cricket, with the captain stepping up to the batsman, and saying to him, 'Play up! Play up! And play the game!' In the second tableau, soldiers in a hard-fought fight are retreating, when an officer stands, and pointing his sword at the enemy, repeats the refrain of the poem. 'Playing up,' they charge. (This is a little different from Newbolt, whose verse suggests the image of the last stand.) The final scene is a procession of men of all ages, conditions, and white nations within the Empire, linked hand-in-hand. Their leader flings out a Union Jack, calling to the rest, 'Play up!' etc., and his words are echoed by the smallest boy, who steps forward and repeats them to the audience.

Besides emphasizing the imperial lesson of 'United We Stand,' Baden-Powell's treatment of the poem attempts to dramatize for an audience outside the class code the meaning of playing the game as a patriotic metaphor. The scene also makes a point of bringing out Newbolt's reference to class hierarchy and leadership, as the captain speaks to his batsman, or the officer rallies his men. And in the final image of imperial duty, the torch of life is passed on, 'to the host behind,' as Newbolt had it, or in Baden-Powell's version, to the youngest Boy Scout on the stage.[48] By this gesture alone the new movement, in the mind of its founder, was joined in spirit to the dominant code of the public schools. In time, too, old Scouts might themselves recognize each other as members of the same brotherhood in some distant outpost of Empire.

Reading *Scouting for Boys* with the benefit of hindsight, one can see the weight its author placed on patriotism. In this he was putting forward quite conventional views for his time; he was worried about the state of the country, and he sought in a straightforward way to provide a remedy. The evocation of the boyhood of Raleigh, calling up images of a glorious history perpetually refreshed and renewed, was an essential part of the ideology of Scouting: it made the movement thoroughly orthodox in its patriotism. 'I am perfectly certain,' Baden-Powell said in

1914, making the point that each generation has to revivify patriotic spirit, 'that bravery and self-sacrifice, the principle among
manly virtues, can be developed in boys, and one of the best
means to this end is to present to them concrete examples not of
dead and gone heroes, but rather of present-day men in the
street, or boys of their own kind who have done great deeds.'[49]
As the next chapter demonstrates, the Scout movement would
add its own heroes to the nation's pantheon, and incorporate its
own history into the myth of the glorious past.

CHAPTER SIX

Mrs Britannia's Youngest Line of Defence: Militarism and the Making of a National Symbol, 1908–1918

In the dim and distant days before the call of the blood had swept [Private McSnape into Kitchener's army] ... he had been a Boy Scout of no mean repute. He was clean in person and courteous in manner. He could be trusted to deliver a message promptly. He could light a fire in a high wind with two matches, and provide himself with a meal of sorts where another would have starved ... In short, he was the embodiment of a system which in times of peace had served as a text for innumerable well-meaning but muddle-headed politicians of a certain type, who made a speciality of keeping the nation upon the alert against the insidious encroachments of – Heaven help us! – Militarism!

(Ian Hay, *The First Hundred Thousand*, 112)

On 4 August 1912 a Boy Scout troop was sailing two miles off the Kent coast near the Thames estuary. Their cutter capsized in a squall, and nine boys, aged between eleven and fourteen, were drowned. The 'Sheppey disaster' was given widespread coverage in the national press, and soon began to assume a symbolic importance. Winston Churchill, First Lord of the Admiralty, ordered the destroyer HMS *Fervent* to carry the dead boys back up the Thames to London, their coffins draped with Union Jacks on the open deck. The newspapers declared that Britain was in mourning for her lost sons; they rejoiced in the improvement that Scouting had already made to the health of the nation. They printed pictures of the 'bluejackets' carrying the coffins ashore at Rotherhithe, just downstream from Tower Bridge, and of the naval guard of honour. They described the dead boys lying in state in Walworth parish church, attended by fellow Scouts from around the country, who stood on vigil, their staves at the reverse. They recorded that forty thousand persons lined up on 8 August to pay their respects, and even more the next day.

The boys were buried on 11 August. The funeral procession was over a mile long, and included local units of the territorial army (members of the Southwark Battalion of the National Reserve), and the Veterans' Corps. *The Times* reported that 'behind the last of the carriages marched the youthful army of Scouts,' recording that the streets along the route to the cemetery were packed more densely than any London street at 'any of the public functions of recent years, festive or mournful.'[1] A week later several newspapers brought out memorial numbers. 'The Nation's Tribute to the Dead Boy Scouts: Warship Brings the Sheppey Disaster Victims to London' ran the *Daily Mirror*'s headline over a picture of HMS *Fervent* docked by the Rotherhithe pier. The newspaper included photographs of the dead boys and their scoutmaster (the inquest had established that he acted heroically, saving other Scouts), a picture of their cutter, and a series of pictures of the funeral procession. The *Daily Mirror* also reported its own gift of a training vessel for Sea Scouts to commemorate the tragedy.

The Sheppey disaster has a number of meanings. The dead boys were from a working-class neighbourhood, their scoutmaster an ex-public schoolboy attached to the Dulwich College mission to the slums: the relationship between a middle-class scoutmaster, a public school mission, and working-class boys typified Scouting's ideal (but uncommon) program of regeneration. The enormous crowds who visited the parish church, and who lined the streets to watch the funeral procession, were clearly touched by the tragic loss of young lives, yet their presence was also testimony to the efficient publicity generated by a modern press, which had cashed in on a sad accident. More significantly – and this is the interpretation that will be insisted upon here – the incident can be read as a step in the legitimation of Scouting as a national institution. The flag-draped coffins, the naval warship, the 'military' funeral, all these trappings transformed the deaths of nine Scouts into a symbol of patriotism and sacrifice for the nation. HMS *Fervent* was the naval Valkyrie carrying the fallen heroes to an English Valhalla; the nation, appropriately, recognized the tribute. *The Times*, praising the honour paid by the Admiralty to the dead boys, noted that it was 'an expression of the public sense of the utility and dignity of the functions of the Boy Scouts.'[2]

In the pages that follow, Scouting will be read as sign in popular culture, as a new element in a symbolic system whose concern is the creation and preservation of an ideal national history. Scouting, this chapter will argue, took on public meanings in the first years of its life. In a context of popular imperialism, patriotic enthusiasm, and the cult of national efficiency, the movement became a symbol of all that was right with Britain. This process had two dimensions: Scouting helped form its own image, but in turn it fed on the mythology and iconography which, through the media, and through public response to the media, grew up around the movement. As the Sheppey disaster indicates, the process frequently involved other national institutions, such as the Royal Navy and the army, and typically, it was associated with that most topical of contemporary questions, the urgency of military preparedness. This analysis of Scouting as sign begins with the controversy over militarism, for the transformation of the Boy Scout into a national symbol paralleled the growing militarism of pre-war British society, and mirrored the movement's own involvement in the production of a masculine ethic.

The Boy Scout organization, in the six and half years before the First World War, was thought of by members of the British public in a number of ways. Some people took it at face value, as simply good fun for boys; others accepted Baden-Powell's declaration that it was a training in citizenship. To Tory imperialists it was a patriotic enterprise, a chance to prepare youth for the war that was coming; to many Liberals and Radicals it was a symptom of the mentality that was making war certain. To most trade unionists and organized members of the working class it was yet another oppressive symbol of class authority, and to many working people it was an irrelevance. From the first, Baden-Powell had been self-conscious about the note of militarism in his movement. He had denied it, excused it, defended it, and at the same time he had exploited the possibilities of martial images in the preparation of his boys.

Late in the 1920s Ernest Thompson Seton, embittered by his long quarrel with the Boy Scouts of America, and recollecting his first meeting with Baden-Powell in 1906, noted that he and Baden-Powell had differed from the beginning in their aims. He had based his character building on woodcraft, nature, and the Indian, Baden-Powell his training in citizenship on military features and the scout. He had stressed independence, romance, and play, Baden-Powell obedience, duty, and work. What should a boy be prepared for, he remembered asking. '"Frankly," B.P. said, "War."'[3] In hindsight the difference between their positions was clear-cut, but in the years before 1914 the issues were confused.

To Baden-Powell, the idealism of Scouting met all objections. Some voices in the Liberal and Radical press might object to his methods, parents might misunderstand his intentions, some non-conformists distrust his lack of emphasis on religion, but his answer was simple: better a worker than a shirker; it seemed certain there was a war coming, and the Boy Scout was first of all a patriot. As he said in *Scouting for Boys*, 'we ought really not to think too much of any boy, even though a cricketer and footballer, unless he can also *shoot*, and *can drill* and *scout*.'[4]

The question of militarism within the movement surfaced from the start. Baden-Powell defended himself in *Scouting for Boys*, most obviously in the last part, which was specifically addressed to adults. Replying to 'two or three prominent authorities,' who had written to him saying he was trying 'to foster among the boys of Britain a bloodthirsty and warlike spirit,' he answered that either they had not read his handbook carefully, or that he had expressed himself very badly. 'The whole intention of the Boy Scouts' training scheme is for peaceful citizenship.' He then went on to argue that even if he had trained the lads in a military way (which he had not), 'I am impenitent enough to see no harm in it.' The soldier was taught obedience and self-sacrifice, he was usually sober, clean, and active, made the best of things as he found them, and was loyal to his officers. These were all assets in a good citizen. He then restated his position – namely, that war could only be prevented by preparing for war, that to shut one's eyes to the obvious danger would tempt the enemy to attack. The sensible course was to train the rising generation as good citizens, sensible of their responsibilities.

For the most part, and especially in addressing the Scouts themselves, Baden-Powell put the argument in a different form, returning again and again to that distinction he had made in his public lectures, and had repeated in *Scouting for Boys.* There were war scouts and 'peace scouts.' War scouting was the military work of active service; Boy Scouting had nothing to do with this; the movement was linked instead to the lives of 'frontiersmen of our Empire,' 'pioneers of civilization,' men 'accustomed to taking their lives in their hands, brave and loyal to their employers, chivalrous and helpful to each other, unselfish and reliable; men, in fact of the best type.' The Boy Scouts 'should follow in their footsteps as regards character and manliness.'[5]

Yet the movement was hardly a year old before it had its first schism: the Battersea Boy Scouts seceded to form the British Boy Scouts, their scoutmasters disenchanted with Scouting's apparent flirtation with military organizations. Sir Francis Vane, the Scout Commissioner for London, whose sympathies were towards the pacifist side of Scouting, became involved in a power struggle with the staff at Scout headquarters. He was forced to resign his position, and in December 1909 he organized a public meeting to protest the autocratic way Scouting was being run. The affair was publicized by the press, who were largely sympathetic to Vane.[6] Taking many of the London Scout troops with him, Vane afterwards accepted the presidency of the new rival organization, the British Boy Scouts, which had on its guiding committee many prominent Liberals, men such as W.T. Stead and Charles Masterman. It was only with difficulty that Baden-Powell's movement was able to reassert itself. It had a superior organization, it had the support of Pearson's press, and it had, when all was said and done, the sympathy of those who felt that a little militarism was not necessarily a bad thing.

The quarrel left scars. In subsequent years Scout headquarters was nervous about hostile criticism, and the ambiguity of many of its statements reveals the difficulty it had in reconciling the several official aims of Scouting. 'It is not part of our policy to teach boys soldiering, for there is a strong objection to it on the part of some parents,' the third annual report in 1912 stated, going on to argue that soldiering 'does not develop individual character as we desire to do.' 'At the same time,' the report continued, 'our training instills the spirit of patriotism and discipline and lays such foundation of manliness as will be of the highest value for a soldier's as for any other career.' In 1914 the annual report returned to this question, listing the reasons against having military training as part of Scouting, and reaffirming the particular emphasis of the movement. Many churches and parents objected to it, drill made the boy part of a machine, military discipline was repressive; all this from an 'education point of view.' From the military point of view, an excess of military training bored a boy, and Scouts' training was 'a better foundation for soldiering.'[7]

The extent and importance of militarism in Scouting has been debated at some length by modern historians. To a degree, interest in this question can be attributed, in modern eyes, to an ironical contrast between the pacific and international character of Scouting in the last three-quarters of the twentieth century,[8] and the rather different, and often militaristic behaviour of the movement in its years before and during the First World War. For whatever motive, consideration of the controversy over militarism in Scouting has led to a thorough examination of the social and political nature of groups advocating preparedness, the different interests and conflicts of class, and the place of

Scouting in relation to other youth organizations. The historio-graphical debate over Scouting's first intentions has tended to concentrate on hard historical evidence: the records of quarrels within the movement itself, the statements, published and unpublished, of its leaders, and the general historical context. A new focus, not fully developed, has been on the activities of the boys themselves. It is certainly not possible now to dismiss the question of militarism as irrelevant to the social history of pre-war Britain. The Scout movement, as has already been sug-gested, had many meanings: to the recruits as individuals, to dif-ferent leaders of the organization, to several constituencies, supportive or hostile.

John Springhall, in the first substantial scholarly analysis of the Boy Scouts and militarism (1971), pointed to the important links between the major youth movements and the imperialist, military, and political elites of the Edwardian ruling class. These he found constituted in such organizations as the Tory party, the army, the territorials, and pressure groups such as the Tariff Reform League. The most significant of these groups was the National Service League, which campaigned throughout the pre-war years for conscription and national preparedness for war. Springhall described in some detail the dispute in the Scout movement itself between its para-militarists, especially those at Scout headquarters, and the pacifist rebels, notably Sir Francis Vane. He also described the experience of other youth groups in the pre-war years, from the Boys' Brigade to the Church Lads Brigade, and listed the attempts by militarists and the War Office to engage them in various types of cadet training. Spring-hall's article made other important points. He placed the youth movements in the context of class, noting particularly the manipulation by Baden-Powell (and by the leaders of the Angli-can Church Lads Brigade) of what he called 'cultural code sym-bols' – their use of the words loyalty, patriotism,' and so on – words we would now more usually describe as belonging to the discourse of popular imperialism. This ideology, he noted, was typically in the hands of 'middle-aged, middle-class, ex-Army officers.'9

Some other recent views of militarism before the First World War may be mentioned. Anne Summers (1976) has characterized British militarism as more than a ruling-class ideology; rather, she sees it as a popular cause, an integral part even of liberal political culture, drawing support from a wide spectrum of British society. Her evidence is in the strength of the Volunteer Force (by 1903 some 8 per cent of the male population had undergone military training, and at least 70 per cent of the force came from the working class), and in the substantial memberships of the militaristic leagues: the Navy League, founded to agitate for an increase in British naval strength, had about one hundred thousand members in 1914, the National Service League double that number the same year. An important part of her argument, which documents 'the tremendous upsurge of interest in things military in Edwardian Britain,' was the importance of Protestantism in supplying an idealistic element to militarist themes. Historically, the connection between evangelical Christianity and patriotic heroics went back to the mid-nineteenth century, to the Crimean War and the Indian Mutiny, where the image of the Christian soldier was first given shape. The sacrificial figures of such heroes as Havelock and later Gordon lent sanctity and power to the imperial cause. Summers describes the growing popularity of the army in the Edwardian era, and points to the way in which its supposed virtues, such as discipline, hard work, and loyalty were invested with a moral and religious dimension. The militaristic leagues and their sympathizers idealized the soldier's life; their use of a Protestant imagery of sacrifice and dedication, with its roots deep in the national consciousness, gave their message a wide and potent currency.[10]

In 1986 Allen Warren contrasted his fellow historians' picture of an anxious Edwardian class-ridden society desperately trying to impose social order on the young with the 'enthusiastic and emancipationist tone' of Scouting itself. The 'sombre intonings' of his fellow scholars exaggerated the military element in Scouting, Warren argued, suggesting that the movement was in fact much more pluralistic, and encompassed ideas and enthusiasms from several quarters. He described the important historical connections between Scouting and Christian social idealism, particularly as practised by the Young Men's Christian Association (YMCA), and by the Boys' Brigade. He thought that the lack of an explicit statement of religious aims in *Scouting for Boys* was the source of many of Baden-Powell's difficulties, and that, in fact, this was 'largely responsible for the charges of militarism.'[11] At the centre of Warren's argument was the assertion that Scouting was engaged in character training, and its goal was to produce good citizens rather than future soldiers.

The *English Historical Review*, which had published Warren's article, in 1987 invited a response to his points from both John Springhall and Anne Summers. Springhall began by claiming that Warren's evidence was selective, that he had chosen data that supported his case and had ignored much that was contradictory, such as the Vane controversy. He quoted from the private correspondence of several Scout officials to demonstrate that their soothing words in public to those alarmed by signs of Scout militarism were political and pragmatic rather than heartfelt. Baden-Powell himself was not as guileless as Warren supposed. To establish the military intentions of Scouting 'at the grass roots level of local practice,' he pointed to the fact that many of the early Scout commissioners held military rank, that several chairmen of local Scout associations were advocates of National Service League policy, and that, in a county such as Hampshire, a great many ex-army officers and men helped run the movement. In 1910, out of 250 presidents and commissioners of Boy Scouts listed in the *Headquarters Gazette*, 140 were serving or retired military officers. Two years later the proportion was up to 70 per cent. Springhall concluded by restating the position taken in his earlier essay, that the Scouting movement, in the years before the First World War, should 'be seen in the context of preparing the next generation of British soldiers.' In spite of Allen Warren's argument, Scouting's claim that its goal was citizenship training, and not preparing soldiers, was camouflage.[12]

Anne Summers, in essence, agreed with Springhall. After a

cautionary note that 'simply to assimilate scouting within a monolithic conceptual framework of "militarism" and "social control"' might well ignore the importance of the Scouting experience to the individual boy, she stated that Scouting could not in fact escape the pervasive militarism of the period. Whatever official distance was put between Scouting and military organizations such as the territorial army was as often contradicted by the week-to-week activities of Scouts themselves. Their troops often participated in exercises with territorial units, sometimes directly, but more often as helpers to voluntary aid detachments (VAD), the auxiliary nursing branch of the territorial force. Scouts acted as wounded soldiers, and were bandaged by nursing trainees. 'Boy Scouts could thus be found on weekends and public holidays all over the country, putting the motto "Be prepared" into practice in the service of the Territorial Force, albeit its medical wing.' Girl Guides too were asked to do their bit. Guides were given first aid training along VAD (military) lines, and some units even took part in war games with Scouts. Summers ended her rebuttal with a warning that the historian should not take the statements of Baden-Powell and his officials at face value, but rather, should look more closely at the grassroots activities of Scouts and Guides. These, she thought, suggested that adolescent boys and girls were ready to respond with uncritical enthusiasm to ideas of war.[13]

The case put by Springhall and Summers is strong. Scouting did reflect the general concern in the pre-war years for a greater military efficiency; Scout training was aimed at preparing the next generation of soldiers for a coming war. Yet Allen Warren's point, that Scouting was pluralistic in its meanings, is also valid: Scouting tried to be many things to many people, and different organizations and individuals interpreted Scouting in ways to suit themselves. The work of these historians makes clear the complexity of pre-war British society, and the central role that the youth movements played in the cause of national efficiency.[14] While not discounting the importance of their analysis – in fact, while depending on it to define the parameters of the argument – it is necessary to expand their thesis. The emphasis that both Springhall and Summers place upon the symbolic language and cultural codes shared by both the elites and the middle class at large, and, in Summers's case, on the roots of this imagery in the Protestant ethos, points to the most important (though neglected) element in the early history of the Scout movement – the Boy Scout's very rapid elevation to the status of a patriotic symbol.

What *were* the means which allowed the Scout, in his first years, to become a symbol of the nation? What does this phenomenon add to our understanding of British society? How can Scouting be read as sign? These questions have not been given much consideration. Their answers lie in the ways in which Scouting appeared in the media, and the ways in which the public was encouraged to respond to a constructed image, repeated in ephemerae, in the newspapers, advertisements, boys' magazines, pictures, in a thousand details which alone mean little but together suggest much. By itself such stuff is trivial; considered as a whole it is revealing, because it indicates what Scouting meant as an element in popular culture, and how it came to have that meaning. To be successful in recovering meaning from this material it will be necessary to try to see Scouting as its first audience saw it, and to read it as a natural phenomenon. (It seemed normal in 1912 to make the deaths of nine boys the occasion for national mourning).

The twin images of the Boy Scout in the years 1908–18 were the Little Soldier and the Young Knight. Both of these images had their genesis in Baden-Powell's handbook, and both grew in strength as they were received and augmented by the media. Though the ideals they suggested appeared contradictory, their ideological base was in fact shared. Together they formed a powerful symbol, a fusion of patriotism and Christian idealism. Scouting came to mean King and Country, Duty and Self-sacrifice.

The outward and visible signs of Scouting were military: Scouts were organized in troops, and sub-divided into patrols; they wore uniform, had parades, and did a little drill, they were led by officers, scoutmasters, patrol leaders, corporals. (These were the ranks named in the first edition of the handbook, but the last term was soon changed: the boys' ranks began with tenderfoot, and went on to second and first class scout.) Scouts' activities were also often military: they practised signalling, carried dispatches, went on trek, posted sentries around camp, and fought mock battles.

Baden-Powell's suggestion for a Scouting display to the public (printed at the end of *Scouting for Boys*) is fair evidence of a naive and unambiguous military emphasis. Though he said his intention was to 'demonstrate Scoutcraft, bringing in Drill, Pathfinding, Camping, Pioneering, Life-Saving, Hygiene, etc.,' the display was in fact a war-game. The Scouts entered in patrol formation, 'one scout semaphores to advanced scout, "We camp here. Keep good look-out."' The patrols drilled briefly, then formed camp, and began to demonstrate various camp crafts and activities, cooking bread, performing physical exercises, cleaning teeth. They then all joined in a War Dance, which was interrupted by shots from without.

> Alarm signal given by leaders ... Smoke fire made, alarm signal sent up by one of the patrols, while the other throws down tent and shelter, cuts lashings, and distributes the staves to scouts. One patrol then doubles out in extended formation (right) towards the firing. Sentry staggers in, and falls. One scout attends to him. Second patrol follows the first at a double in close formation. A scout returns from right carrying a wounded one on his shoulder; bandages him. Another scout drags in a wounded one ... firing ceases; both patrols
> Return, cheerful in having driven off the enemy.[15]

Early Scout publications show the same emphasis: the Boy Scouts did play at soldiering. In a pamphlet explaining the aims of the movement, which began by saying that Scouting was not 'in any way connected with Soldiering,' the photograph heading the text illustrated 'Boy Scouts storming a wall.' In the pages of *The Scout*, there were reports of mock attacks, of spying on hos-

tile troops, of invading enemy camps in disguise. The vocabulary used to describe these games was military:

Scotch Scout's Stratagem

We have heard of a clever ruse by a Lochwinnoch Scout, who
was recently entrusted with important dispatches.

Falling into the hands of the enemy, he was thoroughly
searched, but without any result, and was allowed to go on his way.
Upon reaching his destination, he scraped off the mud from the
end of his staff, and drew the despatch out of a slit, in which he
had cunningly hidden it.[16]

To the organization itself, and, in particular, to its boys, the military connection was exciting, and very much in the news. This is
the first answer to why Scouting became a national symbol: war
games were fun for Scouts, they matched the mood of the
moment, and, to those who organized them, they were in the
national interest.

These facts were recognized by the media. Boy Scouts from
the start were thought of as little soldiers, and the movement
was held to have an honorary connection to the military. The
press frequently referred to Baden-Powell's 'Model Army.' Service journals accepted the quasi-military status of Scouting without equivocation: in a portrait of Baden-Powell (one of a series
of 'Military Men of Mark') *The Bluejacket and the Soldier* in 1909
claimed that it took 'the imagination of "B.-P" to see that with
proper organization this "playing at Soldiers" would not only
give pleasure, but lasting benefit to hundreds of thousands of
youngsters.' A popular boys' book on the British army was typical in including a chapter on the Boy Scouts. Gale and Polden,
the military publishers who had published *Aids to Scouting*,
issued *War Games for Boy Scouts* in 1910.[17]

Other forms of popular culture reproduced the military
image, from cigarette cards to advertisements. A 'trade card' for
Carter's Little Liver Pills (c. 1910), had a Boy Scout as a sentry,
saying 'Halt! Give the pass word for tonight.' The ubiquitous
Jessie Pope produced two picture books for little folk, and

showed Cat Scouts and Baby Scouts armed: 'In time of war, a Baby scout named Flo,/Fought with great hardihood, and shelled the foe.' The German firm of Heyde and the British firm of Britain's manufactured model Boy Scouts in the same series as their toy soldiers. War games were something of a craze. H.G. Wells wrote an account of his own version, complete with pictures showing tin soldiers fighting on the carpet. He included Boy Scouts among his tin soldiers, not as auxiliaries, but as combatants, capturing other soldiers, being killed.[18] Other examples could be added, but the point is surely made: in the years before the First World War Boy Scouts had a military character. They were not, of course real soldiers, and their link to the army was often put in a humorous or ironical context, but the link was there, and at a time of heightened interest in things military it added to the status of Scouting. That this happened with only limited opposition was in part due to the sanitizing effect of the second, and complementary, symbol.

The image of the Young Knight came from *Scouting for Boys.* Baden-Powell had explained Scout Law at some length as 'the Chivalry of the Knights': the medieval knights and their squires, he said, were followed by men-at arms, 'stout, hearty warriors'; the knight was like a patrol leader, the men-at-arms his Scouts. The knights had their rule, a code of honour, self-sacrifice, kindness, generosity, politeness, courtesy to women, courage, humility, fortitude, and good temper. This code was also the code of the Scouts.[19] Mark Girouard has described the Victorian enthusiasm for medieval chivalry from which these ideas derived: Baden-Powell's comparison referred to a well-understood moral and patriotic symbolism.* Scouts, as the title of one of Baden-Powell's books made clear, were the *Young Knights of the Empire* (1916). In drawings he made for Scout use, he placed the Boy Scout in a number of chivalric poses, dressed in armour, or guided by a knight. The essence of the Young Knight was his good turn done each day.

*Girouard has argued that the 'Knights' Code' was the source for the Scout Law (*Camelot*, 255), but the reverse seems more probable, with Baden-Powell tailoring his chivalric cloth to suit the cut of his Scouts.

The chivalric image of Scouting was associated, even in the handbook, with the idea of the Peace Scout, and hence with civic duty, with self-sacrifice at home, and heroism in everyday life. The movement quickly exploited the possibilities of exemplary behaviour, publicizing Boy Scouts who had rescued suicides from drowning, or who had saved little girls from the railway tracks. And they had done these things without hope of reward. Even the cartoons, which made fun of the Scout who insisted on taking the old lady across the road against her will, or the Scout who injudiciously helped a not-so-young Young Lady to do the same, helped to familiarize the public with the idea of the good Scout. In the early numbers of *The Scout* peace Scouting was dramatized, with stories of good deeds performed, and pictures of the latest Scout heroes. On the magazine's cover marking George v's acceptance of the honorary office of patron, the King's portrait was surrounded by scenes of Scouts across the Empire doing useful things: in South Africa stopping a runaway horse, in Australia finding someone lost or 'bushed,' in Canada attending to a case of frostbite, in England wheeling a barrow, 'helping the infirm.'[20]

The two images of Scouting, the Young Knight and the Little Soldier, coexisted together, sometimes uneasily. They were different ideals, and they appealed at first to separate parental constituencies, marked very roughly by the allegiances of Nonconformist and Anglican sympathy. The image of the peace Scout carried the weight of Christian idealism, and could be publicized without fear, the only worry for Scout authorities being the negative connotations, for boys, of too much piety. The image of the war Scout, on the other hand, was muted, for Scouting never surrendered wholly to a military program.

As the war approached, and as the middle ground became less hospitable, the two images converged: the Boy Scout became a cadet version of the Christian soldier, borrowing the language and symbolism of that tradition. Baden-Powell himself advanced this synthesis, for he drew the Scout as St George, mounted on horseback, piercing the dragon, or standing in his armour, behind a shield bearing the motto 'Be Prepared,' while the dragon lay caged by the bars of the Scout Law. Such iconography lifted Scouting above the battle, joining it to the sacred purpose of the nation itself. This possibility had been there from the beginning, at least in the minds of the conservative wing of the movement's supporters. The *Daily Telegraph*, a sponsor of Scouting, claimed in 1910 that the Boy Scouts' participation in the army pageant was nothing to do with militarism, for the movement was 'quite non- military, non-political, and unsectarian in character.' The newspaper went on to say, however, that Baden-Powell and his small army of scouts would depict 'the dedication of the boy to the service of the race in peace and war.'[21] This was no more than Baden-Powell's own reminder in *Scouting for Boys* that the knights' code' was harnessed to the duties of national service: Young Knights must be prepared to fight in the defence of England. As the nation moved towards a more militant mood, the twin images of Scouting would come together as a symbol of patriotism.

In the public mind scouting became a significant and accepted organization with remarkable speed. Though this was in the main a phenomenon that took place in the adult and public world, legitimation could not have happened without the participation of the recruits themselves, and here their enthusiasm was charged, if not formed, by their own magazines. We might expect that the juvenile press would exploit the sensational side of the war Scout; what is surprising is the degree to which the magazines were a forum for promoting the controversy over militarism. The popular middle-class boys' magazines divided predictably enough: the *Boy's Own Paper* favoured peace Scouting, while *Chums* began by using the pacifist schism to boost its own circulation, and ended in a more militaristic mood. *Young England*, with its Low Church connections, tried to ignore Scouting, but *The Captain*, a public school magazine, at first favoured the movement, and later when it became too popular, scorned it. *The Captain* had no trouble with militarism, and at one point reported with enthusiasm the formation of a troop of mobile cycle Scouts, their bicycles fitted with a 'rifle bucket and a clip to carry a Martini Henry carbine.'[22]

The Scout fiction which filled the magazines from 1909 on must have had a powerful influence on young readers, for the stories were sensational and the propaganda topical. The new Scout heroes were not just boys out for adventure; rather, they were members of a national organization working with the authorities. They were both little soldiers *and* good citizens: they caught spies, and they took up arms to save their country. They were more than good citizens, they were agents of law and order. They acted as friends of the police and the army, rounding up thieves, investigating crimes, discovering plots. Covers and illustrations in the magazines showed them using their staffs as weapons, and sometimes handling firearms.

The Scout and his patrol fitted nicely into the formula of the adventure story. That Scouts so readily became scouts, an irregular soldiery adept at discovering all sorts of plots apt to threaten the nation, did nothing but good for the circulation of the magazines, whose readership was centred on pre-adolescents of eleven and twelve, precisely the age group to which the Scout movement most appealed. These stories told their readers who they were, and how to behave in a time of national crisis. They told them that the enemy was as often the hooligan as the scheming foreigner, and that the good Scout could floor the thug as easily as he could discover the German spy. They made the fictional Scout an attractive alter ego, a type of ideal middle-class boy, a good citizen in miniature, the policeman's friend, the brave soldier of the future war – in all, a symbol of the nation.

The extent to which militarism and nationalism were dramatized by the juvenile press can be seen in the exploitation of the invasion scare. Invasion stories had been a staple of the boys' magazines since about 1906; coincident with the beginnings of Scouting, they became a spate, and Boy Scouts were in the forefront of the fictional action. Britain was invaded by Germany, by Russia, even by Japan; the invasion was resisted at sea, in the air, and in the streets of London. *Chums* told its readers 'How Britain Might Be Invaded,' and ran a succession of stories and serials that described the efforts of young heroes, Scouts included, to keep England safe and free. Here the competition between *Chums* and the Harmsworth papers (which aimed at a lower middle-class and upper working-class audience), was obvious and fierce, and the readership of these stories was frequently specified. 'A World at War,' for instance, was advertised in the *Boys' Herald* in 1908 as a 'Thrilling Story, written to appeal to Cadets, Brigade Boys, Boy Scouts and British Boys in Every part of the World'; its heroes were the boys of the King's Own Scouts. We may be familiar with these invasion stories now only from the example of P.G. Wodehouse's skit *The Swoop! or How Clarence Saved England* (1909), in which a Boy Scout, single-handed, resisted simultaneous invasions from a collection of unlikely and bizarre forces. A review of *The Swoop* in *The Captain* is a fair gauge of the popular image of Scouting in the years before the Great War: 'the whole thing, of course, is a merry extravaganza dealing with the present wave of patriotic fervour, when every boy wants to have a gun and learn how to go scouting.'[23]

To get the contemporary sense of this patriotic fervour, it is worth going just one step further and, by looking at some of the detail in the Scout stories, speculating about the effect of their brand of social programming on a young reader. The evidence is necessarily anecdotal, but what there is suggests that boys absorbed the ideological lessons. One example may be allowed to make this point, illustrating the particular meaning of these fictions to one individual.

Howard Reid, a young Canadian, learned from some boys' magazines that war was exciting, that it was a grand adventure. And so, as it seemed in his memory, quite simply he marched off to fight. He survived the First World War. Interviewed in his old age, he was asked why he had joined the army in 1914, and his answer was straightforward.

When I was about 12 years of age, I read in a boys' magazine all about the 'Invasion of Britain,' 'Britain at Bay,' and 'Britain's Revenge.' I can remember all the different stories – it was quite a story. I think it was two boy scouts that held up the German army on London Bridge. The pictures of the planes that I saw were very good – there was a plane in it, I remember – like one of our modern planes. I read those stories, and they did something. And I was always a marcher, I guess.[24]

Reid read his stories in the *Boys' Herald* and the *Boys' Friend*, popular papers put out by the Harmsworth press, which featured fiction that was full of action-packed adventure, typically with a patriotic and imperial touch. Red-blooded boys fought for England and the Empire, killing off Zulus in Africa, shooting mutinous Lascars in India, sinking the Russian fleet in the Channel. The language of these stories was xenophobic, masculine, and jingoistic; it is hard not to see it having a powerful effect on a young reader.

This is the synopsis of one of the stories that did something to the young Canadian from Cape Breton, Howard Reid. 'While Britain Slept,' a 'thrilling, new invasion story,' ran in *The Boys' Herald* during 1910 and 1911.

A WARNING DISREGARDED.

Britain was doomed! So said, so hoped, her countless enemies. Whilst those at the head of affairs wasted their time squabbling over unimportant details of domestic government, our enemies had been preparing the blows which struck at Britain's very heart.

The Germans, taking advantage of the fact that a rebellion – even worse than the one in '57 – had broken out in India, dispatched an army of a million to the shores of Old England.

Sweeping through Kent, they are victorious until they are brought to bay by the British Army under Lord Roberts. Scoutmaster Dick Halliday swears that he will deliver a message to Lord Kitchener, who is in London. The message is from Lord Roberts, and runs:

'All's well in Sheppey. Arm every man under seventy, and every boy over fourteen, and the British people will show themselves as unconquerable as of old. That's all.'

Dick Halliday commands the Otter patrol of Boy Scouts, and the little band starts off intent upon a desperate attempt to pierce the German lines.

As the scouts near Orpington they are obliged to fortify themselves in a stone farm-building, as a body of dismounted German cavalry are approaching in skirmishing order from the east.

'Steady boys!' cries Dick Halliday to his brave patrol. 'Don't throw a shot away, and don't fire till I give the word. Now lads, bear yourselves like British boys!'

There is some fairly straightforward indoctrination going on here. Young readers are being taught about patriotism: 'the British people will show themselves as unconquerable as of old'; 'now lads, bear yourselves like British boys!' Even the appeal to Old England is loaded, ringing the familiar note of England's glorious history. And it seems clear that among all the other messages, the readers of these words are being instructed in what it takes be masculine; that is, how they should bear themselves as boys. 'While Britain Slept' was of course illustrated. The magazine came with a picture of 'The Boy Scouts' Brave Defence' and the caption, '"Now lads!" came the Scout-master's cry from the loft, and immediately the spiteful crack of the rifles rang out, and the Germans dropped in a heap upon each other.'

This sort of commercial material, though aimed at a young readership, was not untypical of popular fiction in general. In a society growing increasingly uncritical of things military, the coming war generated much excitement.

If this was what Scouting might mean to the boy, to the public at large the movement could be given a more formal status. The Boy Scout was linked to the national symbols of the flag, the King, and Britannia; to hope, faith, and to charity. Its original adventurous and even unorthodox identity became muted. If it still followed Baden-Powell's ideal frontiersman, whose manhood was strong and rich and whose life was pure, it seemed to incline in spirit towards the last of his virtues; duty, obedience, and cleanliness became its business as well as its image. As much as anything this was a consequence of its bureaucratic growth, for morality was easier to manage than adventures, but the change was accelerated by the atmosphere of the First World War.

The movement's progress towards the dignified status of a patriotic institution can be illustrated in a number of details. From the start it had the support of what is known nowadays as the 'Establishment.' The names of those who, in the pre-war years, gave their blessing to Scouting make up a list of many of the best-known citizens of Britain, from the sovereign and his family to the heads of church and state. In 1912 the Boy Scouts Association was incorporated by royal charter; its patron was His Majesty the King. In 1913 the Chief Scout for Wales was the Prince of Wales. The council of the Association was represented by the archbishops of Canterbury and York, the Roman Catholic Archbishop of Westminster, leaders of the Presbyterian, Methodist, Baptist, and Congregationalist churches, the Lord Chief Justice of England, Field-Marshals Roberts and Kitchener, Admiral Lord Charles Beresford, the Duke of Norfolk, Lord Strathcona, Professors Howard Marsh and M.E. Sadler, along with some forty other persons, including dignitaries such as the Lord Mayor of London.

With this sort of weight the movement sought for privileges, and was given them. Scouts participated in ceremonial occasions, performing as a cadet branch of the armed forces. For King George v's coronation in 1911 they were allotted one hundred and fifty places on Constitution Hill, where, as an honour guard, they joined the soldiers and sailors who lined the procession route. The War Office, in a letter confirming this arrangement, considered the Boy Scouts an organization 'with Service connections.'[25] Boy Scouts were issued with passports so they could use the royal parks in London. This recognition extended to other quarters: Scouting was included under 'Naval and Military Intelligence' in *Palmer's Index to the Times* from as early as the last quarter of 1908, and the editor of the *Teacher's Encyclopaedia* (1912), an expensive and weighty seven-volume survey on the profession and its methods, included a description of Scouting in a special chapter – the only material extraneous to teaching or schools in the entire work.

The process of legitimation, of the movement becoming associated with authority and with its symbols, can be seen most dramatically in the iconography of Scouting. Here the roles played by the media, and by the market-place, are of great importance: Scouting was 'sold' by both. The good favour of the royal family was marked by Bernard Partridge's cartoon in *Punch* in July 1911 which, referring to the King's recent review of 26,000 Scouts at Windsor and to the King's acceptance of the honorary position of patron, showed a Boy Scout storming the wall, in 'The Capture of Windsor Castle.' This nicely joined the quasi-military spirit of Scouting with the patriotic symbol of the King. Two years earlier King Edward had sent a message to Scouts at the Crystal Palace rally, assuring them that the training they were getting would 'enable them to do their duty as men should any danger threaten the Empire.'[26] This thought had been mounted on a patriotic postcard, and was still offered for sale by the firm of Gamages in 1911.

The degree to which the icon forms opinion, or merely crystallizes ideas that are already there, floating in the public mind, is impossible to determine. But it can be assumed that the image is powerful, and does work to shape the response of its audience. Bernard Partridge's earlier and more famous cartoon in *Punch*, coming as it did in September 1909 at the beginning of the movement's history, encapsulated the hopes and fears of the moment, and indelibly linked the Boy Scout to the nation. It was titled 'Our Youngest Line of Defence,' and showed a Boy Scout taking Mrs Britannia by the arm: 'Fear not, Gran'ma,' the Scout said, 'no danger can befall you now. Remember, *I* am with you!' The nuances of both picture and caption are revealing. Mrs Britannia, as suiting the Boy Scout doing his good turn, is an old lady, not the warrior maiden or the defiant matron. Is the Empire in decline? Britannia seems to be in widow's weeds, and her figure if not her face is somewhat reminiscent of the late

Queen Victoria. Is this a note of nostalgia? The caption plays on the irony of the young Scout taking care of the adult – a not uncommon upper middle-class conceit, as A.A. Milne's verse about the child who 'took great care of his Mother, though he was only three,' might remind us – but it is at heart serious. Partridge's cartoon, appearing where it did in the days when *Punch* was an important publication, a barometer of middle-class opinion, reminded readers of what was on their minds: the bogy of national deterioration, the spectre of the coming war. The Boy Scout would grow up to be the nation's Line of Defence.

The image uses a visual shorthand, an iconography that incorporates words of power. The nation, the King, and the flag all stand for a complex set of ideas about patriotism, imperialism, militarism. Loyalty, courage, duty, good citizenship are embodied in these symbols. With the coming of the war the Boy Scout was pictured, again and again, as the image of Britain. He waved the flag, standing by the side of Britannia and John Bull. He was an actor in rituals that referred to the language of imperial history and to the cultural codes of the dominant elites. The audience is expected to believe, and not to think.

By 1914 a mass of details testify to this, and indicate the way in which cultural divisions were broken down in the general war fever. Scouting was able to symbolize the cohesiveness of a society at war. In 1914 the cover of *Mother and Home* showed a young Boy Scout and, under the heading of 'Let *him* be a Boy Scout!' told the reader that 'the success of the nation depends not so much on its armaments as upon the character of its citizens.' In a series of patriotic stamps, along with Nelson, the Dreadnoughts, and a bulldog guarding the old flag, a Boy Scout, waving his staff and hat, shouted 'Goodbye! I'm off to the War!' W.H. Titcomb's oil painting of a group of Scouts cheering the Chief Scout (1913), which pictured the boys, with a drum and bugle band at their centre, and a Union Jack in their midst, had such obvious resonance that it was re-entitled 'Send Us!' and used as a recruiting poster. The *Church Standard* of January 1915 placed on its cover a Scout bugler rallying the nation. The verse, 'The Trumpet Call,' was by Alfred Noyes:

Trumpeter, rally us, rally us, rally us,
On to the City of God.

Here militant evangelism slides into patriotism. The traditional imagery, both as metaphor and as icon, could evoke a powerful response: the young bugler becomes the conscience of Protestant Britain, his youth and purity a call to sacrifice.

Some other treatments of the Boy Scout specifically attached the patriotic sign to the heroic tradition. Baden-Powell had feared, when the war began, that Scouting would lose its independence, and be absorbed into a cadet force.[27] This did not happen, and, as might be expected, the movement threw all its energies into the war effort. Boys assisted the Coastguard, they guarded telephone and telegraph lines and railway bridges, and carried messages in public offices and hospitals. They continued to act as patients for VAD nurses in training, and they were organized to help in gardens and on farms. How could their work be dramatized? Though the boys were not combatants, might they not be included in the imagery of sacrifice and heroism? They could, and some examples suggest how this was done. In the painting 'The Dispatch – Just in Time,' a Boy Scout delivers a sealed envelope to a general, just as the troop train is ready to leave the station. French and Belgian Scouts give their lives for their countries and legends of their exploits are repeated in the British press: for example, a Belgian Scout, 'Pour la Patrie,' refusing to give information to the enemy, his back to a telegraph pole, is shot by an German officer. Here the reference is to the innocent but heroic non-combatant, as with the nurse Edith Cavell, killed in an act of German 'frightfulness.'[28]

The Boy Scout as sign was able to move easily into this larger iconography of national history, which typically displayed in dramatic form the values of society. Boys were taught to be men; the ultimate validity of this training was when they *were* men. The hospital ship *Britannic* was torpedoed with a group of Boy Scouts aboard. The ship began to sink. The caption to the painting that commemorated this episode told the symbolic story: 'As the Cry rings out "Women and Children First," the Scouts on a Doomed

Ship demand to be treated as Men.'[29] It was an exact reprise of the *Birkenhead* disaster, that favourite Victorian morality of perfect discipline, and, significantly, it became another exemplary lesson in a patriotic history for children.

Boys grew up into men, or could enrol as boy sailors or boy soldiers: Jack Cornwell, the sixteen-year-old hero of the naval battle of Jutland, had been a Scout. Cornwell stood by his gun, after all but two of the ten crew were dead or wounded. The gun was knocked out, and he himself was hit, but he knew his duty: 'Jack Cornwell is standing all alone, with nothing to shelter him against the shot and shell, and he has been terribly wounded. Alone. Around him the dead and the dying; himself torn, bleeding, very faint from pain and the horror of the sight ... and he *wouldn't* drop.'[30] Cornwell was awarded the Victoria Cross posthumously, and the words 'Faithful unto Death' were engraved on his coffin. His action, as many of his eulogies pointed out, echoed the faithfulness of the Roman sentry at Pompeii. Several drawings and paintings were made of him at his post, including one by Baden-Powell, and his sacrifice took its place in the emblematic pageant of British heroism.[31]

In every national crisis society reinvents its heroic myth, whose old signs are given renewed life. An iconography does not and cannot survive alone, but is parasitical on the larger (national) growth. The Boy Scout was a potent symbol precisely because he expressed only a little that was new, and for the most part echoed a set of meanings both familiar and, in time of war, highly charged. As sign itself, while the mood of militant patriotism lasted, Scouting had its most formal role: the Boy Scout was duty personified, he was 'Britain's Last Hope.'* The organization celebrated, and magnified, its own character.

Within six years of its founding, recognizing its public role, and moving to appropriate its own share of the nation's history, the Scout movement began to publish its own annals and legends. In 1914 the *Boy Scouts' Roll of Honour* displayed in twenty-

---

*Scout troops were warned to ignore the louts and loungers who called them 'Britain's last hope' as they marched past. 'It's better to be a last hope than no hope at all!'

three chapters 'a simple record of Scout heroism.' The language of this tribute employed all the discourses of power: it spoke of King and Country, of the Empire in its several parts, of duty, courage, sacrifice, of coolness and virility. There were brave scoutmasters and yet braver Scouts; there were Scouts, who 'were not afraid to face angry mobs, so long as they did their duty'; there were Heroes of Bonnie Scotland who 'fear nothing, and do much'; and brave 'Fire Fighters' with courage of a 'virile kind,' who would win for themselves 'a niche in the temple of heroism.'[32] These were the familiar notes of the patriotic vocabulary, tempered by an echo of Christian evangelism; the book itself was an imitation of adult hymnals.

With its place in the constellation of national symbols now assured, Scouting went through the First World War in style. To the boy, as his magazines made clear, war fever was in the air, and he could read tale after tale of bold Scouts who became brave men, who shot down Germans in the air, or bayoneted them in the trenches. Even the moralistic *Boy's Own Paper*, while deploring the conflict, filled its pages with articles on military units of the Empire and the allies, and dramatized glory with pictures of charges and warships. For adults, Scouting's heart was in the right place: it was patriotic, it trained boys to do their duty. Baden-Powell wrote *Marksmanship for Boys*, and invited Scouts to win the Red Feather; he reminded his Scouts that they were *Young Knights of the Empire*. He designed a recruiting poster that showed a Boy Scout taking his place among all the other war workers and servicemen, handing on ammunition in a chain of supply from the workshop to the front. For the general public he wrote *Quick Training for War*, a pamphlet that had enormous sales.

When the conflict was at an end, the organization produced its own record of those who had served it well: the *Scouts' Book of Heroes* described 'Famous Scouts in the War' (Generals Byng, Birdwood, and Plummer, Admiral Beatty), 'Scout Heroes of the Army,' 'Scout Heroes of the Navy,' 'Heroes of the Air Service,' 'The Heroes at Home' (Scouts themselves), and finally, those who were 'Called to Higher Service,' that is, the dead. Baden-

Powell, in a foreword to this record of bravery, noted that Scouting had not needed to go beyond the ranks of its own fraternity to find a 'glorious record of gallantry,' and said that it was the Scouting spirit that was in evidence here, self-discipline and the 'dare to do.'[33] The Scout movement gave thanks in St Paul's Cathedral, the national shrine, on 12 April 1919, and its war effort was honored by a chapter in *The Times History of the War,* as befitted a national institution.

CONCLUSION

Scouting and Myth

A woman applied at the Thames Court for a summons against a man, who had threatened, she said, to 'Baden-Powell' her.

Mr. Mead: What is that?

The Applicant: To kill me.

Mr. Mead: Why is it called 'Baden-Powell?'

The Applicant: I do not know. It is called that.

Mr. Mead: I do not know why he should be introduced into the matter.

(Newspaper cutting, c. 1907)

A myth has its own life. It is born, it thrives; it becomes weak; phoenix-like, it regenerates. In its strength, it seems to sweep all before it; as it dies, only old believers subscribe to its truths. It has an odd and often uneasy relationship with history, for it can create social reality; yet tested by the individual, it is easily found wanting. It can be killed and discredited, but hydra-like it sprouts new heads from the corpse.

The frontier is still alive as an idea in the English-speaking world. It affects our sense of other people, and other places; it allows us to polarize what we do not know into the safe and the dangerous, it encourages us to flirt, as imperialists of the mind, with dreams of order and good government. Out there beyond the geographical or physical limits we can impose our own sense of reality; we test our strength and assert our power. Language mirrors the dominant ideology of the day. Baden-Powell and his contemporaries described the expeditions of Cecil Rhodes's Chartered Company in southern Africa as pioneering work, and opening up the country: these were the terms of imperial adventure. Their vocabulary of conquest gave the possession of native territory an heroic dimension; the dusty veld would become an English Eden. Those who refused to accept the imperialist dream, such as Olive Schreiner in her bitterly critical *Trooper Peter Halket of Mashonaland,* renamed the confrontation between white pioneers and black natives, subscribing to an anti-myth. The killing of unarmed men, women, and children, which imperial discourse termed pacification, was, in her eyes, murder; the scorched earth policy, called 'the denial of resources,' was a system of starvation; the purchase of native lands, named fair trade, became simple theft. But Schreiner spoke for a minority without power.

Kipling's Lost Legion is long gone,* but its mission lives on as images of adventure in places far away, as stories of conquest over nature itself, Everest climbed, the earth circumnavigated single-handed, space conquered. The boundaries can still be defended in the imperial spirit – as in the Falklands – and the rhetoric of duty and moral superiority still has an audience. As Richard Slotkin says, speaking of the American experience, the echoes of nineteenth-century frontier wars, with their collective-memories of civilization versus savagery, of the game of cowboy and Indian, of the heroic sacrifice for the nation (epitomized in Custer's last stand) give meaning to twentieth-century conflicts like Vietnam.[1] And now Vietnam gives meaning to Iraq and Desert Storm. Myth does not need to argue its case. We can still be tempted, in Baden-Powell's words, to make the world *clean.*

The previous pages have argued that the myth of the imperial frontier provided both the context and the material for the construction of Scouting. Glorifying the idea of the frontiersman

*The Legion of Frontiersmen still exists, both in Britain and in Canada.

and the war scout, the myth helped Baden-Powell become a cult hero at Mafeking, and gave inspiration and impetus to the Scout movement itself. Beyond this, it acted as all social myths act: it concealed and made veritable the ideology that lay behind it, justifying imperialism, masculine power, and racial superiority. Western thought had for a long time imagined civilization and savagery as binary opposites; imperialism co-opted this idea, and asserted that the frontier should be ever pushed back, until the barbarians were finally subdued. The alienation created by industrialism forced another adjustment and the two poles switched values: civilization became negative, savagery positive, and the frontier, in its raw power, suddenly seemed redemptory. Whereas the myth began by justifying the conquests of Empire, it moved on to reassure the culture about its own masculinity. Its believers spoke of the Spartan virtues, and made of the frontiers-men and scouts *real* men, whose lives were pure.

Yet it has to be asked what was the result of it all? Myth can only be measured in belief or disbelief, in the commitment of the culture to its story. We would be unwise to take its message literally, which one anti-Scouting pamphleteer did in 1912, when he pointed out that with imperial expansion at an end, only a handful of boys would actually grow up to become frontiers-men.[2] As the last chapter argued, the myth, telling a tale of both power and escape, eased the movement's progress towards the status of a national institution. Its success can gauged in the lay-ers that Scouting itself added to the *mentalité* of British culture, marked – to choose just one significant detail – by Ian Hay's per-fect Scout from the Glasgow slums, Private McSnape, who, it is clear, represents British manhood risen from the ashes.

The myth of the frontier was the dynamo that drove the move-ment on in its first years, but the myth had to be nurtured. Scouting did this with its own publicity, with thousands of publi-cations, manuals, songbooks, and stories, with Gilwell Park, the jamborees, the Gang Shows and their impresario Ralph Reader. The spirit of adventure, the delight in toughness, became ritual-ized; the memory of Baden-Powell's military heroics, as they grew dim, needed repolishing. Scouting followed the path taken by that other contemporary echo of the frontier spirit, James Barrie's *Peter Pan*: Red Indians turned into Piccaninnies, the Lost Boys played happily enough in a Never Land without women to trouble them, and the most threatening of savage beasts came armed, like the crocodile and its alarm clock, with their own early-warning system. There was always something in Scouting of that note of Barrie's: innocent boys led by innocent scoutmasters, boy-men showing the way to a safe and good-natured wilderness.[3]

The experience of the individual could always be ordinary, the power of myth dissipated in the light of day, and the ideal forgotten in a squalid reality. Stanley Hyatt, a Lost Legionary, told a story of returning home from the Rhodesian frontier to England, suffering from boredom in a snobbish Essex village, starting a Scout troop for the sons of labourers, taking the half-starved 'poor little beggars' for bread and cheese and mineral water to an off-licence beer-house, and being denounced by the dissenting preacher the following Sunday. That was the end for him of the Scout movement.[4]

Evelyn Waugh, bound to his wheel of adult irony, recalled joining the Scouts just before the First World War. They 'fell far short of the expectations raised by the books of Baden-Powell. I supposed we should be trained in tracking and wood-craft, in disguising the plans of enemy forts in drawings of butterflies; that we should be inspired by the high sense of honour exemplified by the Pistol Troop. In fact our proceedings were extremely drab.'[5]

Ian Niall, a recruit in the twenties, joined the Scouts to escape from the house in the evenings; he remembered camping in the rain, in a field full of cow-pats. The scoutmaster slept the night at home.[6] The dream could transfigure reality, but it depended on collective belief, and the right circumstances. In the great parades at the jamborees, in the rush of a Zulu horn formation, in the shout of an Een gonyama chorus, myth kept its power; in a dirty field in the rain it was fighting against the odds.

Like any other social organization whose identity rested on an imaginative construct, Scouting attracted its own myth-makers, and they made the founder, with his own help, into a saint. Rival claimants from time to time told the world that they, not Baden-Powell, had started Scouting: Daniel Beard maintained his own prior invention; Ernest Thompson Seton felt cheated of the credit to his deathbed. The history of Scouting, naturally enough, began to resemble the pattern of a religion: there was the true faith, there were the gospels, there were the apostates. R.B. Townshend, Fellow of Wadham College, Oxford, promoted himself – among rival claimants – as John the Baptist to the founder. A devotee of the Wild West, he built a mechanical wooden horse in his Oxford garden; he practised lassoing from its back, he drilled the neighbourhood boys in riding, roping, and shooting. It was he, he said, who in 1905 first gave Baden-Powell the vision:

> we often talked about the weakness of Britain and the softness of the boys, and finally I took him down to the South Coast. He and I walked along above the white cliffs of Dover. I showed him the lights of France across the channel at night. I said, 'The youth of Britain are getting soft and we've got to do something about it!' After we got back to Oxford he often came to watch my boys.[7]

As late as 1917 Lord Lonsdale was still telling the public that Boy Scouts were his at the beginning. Roger Pocock had given him the idea, they agreed the boys would be little soldiers, and he 'at once took it up and kept it going for some time' before surrendering his rights to Baden-Powell.[8] No wonder that one of Baden-Powell's chores was to fight off false prophets, to keep up a prolonged correspondence with officials at the Boy Scouts of America, and to set down, 'to be opened in the event of my death,' a record for posterity of the true and only origins of the movement.

In the Scout biographies, the life of the Chief Scout was celebrated even before his death, in the words of William Hillcourt's title, as the Two Lives of a Hero. The first life had come to its glorious climax at Mafeking; the second was still under way, for the founder, as George v said, announcing Baden-Powell's peerage, 'has been the mainspring of this great adventure.'[9] Legends accumulated, a cult developed. The founder's childhood was reimagined: he had been blessed by Thackeray and by Ruskin; aged eight, he had written 'Laws for me when I grow up.' The feats of his schooldays were woven into the canon, for had he not begun his scouting in the Godalming copse? His military career was reinvented: he had charged the Dervishes single-handed in the battle of Talmai, shouting, in the character of an Irish washerwoman, 'Hurrah for Misthress Mulvaney's washing!' (He was in India at the time.) As the authors added, this tale was probably new to the reader.[10] And his days as the Chief Scout continued to produce exemplary moments of drama, demon-strating that the heroic life was recognized by the smallest Scout, and that the hero himself was touched with divinity. There was the story of the 'little corporal,' a rather unwilling Scout, who, boarding a bus, was shown his leader.

> 'Truly,' it was whispered, 'he is your General – Sir Robert – the Chief Scout.' And then you should have seen the glow that over-spread the boy's face! ... Never have I seen a finer, a prouder, a more splendid salute than this of the little Corporal at the top of the motor-bus to the back of our Chief. It was a pity that the Chief's back was turned to the boy. But the Chief has eyes at the back of his head.[11]

Nor were Baden-Powell's exploits over. When the First World War came, 'what was the Chief Scout doing? ... Was he a spy? Frankly,' said one of the most faithful of old scoutmasters, leav-ing the door to speculation wide open, 'I cannot answer that.'[12]

From its beginnings the Scout movement had been involved in myth-making, even while it used the social codes of the middle class to instruct its recruits in good citizenship. It renewed the child's old game of hide-and-seek; it made a military skill, as practised by children, seem innocuous. For a generation of its first recruits, it gave form to a freedom from adult rules. In its rituals its campfire was an emblem of fellowship, a dream of male innocence in the woods. It was the last significant defensive statement of imperial and conservative values. Yet nothing stays the same. The conditions that produced Scouting changed; what was new became familiar and then stale; the organization imposed its own reality.

The meaning of the words on which Scouting had based its power shifted their position. When war took to the trenches in 1914, and the machine gun, barbed wire, and artillery made movement next to impossible, Baden-Powell's kind of military scouting became a memory: reconnaissance took to the air. In popular culture the word scout changed hands: it was surrendered to Baden-Powell and his boys. Soon a scout was a boy with bare knees, and scouting was what he did in the Scout hut, or round a campfire. The military usage, too, changed with the fashion, and the scout, except in the case of a few frontier units, became a sharpshooter, a ranger, or a commando. Boy Scouting first appropriated the game, then sanitized it.

With the heroics of war over in 1918, the movement shifted direction. Baden-Powell went on to lead the Scouts towards internationalism and brotherhood for all, and, while never abandoning Nation and Empire, gave new meanings to duty and good citizenship. Throughout the growing formalization of the movement he remained the same heroic, even saintly, figure. Like one of his model scoutmasters, he was the eternal boy-man, joining in the Scout games and the Scout chorus, blowing the kudu horn at the jamborees. He told his yarns over and over again as the need for new handbooks multiplied: what had served for the Scouts would serve just as well for the Guides, the Wolf Cubs, the Brownies, and the Rovers. And the advice he gave stayed the same. To his Cubs he said, 'the Old Wolf knows best.' To the Brownies he said 'play the game,' and 'buck up as the King directs,' and he ordered the Guides to 'T.I.B. (Tuck In your Back)' and 'Be Jolly.'

As the Second World War approached, so his cult took on ever more solid form. He reached old age; his wife Olave, a woman of commanding presence, protected him from his public, to whom he had said his formal farewells at the fifth jamboree in 1937.

His biographers added embellishments to his legend: from his home at Pax Hill he became the 'Piper of Pax,' who in 1939 would be nominated for the unawarded Nobel Peace Prize. As one of them somewhat heretically put it, 'there can never be another discoverer of Scouting, any more than there can ever be a second founder of Christianity.'[13]

In Kenya, where he died in 1941, he called his last home Paxtu (Pax 2), and it was from there that he sent his last messages to all Scouts and Guides. The dean and the chapter of Westminster offered the family a place in the Abbey, appropriately enough between the graves of the Unknown Warrior and David Livingstone. But he was buried in Kenya under a stone bearing the Boy Scout sign for 'I have gone home.' His apotheosis was marked by a statue erected outside Baden-Powell House, the London headquarters of Scouting, a statue of monolithic proportions and Pickwickian countenance, which at once captures the paradox of the hero-saint, larger than life, but still warm, friendly, approachable. He had the common touch, and as Winston Churchill hinted, making once more the connection between the two great B.P.s, Baden-Powell and the British Public, he was in a real sense created by popular demand.[14] Scouting was a celebration of the ethos that had produced its leader; the movement, for all its practical good work, was never very far away from the imperatives of its own myths.

Notes

I have used various scrapbooks in the Scout Association Archives as a source of newspaper cuttings and newspaper cartoons. These scrapbooks are described as the Mafeking Scrapbooks 1 and 2 (unnumbered pages), Baden-Powell Scrapbooks 60 ('Inspector General of Cavalry'), 61, 63 (unnumbered pages), and 'Guardbooks' 1 and 2 (unnumbered pages).

Scout Association Archives, Baden-Powell House, London, are abbreviated SAA.

INTRODUCTION

1 Collier, *England and the English*, 271
2 Haggard, *Days of My Life*, 2: 45, 268
3 Baden-Powell, *Rovering to Success*, 24
4 Baden-Powell, 'A New Scheme to Develop Good Citizens,' reported in the *Hereford Times*, 16 November 1907 (see text of speech on p. 243).
5 Jeal, *Baden-Powell*, 398 and 388–9
6 Figures reported by the Scout Association, SAA. A census of enrolments was taken from 1910 on.
7 MacLeod, *Building Character in the American Boy*, 146–67; Jeal, *Baden-Powell*, 498–517
8 Some Scout troops made do on only a token uniform – jersey, hat, and home-made staff – but most troops insisted on more. A patrol leader from the 4th Clapham (London) Troop, described the minimum kit in 1909 as 'Karki Slouch Hat, colored shirt and neckerchief, leather belt, haversack

on back, waterbottle on right side, axe on left side, Short Trousers and
Staff' (Essays on Scouting written by boys, Founder's Files, T.C. 42, SAA).
This would have cost about ten shillings, a sum well beyond the means of
most working-class families, representing about half a week's wages for
some trades in poor economic times (see Tressell, *Ragged-Trousered Philanthropists*, 558–9). Scout regulations added a jersey and great-coat for winter
wear, stockings, boots, a shoulder-knot, a whistle, and a knife. Gamages's
catalogue in 1911 listed a wide variety of additional kit, in a range of quality
and prices. Affluent troops could choose to buy equipment at double or
treble the basic cost, and they could add many additional items to their
personal kit, from oilskins to knife-sheaths and axe-cases.

9 Pelham, *Training of a Working Boy*, 119–21
10 Springhall, *Sure and Steadfast*, 258
11 MacKenzie, *Propaganda and Empire*, 15–38
12 Milner, *Nation and the Empire*, 152
13 Buchan, *Memory Hold the Door*, 124–5
14 Hobson, *Imperialism*, 46–61, 196–222
15 Masterman, *In Peril of Change*, 5
16 Kimmel, 'Contemporary "Crisis" in Masculinity,' 137–43; Showalter, *Sexual
Anarchy*, 1–15
17 Baden-Powell, *Scouting for Boys*, 342
18 Mills, *Decline and Fall of the British Empire*, 46–7
19 Hillcourt, *Baden-Powell*, 287; Jeal, *Baden-Powell*, 398–9
20 Great Britain, *Report on Physical Deterioration*, 91
21 Keeble, *The Citizen of To-morrow*, 279, 280, 276
22 Hynes, *The Edwardian Turn of Mind*, 32–3; Pearson, *Hooligan*, 93
23 Masterman, *Heart of the Empire*, 32–3; Pearson, *Hooligan*, 93
24 Emerson, *Works*, 2: 7–8
25 Gray, *Musings by Campfire and Wayside*, 299, 16
26 Mason, *Home Education*, 42–78
27 Ibid., 88–9
28 Mason, *Parents and Children*, 229; *Home Education*, 161
29 Hewitt, *The Open-Air Boy*, 250–1
30 *Boy's Own Paper*, 14 (1891–2): 776–8

CHAPTER 1. THE LEGION THAT NEVER WAS 'LISTED

1 Whitmore, 'Beard, Boys, and Buckskins,' 452–4; Seton, *Gospel of the Redman*,
103
2 Frye, *The Educated Imagination*, 8–9

3 Kipling, *Five Nations*, 51
4 Cooper, *Leatherstocking Tales*, 1: 362, 1: 1162–3
5 Lawrence, *Studies in Classic American Literature*, 44–60; H.N. Smith, *Virgin Land*, 59–70; Davis, 'The Deerslayer, a Democratic Knight of the Wilderness,' 92; Fiedler, *Love and Death in the American Novel*, 179–214
6 Zanger, 'The Frontiersman in Popular Fiction,' 141–53
7 Lawrence, *Studies*, 60
8 Dodge, *Our Wild Indians*, 596–623
9 Roosevelt, *Winning of the West*, 4: 237, 6: 166; *Wilderness Hunter*, 262–3
10 Russell, *Lives and Legends of Buffalo Bill*, 194–5
11 Cody, *Life and Adventures*, 288–92; Sandoz, *Buffalo Hunters*, 258–9
12 Grey, afterword, *Last of the Great Scouts*, 323
13 Cody, *Life and Adventures*, 334
14 *Times*, 10 May 1887, 10
15 Reddin, 'Wild West Shows,' 106–120
16 Branch, *The Cowboy and His Interpreters*, 20–31; Weston, *The Real American Cowboy*, 11
17 Wister, *The Virginian*, 18–21, 60
18 Quoted in Higgs, 'Yale and the Heroic Ideal,' 165
19 Weston, *The Real American Cowboy*, 11
20 The author was probably Constable T.A. Boys. Quoted in Horrall, *Pictorial History of the Royal Canadian Mounted Police*, 119
21 Walden, *Visions of Order*, 120; Owram, *Promise of Eden*, 125–48
22 Donkin, *Trooper and Redskin*, 223. The stetson was worn officially for the first time by the contingent of North-West Mounted Police who paraded in Queen Victoria's Diamond Jubilee, 1897. Officers and men of Canadian military units wore the British helmet at the Jubilee; the British press, significantly, paid them scant attention, but pictured the police and the colourful Australians instead.
23 Phillips, *A Man's Country?* 26–48
24 Lawson, *Collected Verse*, 1: 65
25 MacKenzie, *Empire of Nature*, 6–53
26 Leonard, *How We Made Rhodesia*, 268. In the 1890s and into the last days of empire, the Ndebele people were known to Europeans as the Matabele. The name Ndebele will be used here.
27 Stent, *A Personal Record*, 30–1
28 Creswicke, *South Africa and the Transvaal War*, 1: 124; Fitzpatrick, *Through Mashonaland with Pick and Pen*, 110–11
29 Haggard, *Allan Quatermain*, 429
30 Pocock, *A Frontiersman*, 174–5

31 Kipling, *Verses*, 188–9

32 Ibid., 254

33 Kipling, *The Light That Failed*, 158–60, 107

34 Service, *Collected Verse*, 12, 14, 93, 78.

35 Rowan, 'Legion of Frontiersmen,' 62

36 *Lloyd's Weekly News*, 25 March 1906

37 *History of the Legion of Frontiersmen*, 5–10. I am most grateful to Geoffrey Pocock, historian of the Legion of Frontiersmen, for permission to read his unpublished manuscript, 'The Road for the Rest.' Mr Pocock has kindly corrected many details in the following account of the Legion's early history.

38 Ibid., 11–15

39 Hill, 'Legion of Frontiersmen,' 236

40 Pocock, *Frontiersmen's Pocket-Book*, 373–4, 239

41 G. Pocock, *Forgotten as Becomes a Frontiersman*, 6–15. In the Thirties the Legion found itself mistaken for Oswald Mosley's British Union of Fascists, who also paraded in black shirts. With some regret it adopted the patrol jacket for ceremonial occasions.

42 Hill, 'Legion of Frontiersmen,' 237

43 See chapter 2.

44 *History of the Legion of Frontiersmen*, 17. The complete Frontiersman outfit, as advertised by Gamages, included leggings, spurs, brown gauntlet gloves, a revolver with lanyard, and whip.

45 Rowan, 'Legion of Frontiersmen,' 64

46 Jeal, *Baden-Powell*, 415

CHAPTER 2. BUCCANEERS: THE WAR SCOUTS

1 Baden-Powell, *Matabele Campaign*, 12–15; *Aids to Scouting*, 124

2 Jeal, *Baden-Powell*, 127, 188

3 Baden-Powell, *Matabele Campaign*, 45

4 Ibid., 56–63; Baden-Powell, *Lessons from the 'Varsity of Life*, 175

5 Baden-Powell, *Matabele Campaign*, 283–5

6 Baden-Powell, *Sport in War*, 19

7 Burnham, *Scouting on Two Continents*, 127

8 Ibid., 159

9 Ibid., 12–17

10 Ibid., 159

11 Jack Carruthers, 'Scouting for Wilson,' typescript, Sterling Memorial Library, Yale University, Howell Wright Collection 565: 1. 3. 49, 4

12 Burnham, *Scouting on Two Continents*, 174–88. Burnham gave testimony to the committee of inquiry into the Shangani affair. See Newman, *Matabeleland*, 131–9. For years afterwards rumours circulated that one of Burnham's companions, W.L. Gooding, had made a death-bed confession that they were not sent back by Wilson. See Jack Carruthers, 'Wilson's Last Stand,' typescript, Sterling Memorial Library, Yale University, Howell Wright Collection, 565: 1. 3. 49, 6.

13 *Illustrated London News*, 11 July 1896, 39; 25 July 1896, 97

14 Selous, *Sunshine and Storm in Rhodesia*, 97, 165

15 Sykes, *With Plumer in Matebeleland*, 261

16 Baden-Powell, *Matabele Campaign*, 268–74. Captain C.F. Stigand, in his *Scouting and Reconnaissance in Savage Countries*, endorsed Baden-Powell's choice of scout kit, even down to rubber-soled boots for scrambling on rocks: this was high praise from one of the best-known of big-game hunters. Interestingly, in the light of Boy Scout uniform, Stigand approved of 'khaki cut-shorts for walking' (Stigand, *Scouting and Reconnaissance*, 84). Baden-Powell in turn recommended Stigand's book to readers of *Scouting for Boys*.

17 Baden-Powell, *My Adventures as a Spy*, 32

18 Baden-Powell, *Matabele Campaign*, 99

19 Ibid., 121

20 Clery, *Minor Tactics*, 60

21 Browne, *A Lost Legionary in South Africa*, 250–1

22 Baden-Powell, *Downfall of Prempeh*, 162–78

23 Callwell, *Small Wars*, 306

24 Bourke, *On the Border with Crook*, 137–8

25 Ibid., v

26 Hamilton, *My Sixty Years on the Plains*, passim

27 Cooper, *Leatherstocking Tales*, 1: 684–7

28 Custer, *My Life on the Plains*, 234–48

29 Walden, *Visions of Order*, 109; Browne, *Camp Fire Yarns of the Lost Legion*, 167

30 Irregular corps of Pathan soldiers, commanded by British officers, were recruited to police the Northwest Frontier of India. The Chitral Scouts were organized in 1900, the Gilgit Scouts in 1913 (Trench, *Frontier Scouts*, 13). In Rhodesia the Selous Scouts took their name from Frederick Selous, the big-game hunter.

31 Steele, *Forty Years in Canada*, 213

32 Roosevelt, *Theodore Roosevelt, an Autobiography*, 225, 227

33 Lorant, *Life and Times of Theodore Roosevelt*, 297

34 *Lloyd's Weekly News*, 28 December 1902

35 Hyatt, *Off the Main Track*, 150–1

36 Kipling, 'The Parting of the Columns,' *Five Nations*, 165–8

37 Churchill, *My Early Life*, 320–1, 333

38 Ibid., 355–6

39 Ibid., 316–17

40 Creswicke, *South Africa and the Transvaal War*, 3: 144

41 Steele, *Forty Years in Canada*, 347–50. Six hundred Arizona stockmen volunteered to join the Canadians but were reluctantly turned down.

42 Phillips, *A Man's Country?* 145

43 Marquis, *Canada's Sons on Kopje and Veldt*, 43

44 Pocock, *A Frontiersman*, 289–90

45 Vachell, *The Hill*, 298; Hornung, *Raffles: The Amateur Cracksman*, 270–88

46 Lindley, *Lord Lovat*, 75–106

47 *Chums*, 8: 583; *Boys of Our Empire*, 2: 137; *Young England*, 22: 117–19; *Public School Magazine*, 10 July 1900, 35–6; *Boy's Own Paper*, 23: 589. The public schools, following the fashion of other smart military units, caught on to the frontier excitement after the Boer War, and some public school cadet brigades equipped themselves with slouch hats ('Schoolboy soldiers,' *Illustrated London News*, 11 August 1906).

48 Haggard, *Allan Quatermain*, 432; Baden-Powell, *Downfall of Prempeh*, 45. 'M'Lala-Pahnsi [*sic*] is the name by which a Zulu describes the man who lays his plans carefully and with full completeness before he embarks on his enterprise' (Baden-Powell, *Prempeh*, 45). In his diary Baden-Powell admitted that many Africans 'Shrieked with laughter' when he mentioned this nickname, probably because it described the comic (phallic) possibilities of a man lying on his back with a rifle between his legs (Jeal, *Baden-Powell*, 120).

49 Baden-Powell, *Matabele Campaign*, 127–8; *Lessons from the 'Varsity of Life*, 139

50 Hyatt, *Off the Main Track*, 185. '-phisi (impisi): 1. spotted hyena, *Crocuta crocuta*; 2. very ugly, vicious-looking creature; 3. plain, brown military blanket; 4. advanced stage of diarrhoea ... ; 5. spy, scout, special messenger' (C.M. Doke and B.W. Vilakazi, *Zulu-English Dictionary*).

51 Baden-Powell, *Aids to Scouting*, ix

52 Vivian, *The British Army from Within*, 12

53 'The Art of Scouting,' *Black and White*, 28 April 1900, 644

54 *M.A.P.*, 13 January 1900, 25

CHAPTER 3. THE WOLF THAT NEVER SLEPT

1 Newspaper cutting, Scrapbook 61, SAA

2 Jeal, *Baden-Powell*, 205–312

3 Ibid., 228–9

4 Ibid., 260–85

5 Hillcourt, *Baden-Powell,* 196

6 *The Times,* 19 May 1900, 11

7 Jeal, *Baden-Powell,* 246–7; Wilson, *South African Memories,* 72–169; Roberts, *Those Bloody Women,* 19–73

8 Hamilton, *Siege of Mafeking,* 120–1, 192–3

9 Ibid., 193

10 Once the story of the siege was underway it became self-defeating from the journalistic point of view not to make the most of a good story. Some of the soldiers and townspeople of Mafeking, however, were critical of Baden-Powell's behaviour (see Ross, *Siege of Mafeking,* 48; Ashworth, 'Siege of Mafeking,' 113–14).

11 Stent, letter, British Library Add. ms. 46848

12 *Pall Mall Gazette,* 19 April 1900, 2

13 Ibid.

14 *The Times,* 26 May 1900, 7

15 Begbie, *The Story of Baden-Powell,* 114–15

16 The press as a whole supported the war enthusiastically. The *Daily Mail,* the *Evening News,* the *Sun* and later the *Daily Express* were identified by the few anti-war Liberal and Radical papers as the leaders of the jingos, but the 'better' Tory newspapers such as *The Times* and the *Standard* were almost as loud and scarcely less 'patriotic.' The Liberal press was divided: some papers, such as the *Daily Chronicle,* which fired its pro-Boer editor in 1899, were firmly imperialist; others, such as the *Westminster Gazette,* the *Morning Leader,* and its evening companion, the *Star,* were vigorously critical of the government. The leading independents, such as the *Pall Mall Gazette,* found it difficult to keep their distance; opposition to the war threatened a drop in circulation (Koss, *Rise and Fall,* 1: 356–435).

17 *Star,* 19 May 1900, 1

18 *Pall Mall Gazette,* 19 May 1900, 1; Fletcher, *Baden-Powell of Mafeking,* 46

19 Fletcher, *Baden-Powell of Mafeking,* 89

20 *Celebrities of the Army*

21 *Under the Union Jack,* 2 June 1900, 717

22 Fletcher, *Baden-Powell of Mafeking,* 125; *Graphic,* 24 March 1900; *Vanity Fair,* 19 April 1911

23 *Manchester Guardian,* 19 May 1900, 2; Aitken, *Baden-Powell, the Hero of Mafeking,* 23; Bremner, *Col. R.S.S. Baden-Powell,* 2

24 Begbie, *The Story of Baden-Powell,* 2, 156

25 *Pall Mall Gazette,* 19 May 1900, 9

26 *Vanity Fair,* 5 July 1900; Baden-Powell, *Aids to Scouting,* 18

27 Begbie, *The Story of Baden-Powell,* 2–4

28 *Vanity Fair,* 5 July 1900

29 Jeal, *Baden-Powell,* 289

30 *Daily Express,* 19 May 1900, 3

31 *M.A.P.,* 27 May 1900, 496

32 *Daily Chronicle,* 2 December 1899; reprinted in *Morning Post, Under the Union Jack*

33 For a more 'selected' audience there were verses on a public school theme: 'Adsum' – the public schoolboy's answer at roll call – was the Reverend A. Frewen Aylward's vision of Baden-Powell at Mafeking, the 'Old Boy' and officer answering the call of duty.

34 Mafeking Scrapbook 1, SAA

35 Some newspapers carried on as long as they dared in this spirit. The *Daily Express* did its damnedest to milk the excitement: it ran a column of 'Mafe-kites,' a list of jokes and anecdotes connected with the celebrations; it collected money from single women for a sword of honour for the hero; it proposed a national monument for the dead, an English Valhalla. The triumph was exploited in the marketplace. Spinks Limited struck a set of medals of Baden-Powell, and Tuck & Sons, the toymakers, made Mafeking No. 1 in their 'Model Relief Series' of the Transvaal Campaign. Messrs. Thomas Webb & Sons of Stourbridge designed a pair of cut-glass cannons in imitation of the Mafeking guns. Madame Tussaud's advertised 'Numer-ous Additions' for the Whitsun holidays to celebrate Mafeking, including a new 'Life-like Portrait Model of Major-General Baden-Powell.'

36 There is still debate about the nature of the crowds in London, and their behaviour: were they working-class hooligans, and were their excesses jin-goistic? Richard Price has claimed that the mafficking was celebratory, not jingoistic (*A Imperial War and the British Working Class,* 133). John Springhall states that the crowd was led by middle and lower middle-class youths, mostly young clerks, medical students, and 'beardless youths' (*Coming of Age,* 39).

37 Newspaper cutting, Scrapbook 63, SAA

38 Maurice, *History of the War in South Africa,* 3: 140–1

39 Jeal, *Baden-Powell,* 330–42

40 Quoted in Hillcourt, *Baden-Powell,* 222

41 To judge from contemporary photographs in the National Army Museum, the more exotic elements of this uniform, such as shorts, short-sleeve shirts, and neckerchiefs, do not seem to have been worn in the field.

CHAPTER 4. ZULU WARRIORS OR 'RED INDIAN' BRAVES?

1 Jeal, *Baden-Powell*, 384–5
2 Hillcourt, *Baden-Powell*, 264–74
3 *Boy's Own Paper*, 12 (1889–90): 410
4 Everett, *Scouts' Book*, 72
5 'Especially did I relish the literature of Vagabondia,' says the hero of Robert Service's novel *The Trail of '98*. 'I had come under the spell of Stevenson. His name spelled Romance to me ... I too would seek these ultimate islands ... I would be a frontiersman, a trail-breaker, a treasure-seeker' (p. 4).
6 Begbie, *The Story of Baden-Powell*, 101–3
7 Jeal, *Baden-Powell*, 5–6
8 Sanderson, *Heroes of Pioneering*, 38
9 Jeal, *Baden-Powell*, 169
10 De Beaumont, *The Wolf That Never Sleeps*, 42–3
11 Jeal, *Baden-Powell*, 390
12 *Scouting for Boys*, 11
13 Puffer, *The Boy and His Gang*, 159
14 Forbush, *The Boy Problem*, 15–16
15 Ibid., 23–4
16 Paul, *Angry Young Man*, 15. Leslie Paul remembers going out and buying one of Dudley Kidd's books (probably *The Essential Kaffir*). Kidd was the authority on South African natives.
17 Haggard, *King Solomon's Mines*, 78. The magnificence of Haggard's 'Zulus' is a comment on the need for English virility. Haggard's fighting Englishman, Sir Henry Curtis, a throwback to the Danish berserker, is a perfect match and companion to the black warrior Umbopa (Umslopogaas in *Allan Quatermain*).
18 Jeal, *Baden-Powell*, 133
19 *Scouting for Boys*, 172–3; *Rovering to Success*, 25. Another story Baden-Powell repeated described the 'test of pluck' that the boys of the Yaghan tribe of Patagonia had to undergo. It consisted of 'the boy driving a spear deep into his thigh and smiling all the time in spite of his pain.' See Founder's Files, following draft of article on 'My Dog,' *c.* 1931, T.C. 21, SAA.
20 Baden-Powell, *Wolf Cub Handbook*, 14
21 Seton, *Two Little Savages*, 45
22 Seton, *Trail of an Artist-Naturalist*, 383–5
23 *Ladies' Home Journal* had a circulation of 800,000. This helped enormously in the recruitment and promotion of Seton's woodcraft 'tribes.' See Keller, *Black Wolf*, 151.

24 Fry, *Life Worth Living*, 154–5
25 Keller, *Black Wolf*, 166–7
26 Seton, *Book of Woodcraft*, 9
27 Forbush, *The Boy Problem*, 100
28 Eastman, *Indian Boyhood*, 43; Seton, *Gospel of the Redman*, 105
29 Quoted in Keller, *Black Wolf*, 169
30 Jeal, *Baden-Powell*, 501–2
31 The emphasis on hardiness was almost certainly even greater in those parts of the Empire, such as New Zealand, in which the 'frontier spirit' was most closely linked to virility and national pride. See Phillips, *A Man's Country?*, 156.
32 Jeal, *Baden-Powell*, 395
33 Dimmock, *Scouts' Book of Heroes*, 17

CHAPTER 5. THE LAWS OF THE JUNGLE

1 Newspaper cutting (New York, 25 September 1910), 'Visit to Canada' Scrapbook, Scouts Canada, Ottawa
2 Browne, *With the Lost Legion in New Zealand*, 47-8
3 Baden-Powell, *Matabele Campaign*, 483
4 Lawson, *Collected Verse*, 2: 12
5 Paterson, *Best of Banjo Paterson*, 279–85
6 Baden-Powell, *Young Knights of the Empire*, 60–1
7 Jeal, *Baden-Powell*, 333
8 Baden-Powell, *Canadian Boy Scout*, xii–xvii
9 Kipling, *Jungle Book*, 105
10 Rosenthal, *Character Factory*, 161–90; Jeal, *Baden-Powell*, 413
11 Rosenthal, *Character Factory*, 113
12 Baden-Powell, *Scouting for Boys*, 49–51
13 Rosenthal, *Character Factory*, 115–16
14 MacKenzie, 'The Boy Scout Experience,' 15
15 Springhall, 'Boy Scouts, Class and Militarism,' 138–41
16 Paul, *Angry Young Man*, 53
17 Dimmock, *Bare Knee Days*, 16
18 Niall, *A London Boyhood*, 115
19 Humphries, *Hooligans or Rebels?*, 122, 134
20 *The Scout*, 7 (1912): 971. Baden-Powell and his staff did not have editorial control over *The Scout*, and deplored its vulgar tone, but the magazine was, in effect, the public voice of Scouting, and both reported on and influenced Scout behaviour.

21 Bradby, *The Lanchester Tradition*, 45

22 Baden-Powell, *Downfall of Prempeh*, 65

23 *Public School Magazine*, July 1900, 35

24 Hay, *The Lighter Side of School Life*, 35

25 Baden-Powell, *Scouting for Boys*, 251–2; *Rovering to Success*, 24

26 Jeal, *Baden-Powell*, 522

27 Hillcourt, *Baden-Powell*, 342

28 Smiles, *Thrift*, 277

29 Thompson, *The Edwardians*, 297–8

30 Smiles, *Thrift*, 277

31 Hall, *Educational Problems*, 1: 464

32 Jeal, *Baden-Powell*, 106

33 Baden-Powell's collaborator on the handbook, Pearson's manager Percy Everitt, may also have had a hand in the frequent references to Keary and his books as a means of promoting Pearson's sales. Yet judging from his other publications for Scouts, Baden-Powell frequently spoke in the same language as Keary. In *Do It Now!* Keary had used Baden-Powell at Mafeking as one of his examples of the value of assertiveness, 'blowing his little tin trumpet' (p. 54).

34 Keary, *Do It Now!* 34

35 Wodehouse, *Mike*, 198

36 *Boy Scouts and What They Do*, 90

37 Baden-Powell, *Scouting for Boys*, 309

38 Ibid., 12–13

39 Ibid., 65, 312, 62

40 See Field, *Toward a Programme*, 26–31.

41 Stable, *Hearts of Oak*, x

42 Miles, *The Imperial Reciter*, preface

43 Kingsley, *Westward Ho!*, 558

44 Hughes, *Tom Brown's Schooldays*, 13–15

45 Kingsley, *Westward Ho!*, 7; Protheroe, *The Empire's Cause*, 52; Stables, *Hearts of Oak*, 81

46 Baden-Powell, *Scouting for Boys*, 319, 327, 334

47 Ibid., 316–18

48 Ibid., 380–1

49 Wood, *Boy Scouts' Roll of Honour*, foreword

CHAPTER 6. MRS BRITANNIA'S YOUNGEST LINE OF DEFENCE

1 *The Times*, 12 August 1912, 6

2 Ibid., 9 August 1912, 6

3 Seton, 'The Woodcraft Movement/History' (a statement to the editorial board of the Boy Scouts of America, forwarded to Baden-Powell and the Boy Scouts Association, 4 May 1927), Founder's Files, T.C. 42, SAA

4 Baden-Powell, *Scouting for Boys*, 321

5 Ibid., 340–1

6 The Vane 'rebellion' was a muddy business, complicated both by happenstance and by the conflicting personalities of Vane and Baden-Powell, and centring on the quarrel over militarism. See Jeal, *Baden-Powell*, 404–9, and Rosenthal, *Character Factory*, 206.

7 *Boy Scout Association: Annual Reports*, 1912, 7; 1914, 8–9

8 The Boy Scout, as patriotic symbol, was resuscitated in the Second World War. See Reynolds, *Boy Scouts*, 42–3.

9 Springhall, 'Boy Scouts, Class and Militarism,' 155–8

10 Summers, 'Militarism,' 119–22

11 Warren, 'Sir Robert Baden-Powell, the Scout Movement and Citizen Training,' 388

12 Springhall, 'Baden-Powell and the Scout Movement,' 939–42

13 Summers, 'Scouts, Guides and VADs,' 945–7

14 Jeal claims that Springhall et al. overstate their case; he insists that Scouting was more civil than military in its aims. He resists too the idea that Scouting was an agency of social control, and, qualifying the taint of militarism, points out the debt that Scouting owed in its first years to Christian philanthropists (*Baden-Powell*, 409–15).

15 Baden-Powell, *Scouting for Boys*, 395

16 *The Scout*, 5 (1910): 20

17 Golding, *Wonder Book of Soldiers*; Holladay, *War Games for Boy Scouts*

18 Wells, *Little Wars: A Game for Boys*

19 Baden-Powell, *Scouting for Boys*, 242–58

20 *The Scout*, 5 (1910): 2 July 1910

21 *Daily Telegraph*, 4 May 1910, 16

22 *The Captain*, 21: 310

23 Ibid., 189

24 *Cape Breton's Magazine*, 33: 1

25 Letter to the secretary, Boy Scout headquarters, signed E.W. Ward, Secretary, War Office, 30 March 1911, 'Guardbook' 2, p. 42, SAA

26 *Daily Telegraph*, 4 May 1910, 16

27 Jeal, *Baden-Powell*, 448–50

28 *Windsor Magazine*, 43: 17; Hope, *The School of Arms*, frontispiece

29 Mee, *Arthur Mee's Hero Book*, facing p. 278

30 *Jack Cornwell*, 59–61
31 Baden-Powell's painting of Cornwell appeared in the *Boy's Own Paper* 39, facing p. 112, and as the frontispiece to Dimmock, *Scouts' Book of Heroes*. The force of this symbolism can be compared to more self-conscious attempts at dramatizing Scouting's image, such as the pre-1914 paintings by Ernest Carlos, which were circulated within the organization, and which have an ersatz myth-making character. 'If I Were a Boy Again' showed a working-class father looking enviously at a smart young Boy Scout, 'Raw Material' showed a working-class boy joining the Scouts, 'Headquarters' pictured Scouts at work in the Scout hut, and 'The Pathfinder' had a young Scout in the protection of the 'original Scout,' Jesus Christ.
32 Wood, *Boy Scouts' Roll of Honour*, vii–ix
33 Dimmock, *Scouts' Book of Heroes*, 10

CONCLUSION. SCOUTING AND MYTH

1 Slotkin, *The Fatal Environment*, 19
2 'Noemo,' *Boy Scout Bubble*, 25–7
3 In confessing to the frontier games that he and his 'adopted' sons played in Kensington Gardens, the games which gave birth to *Peter Pan*, Barrie told a story of meeting Ernest Thompson Seton in the Reform Club in London, and learning from him the proper Indian method of making fire with two sticks.
4 Hyatt, *Off the Main Track*, 233–5
5 Waugh, *A Little Learning*, 89
6 Niall, *A London Boyhood*, 113–26
7 Moran, 'Baden-Powell's Big Idea,' 66
8 *Grimsby Daily Telegraph*, 28 July 1917
9 Hillcourt, *Baden-Powell*, 382
10 Catherall, *Young Baden-Powell*; Batchelder, *Life of Baden-Powell*, 9–10
11 Aitken, *The Chief Scout*, 141–2
12 Dimmock, *Bare Knee Days*, 48–9
13 Wade, *Piper of Pax*, 11
14 Churchill, *Great Contemporaries*, 297

Bibliography

CONTEMPORARY NEWSPAPERS AND PERIODICALS

Black and White
The Bluejacket and the Soldier
The Boys' Friend
The Boys' Herald
Boys of Our Empire
Boy's Own Paper
The Captain
C.B. Fry's The Outdoor Magazine
Chums
The Church Standard
Daily Chronicle
Daily Express
Daily Mail
Daily Mirror
Daily Telegraph
Evening News
The Frontiersman
The Graphic
Grimsby Daily Telegraph
Hereford Times
Illustrated London News
Irish Daily Independent
Lloyd's Weekly News

Manchester Guardian
M.A.P.
Morning Leader
Morning Post
Mother and Home
Navy and Army Gazette
Pall Mall Budget
Pall Mall Gazette
Pearson's Weekly
Public School Magazine
Punch
Reynold's Newspaper
The Scout
The Sphere
The Star
Sunday Times
The Times
Tit-Bits
Under the Union Jack
Vanity Fair
Windsor Magazine
Young England

PRIMARY SOURCES

Adams, Morley. *The Scout's Active Service Book*. London: Frowde, 1916
Adams, Morley, ed. *The Boy Scout's Companion: A Manual of Scoutcraft*. London: RTS, 1912
Aitken, W. Francis. *Baden-Powell, the Hero of Mafeking*. London: Partridge, 1900
– *The Chief Scout: Sir Robert Baden-Powell*. London: Partridge, [1911]
Alexander, John, ed. *Stories of Self-Help*. London: Partridge, n.d.
Ashworth, R.L. 'The Siege of Mafeking.' Ms., SAA
Ayres, Leonard P. *Open-air Schools*. New York: Doubleday, 1910
Baden-Powell, Robert S.S. *Adventuring to Manhood*. London: Pearson, 1936
– *Aids to Scouting for N.C.O.s and Men*. Aldershot: Gale and Polden, [1899]
– *The Canadian Boy Scout: a Handbook for Instruction in Good Citizenship* (Canadian edition of *Scouting for Boys*). Toronto: Morang, 1911
– *The Downfall of Prempeh*. London: Methuen, 1896.
– [With Agnes Baden-Powell.] *The Handbook for Girl Guides or How Girls Can Help Build the Empire*. London: Nelson, 1912.
– *Indian Memories*. London: Jenkins, 1915
– *Lessons from the 'Varsity of Life*. London: Pearson, 1933
– *Life's Snags and How to Meet Them: Talks to Young Men*. London: Pearson, 1930
– *Marksmanship for Boys: The Red Feather and How to Win It*. London: Pearson, 1915
– *The Matabele Campaign*. London: Methuen, 1897
– *My Adventures as a Spy*. London: Pearson, 1915
– *My Hat!* (and Nicholas Palmerston, *A Gentleman of Burgundy*). Oxford: Blackwell, [1927]
– *Pigsticking or Hoghunting*. London: Harrison, 1899
– *Quick Training for War*. London: Jenkins, 1914
– *Reconnaissance and Scouting*. London: Clowes, 1884
– *Rovering to Success*. 1922. London: Jenkins, 1963
– *Scouting for Boys*. London: Cox, 1908
– *Scouting for Boys*. 3rd ed. London: Pearson, 1910
– *Scouting for Boys: An Explanation*. n.p. [c. 1909]
– *Sketches in Mafeking and East Africa*. London: Smith Elder, 1907
– *Sport in War*. London: Heinemann, 1900
– *What Scouts Can Do: More Yarns*. London: Pearson, 1921
– *The Wolf Cub's Handbook*. London: Pearson, 1916
– *Young Knights of the Empire*. 1916. London: Pearson, 1920
Baillie, Frederick D. *Mafeking: A Diary of the Siege*. London: Constable, 1900
Ballantyne, Robert M. *The Coral Island*. London: Nelson, 1901

Barrie, James M. *The Plays*. London: Hodder and Stoughton, 1928

Batchelder, W.J., and David Balfour. *The Life of Baden-Powell*. London: Collins, 1929

Begbie, Harold. *The Story of Baden-Powell: 'The Wolf That Never Sleeps.'* London: Richards, 1900

Bond, Geoffrey. *The Adventures of Baden-Powell*. London: Staples, 1957

– *The Baden-Powell Story*. London: Staples, 1955

Bourke, John G. *On the Border with Crook*. 1891. Lincoln, NE: U. of Nebraska P, 1971

The Boy Makes the Man; or, Stories of the Boyhood and Manhood of Famous Men (Royal Standard Readers). London: Nelson, 1888

Boy Scout Association: Annual Reports, 1910–14

Boy Scouts and What They Do (Record of the Imperial Scout Exhibition and Rally, Birmingham, July, 1913). n.p., n.d.

Boy Scouts Scheme. n.p., n.d. [1907?]

'B.-P.': The Hero of Mafeking. (Tit-Bits Monster Penny Books). London: Newnes, [1900]

Bradby, G.F. *The Lanchester Tradition*. 1913. London: Richards, 1954

Browne, G. Hamilton. *Camp Fire Yarns of the Lost Legion*. London: Laurie, [1913]

– *A Lost Legionary in South Africa*. London: Laurie, [1912]

– *With the Lost Legion in New Zealand*. London: Laurie, [1911]

Buchan, John. *Greenmantle*. 1916. London: Hodder and Stoughton, 1935

– *Memory Hold the Door*. Toronto: Musson, 1940

– *Prester John*. 1910. Harmondsworth: Penguin, 1983

Bullen, Frank T. *The Cruise of the Cachalot*. Philadelphia: McKay, n.d.

Burnham, Frederick R. *Scouting on Two Continents*. Garden City, NY: Doubleday, 1926

Burnham, Roy. *B-P's Life in Pictures*. London: Boy Scouts Assoc., [c. 1952]

Butler, William. *The Campaign of the Cataracts*. London: Sampson Low, 1887

– *Charles George Gordon* (English Men of Action Series). London: Macmillan, 1911

Cadett, Herbert. *The Boys' Book of Battles*. London: Pearson, 1903

Callwell, Charles. *Small Wars: Their Principles and Practice*. 1896. London: HMSO, 1899

Carlyle, Thomas. *Heroes, Hero Worship and the Heroic in History*. New York: Burt, n.d.

Carter, F.C. *The Training and Use of Scouts*. London: HMSO, 1904

Carter, M.E. *Life of Baden-Powell*. London: Longmans, 1956

Catherall, Arthur. *The Young Baden-Powell*. Toronto: Clarke, Irwin, 1961

Celebrities of the Army. n.p., n.d. [c. 1900]

Churchill, Winston S. *Frontiers and Wars* (*The Malakand Field Force, The River War, London to Ladysmith, Ian Hamilton's March*). London: Eyre and Spottiswoode, 1962

– *Great Contemporaries.* 1937. London: Collins, 1962

– *My Early Life* (*A Roving Commission*). 1930. Montreal: Reprint Society, 1948

Clery, Cornelius. *Minor Tactics.* 1874. London: Kegan Paul, 1880

Cody, William. *Life and Adventures of 'Buffalo Bill.'* Chicago: Stanton, 1917

Collier, Price. *England and the English from an American Point of View.* New York: Scribner, 1909

Connor, Ralph. *The Patrol of the Sun Dance Trail.* Toronto: Westminster, 1914

Cooper, J. Fenimore. *The Leatherstocking Tales.* 2 vols. New York: Library of America, 1985

Cornford, Leslie Cope. *The Canker at the Heart.* London: Grant Richards, 1905

Couch, Arthur Quiller. *The Roll Call of Honour: A New Book of Golden Deeds.* London: Nelson, [1911]

Creswicke, Louis. *South Africa and the Transvaal War.* 6 vols. Edinburgh: Jack, 1900

Custer, George A. *My Life on the Plains.* 1874. Lincoln, NE: U of Nebraska P, 1971

Davitt, Michael. *The Boer Fight for Freedom.* New York: Funk and Wagnalls, 1902

De Beaumont, Marguerite. *The Wolf That Never Sleeps.* London: Girl Guides, 1944

Deeds of Glory: Stories of Our Empire. London: Jarrold, 1901.

Dimmock, F. Haydn. *Bare Knee Days.* London: Pearson, 1939

[Dimmock, F. Haydn, ed.] *The Scouts' Book of Heroes: A Record of Scouts' Work in the Great War.* London: Pearson, 1919

Dodge, Richard Irving. *Our Wild Indians: Thirty-three Years Personal Experience.* 1882. Williamstown, MA: Corner House, 1978

Donkin, John G. *Trooper and Redskin in the Far North-West.* London: Sampson Low, 1889

Doyle, Arthur Conan. *The Complete Sherlock Holmes.* 2 vols. New York: Doubleday, 1953

– *The Great Boer War.* London: Nelson, 1903

– *Historical Romances* (*The White Company, Sir Nigel,* etc.). London: Murray, 1962

Drannan, W.F. *Chief of Scouts.* Chicago: Rhodes and McClure, n.d.

Drewery, Mary. *Baden-Powell: The Man Who Lived Twice.* Ottawa: Boy Scouts of Canada, 1975

Eastman, Charles A. [Ohiyesa]. *Indian Boyhood.* 1902. New York: Dover, 1971

Emerson, Ralph Waldo. *The Works.* Philadelphia: Nottingham Society, 1900

The Empire Reciter. London: Sunday School Union, [1898]

Everett, Bernard, ed. *The Scout's Book.* London: Pearson, 1920

Fitchett, William H. *Deeds That Won the Empire* (Bell's Literature Readers.) London: Bell, [1908]

– *Fights for the Flag* (Bell's Literature Readers). London: Bell, [1908]

Fitzpatrick, James Percy. *Jock of the Bushveld.* 1907. London: Longmans, 1941

– *Through Mashonaland with Pick and Pen.* 1892. Johannesburg: Donker, 1973

Fletcher, J.S. *Baden-Powell of Mafeking.* London: Methuen, 1900

Forbush, William B. *The Boy Problem.* 1901. New York: Westminster, 1907

Forster, H.O. Arnold. *The Citizen Reader.* 8th ed. London: Cassell, 1887

– *In Danger's Hour, or, Stout Hearts and Stirring Deeds.* London: Cassell, 1899

– *Things Old and New; or, Stories from English History* (Cassell's Modern School Series.) London: Cassell, 1893

Froude, James Anthony. *English Seamen in the Sixteenth Century.* London: Longmans, 1895

Fry, Charles B. *Life Worth Living.* London: Eyre and Spottiswoode, 1939

Golding, Harry, ed. *The Wonder Book of Soldiers for Boys and Girls.* London: Ward Lock, [1914]

'Good Turns,' by the Digbeth Boy Scouts. Birmingham: Parkins, n.d.

Gorst, Sir John Eldon. *The Children of the Nation: How Their Health and Vigour Should Be Promoted by the State.* Ed. C.W. Saleeby. London: Methuen, 1906

Goulding, Francis R. *The Adventures of the Young Marooners: or, Robert and Harold on the Florida Coast. A Tale for Boys.* 1853. London: Ward, [1882]

Grahame, Kenneth. *The Wind in the Willows.* 1908. New York: Bantam, 1982

Gray, Herbert B. *The Public Schools and the Empire.* London: Williams, 1913

Gray, William C. *Musings by Campfire and Wayside.* New York: Revell, 1902

Great Britain. *Report of the Inter-departmental Committee on Physical Deterioration.* British Sessional Papers. House of Commons (1904). Vol. 32

Greene, Graham. *A Sort of Life.* New York: Simon and Schuster, 1971

Grey Owl. *Men of the Last Frontier.* London: Country Life, 1934

Grey, Zane. Introduction and Afterword. *Last of the Great Scouts.* Helen Cody Wetmore. New York: Grosset and Dunlap, 1918

Grinnell-Milne, Duncan. *Baden-Powell at Mafeking.* London: Bodley Head, 1957

Gross, Hans. *Criminal Investigation: A Practical Textbook for Magistrates, Police Officers and Lawyers.* Trans. 1906. Adapted by John Adam and J. Collyer Adam. Ed. Norman Kendal. London: Sweet and Maxwell, 1934

Haggard, H. Rider. *Allan Quatermain.* 1887. London: Octopus, 1979

– *The Days of My Life.* 2 vols. London: Longmans, 1926

– *King Solomon's Mines.* 1885. London: Octopus, 1979

– *Nada the Lily.* London: Longmans, 1892

Hall, G. Stanley. *Adolescence.* New York: Appleton, 1904

— *Educational Problems.* 2 vols. New York: Appleton, 1911

Hamilton, J. Angus. *The Siege of Mafeking.* London: Methuen, 1900

Hamilton, William T. *My Sixty Years on the Plains.* Ed. E.T. Sieber. Ill. Charles M. Russell. 1905. Columbus, OH: Long, 1951

Hargrave, John. *Lonecraft: The Handbook for Lone Scouts.* London: Constable, 1913

— *Tribal Training.* London: Pearson, 1919

— *The Wigwam Papers.* London: Pearson, n.d. [1916?]

Harris, Frank. *My Life and Loves.* New York: Grove, 1963

Hay, Ian [John Beith]. *The First Hundred Thousand.* London: Toronto, Briggs, 1916

— *The Lighter Side of School Life.* 1914. London: Foulis, 1919

Hayens, Herbert. *With Sword and Ship.* London: Collins, 1906

Henty, George A. *Among Malay Pirates: A Tale of Adventure and Peril.* New York: Mershon, n.d.

— *In Times of Peril: A Tale of India.* New York: Burt, n.d.

— *Jack Archer. A Tale of the Crimea.* New York: Mershon, n.d.

— *St. George for England: A Tale of Cressy and Poitiers.* London: Blackie, n.d.

— *With Wolfe in Canada, or, the Winning of a Continent.* London: Blackie, n.d.

Hewett, G.M.A. *The Open-Air Boy.* London: Allen, 1901

Highton, E. Gilbert. *The Siege of Mafeking: A Patriotic Poem.* [London?]: Harrison, 1900

The History of the Legion of Frontiersmen. Regina: n.p., n.d. [1970?]

Hobson, J.A. *Imperialism: A Study.* 1902. Ann Arbor: U of Michigan P, 1965

Hole, H. Marshall. *The Making of Rhodesia.* London: Macmillan, 1926

Holladay, A.J. *War Games for Boy Scouts.* Aldershot: Gale and Polden, 1910

Hope, Ascott. *The School of Arms: Stories of Boy Soldiers and Sailors.* London: Routledge, n.d.

Hornung, E.W. *Raffles: the Amateur Cracksman (The Amateur Cracksman* 1899; *The Black Mask* 1901). London: Chatto and Windus, 1972

Hughes, Thomas. *Tom Brown's Schooldays.* 1857. Harmondsworth: Puffin, 1985

Hyatt, Stanley. *The Diary of a Soldier of Fortune.* New York: Lane, 1911

— *Off the Main Track.* London: Laurie, n.d.

Jack Cornwell. By the author of *Where's Master?.* London: Hodder and Stoughton, n.d.

Jefferies, Richard. *Bevis: The Story of a Boy.* 1882. London: Duckworth, 1913

Jones, George C.G. [afterwards Griffith]. *Men Who Have Made the Empire.* London: Pearson, 1897

Jones, L.E. *An Edwardian Youth.* London: Macmillan, 1938

Keary, Peter. *Do It Now!* London: Pearson, 1908

— *The Secrets of Success.* London: Pearson, 1906

Keeble, Samuel E., ed. *The Citizen of To-morrow: A Handbook on Social Questions.* London: Kelly, 1906

Kidd, Dudley. *The Essential Kaffir.* London: Black, 1904

– *Savage Childhood.* 1906. New York: Negro UP, 1969

Kingsley, Charles. *Westward Ho!* 1855. London: Collins, n.d.

Kipling, Rudyard. *The Day's Work.* Part 2. New York: Scribner, 1916

– *The Five Nations.* New York: Scribner, 1917

– *The Jungle Book.* 1894. (*The First Jungle Book*). New York: Scribner, 1917

– *Kim.* New York: Scribner, 1916

– *The Light That Failed.* New York: Scribner, 1917

– *Puck of Pook's Hill.* New York: Scribner, 1916

– *Stalky & Co.* New York: Scribner, 1913

– *Verses 1889–1896.* New York: Scribner, 1916.

Laurie, A.P., ed. *The Teacher's Encyclopaedia.* 7 vols. London: Caxton, 1912

Lawson, Henry. *Collected Verse.* 3 vols. Ed. Colin Roderick. Sydney: Angus and Robertson, 1967

The Legion of Frontiersmen: Its History, Aims, Objects, Organization, Regulations, Etc. Calgary: n.p., n.d. [1916?]

Leonard, Arthur G. *How We Made Rhodesia.* London: Kegan Paul, 1896

Long, William J. *School of the Woods.* Boston: Ginn, 1903

Longfellow, Henry W. *The Writings.* 11 vols. Cambridge: Riverside, 1886

Macdonald, Donald. *Baden-Powell: Soldier and Scout.* Melbourne: Lake, 1912

MacKenzie, R.H. 'The Boy Scout Experience.' A.P. Laurie, ed. *The Teacher's Encyclopaedia.* 7 vols. Vol. 5. London: Caxton, 1912

Mackie, John. *The Life Adventurous.* London: Jarrold, [1907]

MacLaren, Ian [John Watson]. *Young Barbarians.* Toronto: Copp Clark, 1901

Marquis, T.G. *Canada's Sons on Kopje and Veldt.* Toronto: Canada's Sons, 1900

Mason, Charlotte. *Home Education.* 1886. London: Kegan Paul, 1926

– *Parents and Children.* London: Kegan Paul, 1897

Masterman, Charles F.G. *The Condition of England.* 1909. Ed. J.T. Boulton. London: Methuen, 1960

– *In Peril of Change.* London: Fisher Unwin, 1905

Masterman, Charles F.G., ed. *The Heart of the Empire.* 1901. Brighton: Harvester, 1973

Maugham, W. Somerset. *The Collected Short Stories.* 4 vols. London: Pan, 1979

Maurice, Frederick, et al. *History of the War in South Africa, 1899–1902.* 8 vols. London: Hurst and Blackett, 1906–10

Mee, Arthur. *Arthur Mee's Wonderful Day.* London: Hodder and Stoughton, n.d.

– *Arthur Mee's Hero Book.* London: Hodder and Stoughton, n.d

Miles, Alfred H., ed. *The Imperial Reciter.* London: Cassell, n.d.

Millin, Sarah Gertrude. *Rhodes.* London: Chatto and Windus, 1934

Mills, Elliot. *The Decline and Fall of the British Empire.* Oxford: Alden, [1905]

Milner, Alfred. *The Nation and the Empire* (speeches and addresses). London: Constable, 1913

Neilly, J. Emerson. *Besieged with B.-P.* London: Pearson, 1900

Newman, Charles L.N. *Matabeleland and How We Got It.* London: Fisher Unwin, 1895

Niall, Ian. *A London Boyhood.* London: Heinemann, 1974

'Noemo, Captain' [pseud.]. *The Boy Scout Bubble: A Review of a Great Futility.* London: Allen, 1912

Nordau, Max. *Degeneration.* London: Heinemann, 1895

O'Moore, MacCarthy. *The Romance of the Boer War.* London: Stock, 1901

Our Heroes of the South African War. n.p. [1900?]

Our Scouts at Work and Play: A Picture Book for Boys and Girls. London: Ward, Lock, n.d.

Parry, D.H. *The V.C.: Its Heroes and Their Valour.* London: Cassell, 1913

Paterson, Andrew B. *The Best of Banjo Paterson.* Selected by Walter Stone. Sydney: Summit, 1977

Paul, Leslie. *Angry Young Man.* London: Faber, 1951

Pelham, Henry. *The Training of a Working Boy.* London: Macmillan, 1914

Peril and Patriotism: True Tales of Heroic Deeds and Startling Adventures. London: Cassell, 1901

Plaatje, S.T. *The Boer War: A Diary of the Siege of Mafeking.* Ed. John Comoroff. Cape Town: Macmillan, 1973

Pocock, Roger. *The Blackguard.* London: Beeman, 1896

– *A Frontiersman.* London: Methuen, 1903

– *Rottenness: A Study of America and England.* London: Beeman, 1896

Pocock, Roger, ed. *The Frontiersman's Pocket-Book.* 1909. London: Murray, 1911

Pope, Jessie. *The Baby Scouts.* London: Blackie, [1912]

– *The Cat Scouts: A Picture-Book for Little Folk.* London: Blackie, [1912]

Poyser, Arthur, ed. *The Scout Song Book.* London: Pearson, 1917

Protheroe, Ernest. *In Empire's Cause.* London: Guy, 1908

Puffer, J. Adams. *The Boy and His Gang.* Boston: Houghton Mifflin, 1912

Raymond, Ernest. *Tell England: A Study in a Generation.* 1922. London: Cassell, 1927

Reynolds, E.E. *Boy Scouts.* London: Collins, 1944

– *Stories to Tell to Scouts and Guides.* London: Harrap, 1933

Roberts, Robert. *The Classic Slum.* Manchester: Manchester UP, 1971

Roosevelt, Theodore. *Theodore Roosevelt, an Autobiography.* New York: Scribner, 1924

– *The Wilderness Hunter.* New York: Putnam, 1900

– *The Winning of the West.* 6 vols. New York: Putnam, 1900

Ross, Edward. *Diary of the Siege of Mafeking.* Ed. Brian P. Willan. Cape Town: Van Riebeeck Society, 1980

Rowan, Hill. 'The Legion of Frontiersmen.' *C.B. Fry's The Outdoor Magazine* 6, no. 31 (October 1906): 62–4

Sanderson, Edgar. *Heroes of Pioneering.* London: Seeley, 1908

Sassoon, Siegfried. *The Old Century.* 1938. London: Faber, 1986

Schreiner, Olive. *Trooper Peter Halket of Mashonaland.* London: Fisher Unwin, 1897

Scott, Walter. *The Talisman.* Edinburgh: Jack, 1902

Selous, Frederick C. *A Hunter's Wanderings in Africa.* London: Bentley, 1881

– *Sunshine and Storm in Rhodesia.* London: Ward, 1896

Service, Robert W. *Collected Verse.* London: Benn, 1935

– *The Trail of '98.* London: Fisher Unwin, 1911

Seton, Ernest Thompson. *The Book of Woodcraft.* 1912. Garden City, NY: Garden City, 1921

– *The Gospel of the Redman.* 1937. London: Psychic Press, 1970

– *How to Play Indian.* Philadelphia: Curtis, 1903

– *The Natural History of the Ten Commandments.* New York: Scribner, 1907

– *Rolf in the Woods.* New York: Grosset and Dunlap, 1911

– *Trail of an Artist-Naturalist.* New York: Scribner, 1940.

– *Two Little Savages.* 1903. Garden City, NY: Doubleday, 1959

– *The Gospel of the Redman.* 1937. London: Psychic Press, 1970

– *The Wild Animal Play for Children.* Philadelphia: Curtis, 1900

– *Wild Animals I Have Known.* 1898. London: Nutt, 1903

– *Woodmyth and Fable.* London: Hodder and Stoughton, 1905

Seton, Ernest Thompson, and Robert S.S. Baden-Powell. *Boy Scouts of America.* New York: Doubleday, 1910

Sherard, Robert H. *The Child-Slaves of Britain.* London: Hurst and Blackett, 1905

Smiles, Samuel. *Character.* New York: Allison, n.d

– *Duty.* 1880. Chicago: Donohue, n.d.

– *Self-Help.* Introduction by Asa Briggs. London: Murray, 1958

– *Self-Help.* Chicago: Belford, 1883

– *Thrift.* Toronto: Belford, 1876

Smith, R.J. Bremner. *Col. R.S.S. Baden-Powell* (Soldiers of the Queen Library). London: London Publishing Co., [1900]

Stables, Gordon. *For Honour: Not Honours.* London: Shaw, [1896]

– *Hearts of Oak: A Story of Nelson and the Navy.* London: Shaw, [1893]

Steele, Samuel B. *Forty Years in Canada.* Toronto: McClelland, 1915

Stelzle, Charles. *Boys of the Street: How to Win Them.* New York: Revell, 1904

Stent, Vere. Letter. British Library Add. ms. 46848

– *A Personal Record of Some Incidents in the Life of Cecil Rhodes.* 1925. Bulawayo: Books of Rhodesia, 1970

Stevenson, Robert L. *Kidnapped.* Edinburgh: Cassell, 1907

– *Treasure Island.* Edinburgh: Cassell, 1907

Stigand, Chauncy H. *Scouting and Reconnaissance in Savage Countries.* London: Rees, 1907

Stoker, Bram. *Dracula.* 1897. New York: Dell, 1977

Strachey, Lytton. *Eminent Victorians.* 1918. Harmondsworth: Penguin, 1981

Strang, Herbert. *Rob the Ranger.* London: Frowde, 1908

Sykes, Frank W. *With Plumer in Matabeleland.* London: Constable, 1897

Things All Scouts Should Know. London: Pearson, 1910

The Times History of the War [i.e., 1914–18]

Tressell, Robert [Robert Noonan]. *The Ragged Trousered Philanthropists.* London: Grafton, 1988

Vachell, Horace. *The Hill: A Romance of Friendship.* London: Murray, 1905

Vane, Francis P.F. *The Boy Knight.* n.p.: Council of National Peace Scouts, n.d.

Vivian, E. Charles. *The British Army from Within.* London: Frowde, [1914]

Wade, A.G. *'Counterspy!'* London: Paul, 1938

Wade, E.K. *The Piper of Pax: The Life Story of Lord Baden-Powell of Gilwell.* London: Pearson, 1931

– *The Story of Scouting.* London: Pearson, 1935

Weir, C.J. *The Boer War: A Diary of the Siege of Mafeking.* Edinburgh: Spence and Phimister, 1901

Wells, H.G. *Little Wars: A Game for Boys from Twelve Years of Age to One Hundred and Fifty …* London: Palmer, 1913

White, George S. 'The Siege of Mafeking.' Ms., SAA

White, Stewart E. *The Cabin.* New York: Grosset and Dunlap, 1911

– *Camp and Trail.* Toronto: Musson, 1907

– *The Forest.* New York: Outlook, 1903

– *The Magic Forest.* New York: Macmillan, 1903

– *The Mountains.* New York: McClure, Phillips, 1904

Wills, W.A., and L.T. Collingridge. *The Downfall of Lobengula.* 1894. Bulawayo: Books of Rhodesia, 1971

Wilson, H.W. *With the Flag to Pretoria.* 2 vols. London: Harmsworth, 1901

Wilson, Sarah. *South African Memories.* London: Arnold, 1909.

Wister, Owen. *The Virginian.* 1902. New York: Signet, 1979.

Wodehouse, P.G. *Mike: A Public School Story.* 1909. London: Black, 1924

– *The Swoop! or How Clarence Saved England.* London: Alston Rivers,1909
Wood, Eric. *The Boy Scouts' Roll of Honour.* London: Cassell, 1914
Yonge, Charlotte. *A Book of Golden Deeds.* London: Macmillan, 1883
Young, Ernest, ed. *Scout Pie.* London: Pearson, n.d
Young, F. *The Relief of Mafeking.* London: Methuen, 1900

SECONDARY SOURCES

Anderson, Olive. 'The Growth of Christian Militarism in Mid-Victorian
 Britain.' *English Historical Review* 86 (1971): 46-72
Anthony, P.D. *The Ideology of Work.* London: Tavistock, 1977
Barthes, Roland. *Mythologies.* Trans. Annette Lavers. St Albans: Paladin, 1973
Behrman, Cynthia F. *Victorian Myths of the Sea.* Athens, OH: Ohio UP, 1977
Berkhofer, Robert F., Jr. *The White Man's Indian.* New York: Vintage, 1979
Best, Geoffrey. 'Militarism and the Victorian Public School.' In *The Victorian
 Public School,* ed. Brian Simon and Ian Bradley. Dublin: Gill and Macmillan,
 1975
Branch, Douglas. *The Cowboy and His Interpreters.* 1926. New York: Cooper
 Square, 1961
Brantlinger, Patrick. *Rule of Darkness: British Literature and Imperialism, 1830–
 1914.* Ithaca: Cornell UP, 1988
Bratton, J.S. 'Of England, Home and Duty: The Image of England in Victorian
 and Edwardian Juvenile Fiction.' In *Imperialism and Popular Culture,* ed. John
 M. MacKenzie. Manchester: Manchester UP, 1986
Briggs, Asa. *Victorian People.* London: Odhams, 1954
Brown, Dee. *Bury My Heart at Wounded Knee.* New York: Holt, Rinehart, 1970
[Carpenter, K.]. *Penny Dreadfuls and Comics.* London: Victoria and Albert
 Museum, 1983
Chancellor, Valerie E. *History for Their Masters: Opinion in the English History Text-
 book: 1800–1914.* Bath: Adams and Dart, 1970
Coffin, Tristram P., and Hennig Coffin. *The Parade of Heroes: Legendary Figures in
 American Lore.* Garden City, NY: Doubleday, 1978
Connell, Evan S. *Son of the Morning Star.* New York: Harper, 1985
Cowper, H.E. 'British Education, Public and Private, and the British Empire,
 1880–1930.' Dissertation, U of Edinburgh, 1980
Davis, David B. 'The Deerslayer, a Democratic Knight of the Wilderness.' In
 Leatherstocking and the Critics, ed. Warren S. Walker. Chicago: Scott Foresman,
 1965
Drotner, Kirsten. *English Children and Their Magazines, 1751–1945.* New Haven
 and London: Yale UP, 1988
Dunae, Patrick A. 'Boys' Literature and the Idea of Empire, 1870–1914.' *Victo-
 rian Studies* 24 (1980): 105–58

Eksteins, Modris. *Rites of Spring: The Great War and the Birth of the Modern Age.* Toronto: Lester and Orpen Dennys, 1989

Fiedler, Leslie. *Love and Death in the American Novel.* London: Cape, 1967

– *The Return of the Vanishing American.* London: Cape, 1968

– *Waiting for the End.* Harmondsworth: Penguin, 1967

Field, H. John. *Toward a Programme of Imperial Life.* Westport, CT: Greenwood, 1982

Frye, Northrop. *Anatomy of Criticism.* New York: Atheneum, 1967

– *The Educated Imagination.* Toronto: CBC, 1963

Fussell, Paul. *The Boy Scout Handbook and Other Observations.* Oxford: Oxford UP, 1982

– *The Great War and Modern Memory.* Oxford: Oxford UP, 1979

Gardner, Brian. *Mafeking: A Victorian Legend.* New York: Harcourt, Brace, 1967

Gathorne-Hardy, Jonathan. *The Old School Tie: The Phenomenon of the English Public School.* New York: Viking, 1978

Girouard, Mark. *The Return to Camelot.* New Haven and London: Yale UP, 1981

Goetzmann, William H., and William N. Goetzmann. *The West of the Imagination.* New York: Norton, 1986

Green, Martin. *Dreams of Adventure, Deeds of Empire.* New York: Basic Books, 1979

Gwyn, Sandra. *The Private Capital.* Toronto: McClelland and Stewart, 1984

Haley, Bruce. *The Healthy Body and Victorian Culture.* Cambridge, MA: Harvard UP, 1975

Higgs, Robert J. 'Yale and the Heroic Ideal, *Gotterdammerung* and Palingenesis, 1865–1914.' *Manliness and Morality,* ed. J.A. Mangan and James Walvin. Manchester: Manchester UP, 1987

Hill, R.M. 'The Legion of Frontiersmen.' *The Cadet Journal* 13, no. 10 (1951): 236–7; 13, no. 11 (1951): 267–8

Hillcourt, William. *Baden-Powell: The Two Lives of a Hero.* London: Heinemann, 1964

Hobsbawn, Eric. *The Age of Empire 1875–1914.* London: Weidenfeld and Nicolson, 1987

Hobsbawm, Eric, and Terence Ranger, eds. *The Invention of Tradition.* Cambridge: Cambridge UP, 1983

Honey, J.R. de S. *Tom Brown's Universe: The Development of the Victorian Public School.* London and Blandford: Millington, 1977

Horn, Pamela. 'English Elementary Education and the Growth of the Imperial Ideal: 1880–1914.' In *'Benefits Bestowed'? Education and British Imperialism,* ed. J.A. Mangan. Manchester: Manchester UP, 1988

Horrall, S.W. *The Pictorial History of the Royal Canadian Mounted Police.* Toronto: McGraw-Hill, 1973

Houghton, Walter E. *The Victorian Frame of Mind 1830–1870*. 1957. New Haven: Yale UP, 1985

Humphries, Stephen. *Hooligans or Rebels? An Oral History of Working-Class Children and Youth 1889-1939*. Oxford: Blackwell, 1981

Hynes, Samuel. *The Edwardian Turn of Mind*. Princeton: Princeton UP, 1968.

James, Louis. 'Tom Brown's Imperialist Sons.' *Victorian Studies* 17 (1973–4): 89–99

Jeal, Tim. *Baden-Powell*. London: Hutchinson, 1989

Jones, Gareth Stedman. *Outcast London: A Study in the Relationships between Classes in Victorian Society*. Oxford: Clarendon P, 1971

Jones, Virgil C. *Roosevelt's Rough Riders*. Garden City, NY: Doubleday, 1971

Katz, Wendy R. *Rider Haggard and the Fiction of Empire*. Cambridge: Cambridge UP, 1987

Keller, Betty. *Black Wolf: The Life of Ernest Thompson Seton*. Vancouver and Toronto: Douglas and McIntyre, 1986

Kiernan, V.G. *The Lords of Human Kind: European Attitudes towards the Outside World in the Imperial Age*. London: Weidenfeld and Nicolson, 1969

Kimmel, Michael S. 'The Contemporary "Crisis" in Masculinity in Historical Perspective.' In *The Making of Masculinities*, ed. Harry Brod. Boston: Allen and Unwin, 1987

Koss, Stephen. *The Anatomy of an Antiwar Movement: The Pro-Boers*. Chicago: U of Chicago P, 1973

– *The Rise and Fall of the Political Press in Britain*. 2 vols. London: Hamilton, 1981, 1984

Lawrence, D.H. *Studies in Classic American Literature*. London: Heinemann, 1971

Lee, Emanoel. *To the Bitter End: A Photographic History of the Boer War 1899–1902*. Harmondsworth: Penguin, 1986

Lindley, Francis. *Lord Lovat*. London: Hutchinson, [1936]

Lorant, Stefan. *The Life and Times of Theodore Roosevelt*. Garden City, NY: Doubleday, 1959

MacDonald, Robert H. 'Reproducing the Middle-class Boy: From Purity to Patriotism in the Boys' Magazines, 1982-1914.' *Journal of Contemporary History* 24 (1989): 519–39

– 'The Revolt against Instinct: The Animal Stories of Seton and Roberts.' *Canadian Literature* 84 (1980): 18–29

– 'Signs from the Imperial Quarter: Illustrations in *Chums*, 1892–1914.' *Children's Literature* 16 (1988): 31–55

MacDougall, Hugh A. *Racial Myth in English History*. Montreal: Harvest House; Hanover: UP of New England, 1982

McFarlan, D.M. *First for Boys: The Story of the Boys Brigade 1883–1983.* Glasgow: Collins, 1982

MacKenzie, John M. *The Empire of Nature: Hunting, Conservation and British Imperialism.* Manchester: Manchester UP, 1988.

– *Propaganda and Empire: The Manipulation of British Public Opinion 1880–1960.* Manchester: Manchester UP, 1984

MacKenzie, John M., ed. *Imperialism and Popular Culture.* Manchester: Manchester UP, 1986

MacLeod, David I. *Building Character in the American Boy: The Boy Scouts, YMCA, and Their Forerunners, 1870–1920.* Madison: U of Wisconsin P, 1983

Mangan, J.A. *Athleticism and the Edwardian Public School.* Cambridge: Cambridge UP, 1981

– *The Games Ethic and Imperialism.* Harmondsworth: Viking, 1986

Mangan, J.A., ed. *'Benefits Bestowed?' Education and British Imperialism.* Manchester: Manchester UP, 1988

– *Making Imperial Mentalities: Socialisation and British Imperialism.* Manchester: Manchester UP, 1990

Mangan, J.A., and James Walvin, eds. *Manliness and Morality: Middle-class Masculinity in Britian and America 1800–1940.* Manchester: Manchester UP, 1987

Moran, Hugh. 'Baden-Powell's Big Idea.' *American Oxonian* 45, no. 2 (1958): 63–7

Moyles, R.G., and Doug Owram. *Imperial Dreams and Colonial Realities: British Views of Canada, 1880–1914.* Toronto: U of Toronto P, 1988

Nerlich, Michael. *Ideology of Adventure: Studies in Modern Consciousness, 1100–1750.* Vol. 1. Trans. Ruth Crowley. Minneapolis: U of Minnesota P, 1987

Nordon, Pierre. *Conan Doyle.* Trans. Frances Partridge. London: Murray, 1966

Opie, Robert. *Rule Britannia: Trading on the British Image.* Harmondsworth: Viking Penguin, 1985

Orwell, George. *Collected Essays, Journalism, Letters.* 2 vols. London: Secker, 1968

Owram, Doug. *Promise of Eden: The Canadian Expansionist Movement and the Idea of the West, 1856–1900.* Toronto: U of Toronto P, 1980

Pakenham, Thomas. *The Boer War.* London: Weidenfeld, 1979

Pearce, Roy Harvey. *Savagism and Civilization.* 1953. Baltimore: Johns Hopkins UP, 1977

Pearson, Geoffrey. *Hooligan: A History of Respectable Fears.* London: Macmillan, 1983

Pearson, Hesketh. *Labby.* London: Hamilton, 1936

Phillips, Jock. *A Man's Country? The Image of the Pakeha Male – a History.* Auckland: Penguin, 1987

Pocock, Geoffrey A. *Forgotten as Becomes a Frontiersman.* n.p.: n.p., 1991

Price, Richard. *An Imperial War and the British Working Class.* London: Routledge, 1972

Pugh, David G. *Sons of Liberty: The Masculine Mind in Nineteeth-Century America.* Westport, CT: Greenwood Press, 1983

Quigley, Isabel. *The Heirs of Tom Brown: The English School Story.* Oxford: Oxford UP, 1984

Reader, W.J. *At Duty's Call: A Study in Obsolete Patriotism.* Manchester: Manchester UP, 1988

Reddin, Paul L. 'Wild West Shows: A Study in the Development of Western Romanticism.' Dissertation, U of Missouri, 1970

Roberts, Brian. *Those Bloody Women: Three Heroines of the Boer War.* London: Murray, 1991

Roper, Michael, and John Tosh. *Manful Assertions: Masculinities in Britain since 1800.* London: Routledge, 1991

Rosenthal, Michael. *The Character Factory. Baden-Powell and the Origins of the Boy Scout Movement.* New York: Pantheon, 1986

Russell, Don. *The Lives and Legends of Buffalo Bill.* Norman, OK: U of Oklahoma P, 1960

Sandoz, Mari. *The Buffalo Hunters.* New York: Hastings House, 1954

Searle, Geoffrey R. *The Quest for National Efficiency.* Berkeley: U of California P, 1971.

Showalter, Elaine. *Sexual Anarchy: Gender and Culture at the Fin de Siècle.* Harmondsworth: Penguin, 1990

Slotkin, Richard. *The Fatal Environment: The Myth of the Frontier in the Age of Industrialization, 1800–1890.* Middletown, CT: Wesleyan UP, 1986

Smiles, Aileen. *Samuel Smiles and His Surroundings.* London: Hale,1956

Smith, Donald B. *From the Land of Shadows: The Making of Grey Owl.* Saskatoon: Western Producer Prairie Books, 1990

Smith, Henry Nash. *Virgin Land: The American West as Symbol and Myth.* 1950. Cambridge, Mass.: Harvard UP, 1970

Springhall, John O. 'Baden-Powell and the Scout Movement before 1920: Citizen Training of Soldiers of the Future?' *English Historical Review* 102 (1987): 934–42

– 'The Boy Scouts, Class and Militarism in Relation to British Youth Movements 1908–1930.' *International Review of Social History* 16 (1971), 125–58

– 'Building Character in the British Boy: The Attempt to Extend Christian Manliness to Working-class Adolescents, 1880–1914.' *Manliness and Morality*, ed. J.A. Mangan and James Walvin. Manchester: Manchester UP, 1987

– *Coming of Age: Adolescence in Britain 1860–1960.* Dublin: Gill and Macmillan, 1986

- '"A Life Story for the People"? Edwin J. Brett and the London "Low-Life" Penny Dreadfuls of the 1860s.' *Victorian Studies* 33 (1990): 223–46
- '"Up Guards and at them!" British Imperialism and Popular Art, 1880–1914.' In *Imperialism and Popular Culture*, ed. John M. MacKenzie. Manchester: Manchester UP, 1986
- *Youth, Empire and Society: British Youth Movements 1883–1942*. London: Croom Helm, 1977
Springhall, John O., Brian Fraser, and Michael Hoare. *Sure and Steadfast: A History of the Boys' Brigade*. London: Collins, 1983.
Summers, Anne. 'Militarism in Britain before the Great War.' *History Workshop* 1, no. 2 (1976): 104–23
- 'Scouts, Guides and VADS: A Note in Reply to Allen Warren.' *English Historical Review* 102 (1987): 943–7
Tanner, Ogden. *The Canadians*. Chicago: Time-Life, 1977
Thompson, Paul. *The Edwardians: The Remaking of British Society*. London: Weidenfeld, 1975
Trench, Charles C. *The Frontier Scouts*. London: Cape, 1985
Trigger, Bruce G. *Natives and Newcomers: Canada's 'Heroic Age' Reconsidered*. Kingston and Montreal: McGill-Queen's UP, 1985
Usherwood, Paul, and Jenny Spencer-Smith. *Lady Butler – Battle Artist 1846–1933*. London: National Army Museum, 1987
Utley, Robert M. *Frontier Regulars: The United States Army and the Indian 1866–1891*. New York: Macmillan, 1973
Vansittart, Peter. *Voices from the Great War*. Harmondsworth: Penguin, 1983
Van Wyk Smith, M. *Drummer Hodge: The Poetry of the Anglo-Boer War*. New York: Oxford UP, 1978
Wadland, J.H. *Ernest Thompson Seton: Man in Nature and the Progressive Era, 1880–1915*. New York: Arno, 1978
Wagner, Carolyn D. 'The Boy Scouts of America: A Model and a Mirror of American Society.' Dissertation, U of Michigan, Ann Arbor, 1978
Walden, Keith. *Visions of Order*. Toronto: Butterworth, 1982
Wallace, Paul A.W. 'Cooper's Indians.' In *Leatherstocking and the Critics*, ed. Warren S. Walker. Chicago: Scott Foresman, 1965
Walvin, James. *Victorian Values*. London: Sphere, 1988
Ward, Russel. *The Australian Legend*. Melbourne: Oxford UP, 1958
Warren, Allen. 'Citizens of the Empire: Baden-Powell, Scouts and Guides, and an Imperial Ideal.' In *Imperialism and Popular Culture*, ed. John M. MacKenzie. Manchester: Manchester UP, 1986
- 'Popular Manliness: Baden-Powell, Scouting and the Development of Manly

Character.' *Manliness and Morality,* ed. J.A. Mangan and James Walvin. Manchester: Manchester UP, 1987
– 'Sir Robert Baden-Powell, the Scout Movement and Citizen Training in Great Britain, 1900–1920.' *English Historical Review* 101 (1986): 376–98
Weston, Jack. *The Real American Cowboy.* New York: Schocken, 1985
Whitmore, Allan R. 'Beard, Boys, and Buckskins: Daniel Carter Beard and the Preservation of the American Pioneer Tradition.' Dissertation, Northwestern U, 1970
Zanger, Jules. 'The Frontiersman in Popular Fiction, 1820–60.' In *The Frontier Re-examined*, ed. John H. McDermott. Urbana, IL: U of Illinois P, 1967

Appendix 1

Baden-Powell's 'Boy Scouts Scheme'

From a report in the *Hereford Times*, 16 November 1907. Baden-Powell gave this lecture on more than fifty occasions between November 1907 and February 1908.

HEREFORD Y.M.C.A. ANNIVERSARY

VISIT OF MAJOR-GENERAL R.S. BADEN-POWELL, C.B. 'BOY SCOUTS.'

'A NEW SCHEME TO DEVELOP GOOD CITIZENS.'

The meeting opened with the singing of the hymn 'All hail the power,' after which the dean offered prayer. A portion of Scripture was read by the Rev. J. Meredith, and a special choir under Mr F. Barrass gave a rendering of the anthem, 'The City Beautiful.' At this stage Major-General Baden-Powell, C.B., the hero of Mafeking, made his appearance on the platform, and received a great ovation, the assembly rising to their feet and cheering again and again. The reception was worthy of the man and the occasion.

The MAYOR said he next came to one of the greatest pleasures of his life, and that was to introduce to them Major-General Baden- Powell, the hero of Mafeking (great and prolonged applause). They had all heard so much about him, and they all very much wanted to see him (applause). He called the General one of his heroes. He followed every detail of the siege of Mafeking, and nothing pleased him better than to find what a tough customer the General was (cheers and applause). He held on like grim death, and fought for his King and country in a manner that won the admiration of all his countrymen (applause). When relief came, all their hearts gave a sigh of relief (applause). The General came to them, he understood, that evening on a behalf of a work into which he was infusing as much ardour as he had shown during the siege of Mafeking (applause). It was to raise men to a higher level, to make them what he wished them to be, real citizens of a great Empire (applause).

Major-General BADEN-POWELL, who was received with tremendous enthusiasm, said he must thank the Mayor for the more than generous words with which he had introduced him, and his hearers for their kindly reception (applause). He should like to say a few words in continuation of what the Mayor had said about the Y.M.C.A. for he, like him, was a firm believer in that institution (applause), and in the good it was doing, not only to its members but to the country at large (applause). He really looked on it as a great national asset, because it aimed at raising the standard of citizenship, not only in England, but in their Colonies and in the farthest parts of the earth (applause). Some people looked on the Y.M.C.A. as a place of tears and texts, but he could heartily assure them that it was an institution established for the making of real true Christian men, and a man who was not a Christian could only be half a man (applause). He was there that evening to put forward a scheme for the development of good citizenship and good men, a scheme which he believed the Y.M.C.A. ought to take up and carry through. The same causes which brought about the downfall of the Roman Empire (and of many others of the empires of antiquity) were working to-day in Great Britain, and this truth was practically admitted by those who studied the general conditions of both countries. The main cause of the downfall of Rome was the decline of good citizenship among its subjects, due to want of energetic patriotism, to the growth of idleness and luxury, and the exaggerated importance of local party politics. The General was not so pessimistic as to believe that we are in this country so far on the downgrade as to be hopeless; but he was strongly of the opinion that we are only near to the parting of the ways, where it becomes incumbent upon every one of us who has the slightest patriotism in him to earnestly help, in however small a way, to turn the rising generation on the right road for good citizenship. There was no use pottering away at the present generation, the hope of the country was in the boys of to-day who would become the citizens of tomorrow. Believing this, he had carefully thought out a scheme for the training and development of boys of all creeds and classes, which he was sure if put into practice would help the rising generation to become better citizens and better men. This scheme he had termed 'Scouting,' or 'Boy

Scouts,' and he was glad to say that an experimental trial had recently been made in working out the details, and with very satisfactory results. Scouts, he said, were of two kinds – war scouts and peace scouts. A war scout was a man selected for his reliability, courage, and intelligence to go ahead of a force to find out all about the enemy and the country. On his good work and sense of duty depended very largely the success or failure of the expedition. A peace scout was a different kind of man – he was to be found amongst the pioneers and trappers of North-West Canada, the explorers and hunters of Africa, prospectors, drovers, and bushmen of Australia, and above all in the Canadian North-West Mounted Police, the South African Constabulary, Royal Irish Constabulary, British South African and numerous other police forces. It was the examples of men such as these that boys should be set to follow – these were the men whose manhood was strong and rich, and whose lives were pure, and in them were combined the many qualities that go to make good citizens as well as good scouts. There were certain qualities absolutely essential in a good scout, and these were also the qualities which made the best citizens in a peaceful community. These could all be acquired under instruction, and this scheme was offered as a step in educating boys in these qualities. Scoutcraft included many subjects, and their respective details after being taught theoretically were worked out in practice by certain tests and games. The instruction was partly indoor but mostly outdoor, and was adapted to towns as well as to country – it was easy, inexpensive, and useful, and developed character and health not only in boys but in the instructor as well. Badges with the scouts' motto, 'B.P.' (Be Prepared) were given to each scout on proficiency, and the examination set for the boys was by no means easy. The General went on to give fuller details of the programme of instruction which we tabulate below:

1. Discipline. – Self-discipline, obedience to scout law and to officers, self-sacrifice and duty.

2. Observation. – Noticing and memorizing details, tracking, quick sight, judging distances, heights and numbers, reading signs etc.

3. Woodcraft. – Natural history, astronomy, map-reading, finding way in strange country, boat management, swimming, carpentering, cycling, cooking, camping, resourcefulness, the making of huts and mats, tying various knots, reading character and condition of people, thereby gaining sympathy.

4. Health and Endurance. – Physical culture, exercises and games, cleanliness, non-smoking, continence, sobriety, food and sanitation, etc.

5. Chivalry. – Courtesy, honour, code of the knights, charity, thrift, courage, cheerfulness, unselfishness, loyalty to King and employers or officers, practical chivalry to women, obligation to do a good turn daily and how to do it, etc.

6. Patriotism. – History and geography of Britain and her Colonies, flags, medals, H.M. Services, deeds that won the Empire, marksmanship, duties as citizens, helping police, etc.

7. Saving Life. – From fire, drowning, sewer gas, runaway horses, panic, street accidents, etc. First Aid. Albert medal, etc.

The experiment of putting boys of all classes to live and work together had succeeded beyond expectation. All were treated exactly alike, whether they were from Eton or from the London slums, and the effect for good on their character which became visible in the first few days of the trial camp was surprising. Altogether the scheme was one admirably fitted to develop character, manliness, honour, endurance, patriotism, and good citizenship in boys, and he appealed to the men present to take up the scheme and carry it through in the city of Hereford. When he took into consideration the fact that there were to-day in this country one and three-quarter millions of boys drifting into hooliganism for want of guiding hands to set them on the right road, it was incumbent on all interested in the welfare of the nation – and who was not – to do something to rescue the lads. Mr Dandie had consented to act as local hon. secretary for Hereford county, to collect names of those in sympathy with the scheme, and willing to take up the training of a patrol of six boys. Hereford was the first town he had visited on this crusade and he was now on his way to Wales. He was by nature a Welshman. His forbears lived on the border, and he had no doubt did a lot of scouting after other people's cattle (laughter). He was glad to have had recognition by a gentleman in the city who was the father of one of their most famous citizens, Miss Evangeline Anthony (great applause). He was delighted to be a relative of hers, and so could look upon himself as having a connection with Hereford (renewed applause). He wished to have a still closer connection with them all (loud and prolonged applause).

Appendix 2

Lists of 'Books to Read' in *Scouting for Boys* (1908)

PART I
SCOUTCRAFT

Stevenson, R.L.	*Kidnapped*
Kipling, R.	*Kim*
Baillie, F[rederick]	*Siege of Mafeking*
Seton, E[rnest] Thompson	*Two Little Savages*
Mason, Charlotte	*Parents and Children*
Couch, L[illian] Quiller	*The Romance of Everyday*
Sanderson, Edgar	*Heroes of Pioneering*

PART II
TRACKING AND WOODCRAFT

Gross, Dr [Hans]	*Criminal Investigation*
Baden-Powell, R.S.S.	*Aids to Scouting*
Baden-Powell [?]	'Lectures on Tracking' in *Cavalry Journal,* Oct. 1907
Stigand, Capt. [Chauncy]	*Scouting and Reconaissance in Savage Countries*
Baden-Powell [?]	'Tracks of Wild Animals'

Doyle, A. Conan	*Memoirs of Sherlock Holmes*
–	*Adventures of Sherlock Holmes*
[?]	*The Thinking Machine*
[?]	*Deer Stalking*
Westall, W.P.	*Every Boy's Book of British Natural History*
Schilling, [Carl G.]	*With Flashlight and Rifle in Africa*
Smiles, S[amuel]	*Duty*
Westall, W.P.	*A Year with Nature*
Long, W[illiam P.]	*Beasts of the Field*
	Countryside [ill. weekly]
St. John, C[harles]	*Wild Sports of the Highlands*
Johns, Rev. C[harles]	*I Go A-Walking Through Lanes and Meadows*
Kipling, R.	*The Jungle Book*
Fitzpatrick, Sir Percy	*Jock of the Bushveld*
Seton, Mrs [sic] E. Thompson	*The Wild Animal Play*
Watkins, W[illiam] E.	*School Gardening*

PART III
LIFE IN THE OPEN

Stewart, Bertrand	*Manual of Military Engineering*
	Active Service Pocket Book
	Romance of Engineering and Mechanism
[Williams, Archibald]	*How It Works*
	'1s. books on Carpentering, Joinery, Engine-driving, etc.'
Nessmuk [George W. Sears]	*Woodcraft*
Seton, Mrs E. Thompson [Grace]	*A Woman Tenderfoot*
Seton, E. Thompson	*Two Little Savages*
	Mountaineering [Badminton Libr.]
MacEwan, D[uncan]	*Guide to the Umbrella Star Map*
Baden-Powell, Major [Baden]	*The Science Year Book*
Gall, Rev. James	*An Easy Guide to the Constellations*
Newcomb, Simon	*Astronomy for Everybody*

'Also books on astronomy by
Professors Ball, Heath, Maunder,
and Flammarion.'

PART IV
ENDURANCE FOR SCOUTS

Miles, E[ustace]	*Cassell's Physical Educator*
[Hancock, Harrie?]	*Ju-jitsu*
Chesterton, T[homas]	*School Games*
Newton, A.J.	*Boxing*
Barbour, B. McCall	*What's the Harm in Smoking?*
– . [?]	*In My Youth* [Practical Hints on Purity]
Stall, Sylvanus	*What a Young Boy ought to Know*
Bradley, J.H.	*A Note for Parents* [teaching children about eproduction]
Hancock, Irving	*Japanese Physical Training*
Edwards, W[alter]	*How to be Well and Strong*
Neil, C. Lang	*Walking*
– .	*Modern Physical Culture Health and Strength* [monthly]

CHIVALRY OF THE SCOUTS

Scott, Sir Walter	*Ivanhoe*
[Cutler, Uriel W.]	*Stories of King Arthur*
Doyle, Sir Conan	*The White Company*
Digby, Kenelm	*The Broad Stone of Honour*
[Miles, Alfred H., ed.?]	*Fifty-two Stories of Chivalry*
Kipling, Rudyard	*Puck of Pook's Hill*
Wagner, Charles	*Courage*
[Yonge, Charlotte]	*[A Book of] Golden Deeds*
Mason, Charlotte	*Parents and Children*
Smiles, Samuel	*Duty*
Smiles, Samuel	*Thrift*
[?]	*One Hundred and One Ways of Making Money*
Keary, Peter	*Do It Now*

– .	*The Secrets of Success*
Brod, J.	*Rabbits for Profit*
Swanson [George Samson]	*Bees for Pleasure and Profit*
[?]	*Esperanto for the Million*
	Cassell's Handbooks [joinery, pottery, painters' works, etc.] *Work Handbooks* series [on harness-making, tinplate, pumps, bookbinding, signwriting, beehives, etc.]
White, Miss [Mary]	*Basket-making*
Swannell, M[ildred]	*Rafia Work*
Smiles, S.	*Self Help*
	Papers on trades for boys in the *Boys Brigade Gazette*

PART V
SAVING LIFE

	Manual of Boys' Life Brigade
	Manual of Fire Drill
Holbein, Prof. [Montague]	*Swimming*
Gell, H[enry] W.	*Aid to the Sick or Injured*
	National Health Society's booklets on hygiene and sanitation.

PATRIOTISM

Lord, Mrs Frewen [Millicent]	*[Tales from] St. Paul's Cathedral*
– .	*[Tales from] Westminster Abbey*
Rouse, Dr	*Travels of Captain John Smith*
Lang, John, ed.	*The Story of Captain Cook*
Fitchett [William]	*Deeds That Won the Empire*
Berry, Power	*The Boys' Book of Bravery*
Cadett, Herbert	*The Boys' Book of Battles*
	Rules for Miniature Rifle Clubs
Wintour, F.	*The Union Jack and How it was Made*
	Leaflets from the Empire Day Association.
Forster, Arnold	*History of the British Empire*

PART VI
NOTES FOR INSTRUCTORS

Stelzle, Charles	*Boys of the Street and How to Win Them*
Forbush, W[illiam] B.	*The Boy Problem*
[?]	*The Teacher's Problem*
Smiles, Samuel	*Duty*
Gorst, Sir John	*The Children of the Nation*
Keeble, Samuel	*The Citizen of Tomorrow*
Cornford, L[eslie] Cope	*The Canker at the Heart*
Sherard, M. [Robert H.]	*The Child Slaves of Britain*
Booth, Bramwell	*The Abandoned Child*
	Pamphlets on training of children published by the Moral Education Committee.
Holding, T[homas] H.	*The Camper's Handbook*
Goulding, F[rancis]	*The Young Marooners*
Oakwood, W.M.	*Carpentering and Cabinetmaking*
Hall, Cyril	*Models and How to Make Them*
Sanderson, E[dgar]	*Heroes of Pioneering*
Jenks, Tudor	*Boys' Book of Exploration*
Rooper, W[ilhelmina] L.	*Healthful, Physical Exercises*
Watts, Mrs Roger [Emily]	*The Fine Art of Ju Jitsu*
[Protheroe, Ernest?]	*Heroic Deeds Simply Told*
Protheroe, Ernest	*Heroes and Heroines of Everyday Life as well as those of War*
Forster, H.O. Arnold	*History of England*
Thomson, C[lara] L.	*Adventures of Beowulf*
Forster, H.O. Arnold	School Atlas
Vincent, Sir [Charles] Howard	*Through the British Empire in a Few Minutes*
Chesterton, T.	*School Games*
Alexander, H.	*New Games and Sports*
Aldrich, Mrs	*Industrial Games*
[?]	*Social – to Save* [New York]
[?]	*Finger Problems* [games with string]

Books recommended or cited in the text of *Scouting for Boys* [1908]

Boyd, Alexander, Lt.	*From the Niger to the Nile*
Catlin, [George]	*Shut Your Mouth and Save Your Life*
Cooper, Fenimore	*The Pathfinder*
Cornish, C[harles] J.	*Animal Artisans*
Gibson, Hamilton	*Camp Life*
Hamilton, Bill	*My Sixty Years in the Plains*
How, F[rederick] D.	*The Book of the Child*
Long, William	*Beasts of the Field*
–	*School of the Woods*
Millais [John G.]	*Mammals of Great Britain and Ireland*
Seton, E. Thompson	*Birchbark [Roll] of the Woodcraft Indians*
Scott, Walter	*The Talisman*
Smith, Richmond	*The Siege and Fall of Port Arthur*

Books added in 1910 edition

Strang, Herbert	*Rob the Ranger*
Pocock, Roger	*The Frontiersman's Pocket Book*
[?]	*The ABC of the Royal Navy*
Hurd, A[rchibald] S.	*How Our Navy is Run*
Stables, Gordon	*Hearts of Oak*
Protheroe, E[rnest]	*In Empire's Cause*
Bullen, Frank	*The Cruise of the 'Cachelot'*
[?]	*Signalling for Boy Scouts*
	'Scout Chats' No. 14: Morse Signalling Code [*The Scout*]
Garnett, J.H.	*Wood-Carving*
Day, George	*Metal Work*
Bridges, Victor	*Camping Out for Boy Scouts*
Corbin, T[homas] W.	*The 'How Does It Work' of Electricity*
–	*Modern Engines*
	'Scout Charts' on physical exercise [*The Scout*]

Bisseker, H[arry].	*In Confidence [: to Boys]*
Waite, Surgeon-Captain [Henry]	*How to Keep Fit*
	Bradshaw's Railway Guide
Keary, Peter	*Get On or Get Out*
Gardner, George	*Rabbit Keeping*
	First Aid to the Injured
Wilson, Dr Andrew	*What to do in Emergencies*
Cullen, Dr	*Ambulance Illustrated*
	R.E.P. [Elliman's handbook]

Some books omitted from 1910 edition [out of print?]

Miles, Alfred H., ed.	*Fifty-two Stories of Chivalry*
Smiles, Samuel	*Duty*
Berry, Power	*The Boys' Book of Bravery*
Cadett, Herbert	*The Boys' Book of Battles*
	The Teacher's Problem
Sherard, Robert	*The Child Slaves of Britain*
Jenks, Tudor	*Boys' Book of Exploration*
Forster, H.O. Arnold	*History of England*
Chesterton, T.	*School Games*
Alexander, H.	*New Games and Sports*
Aldrich, Mrs	*Industrial Games*
	Social – to Save
	Finger Problems

Index

adventure 119–20; fiction of 121; and imperialism 121; and the yarn 121–2

Aids to Scouting 23, 82, 84–5, 93

Baden-Powell, Olave 209

Baden-Powell, Robert S.S.: on Canadian boys 148; and Charterhouse School 104, 159; on degeneracy 20; on frontiersmen, 8–9, 145–8; heroic image, 88–90, 96–114, 208–10; honorific names 83–4; *impeesa* story 84, 98–9; in Mafeking 91–5; in Matabeleland 62–4, 68–70; as myth-maker 124–6; on obedience 147–50; scouting 68–70; on virility 5, 123–4, 163; and 'Wild West' 63. See also *Aids to Scouting, Scouting for Boys*

Barrie, James 206

Beard, Daniel 13, 33, 207

Begbie, Harold 99, 101, 121, 159

Birkenhead disaster 173, 199–200

Boer War 77–82, 90–1

Boone, Daniel 37–8

Booth, Charles 163–4

Boy Scout movement: Birmingham exhibition 10, 167–8; Brownsea Camp 118; and class 153–8; and First World War 198–202; founding of 7; and frontier myth 8–9, 205–6; growth of 10–11; images of 186–91; and imperialism 168–74; legitimation of 195–202; and militarism 178–86; mythologized 205–10; and public school code 158–62; and religion 160–1; rites and rituals 122–3; and self-help 162–8; and sex 165–6; Sheppey disaster 176–8; talismans 124–6; uniform 124–5, 211–12; values 8

Boy Scouts' Roll of Honour 200–1

Boys' Brigade 12, 148, 182, 184. *See also* Smith, William

Boy's Own Paper 119–20, 191, 201

boys' periodicals: and Boy Scout movement 191–5; and scouting 81–2

British Boy Scouts 190–1

Browne, G. Hamilton 53n, 146

Buchan, John 14
Buffalo Bill. *See* Cody, William
Burnham, Frederick R. 64–8, 82

Callwell, Maj. Charles 72
The Captain 191–2, 193
children: and health 19, 24; and
  poverty 19–20, 163–4
Chingachgook 37, 74
Chums 16, 82, 191, 192–3
Church Lads Brigade 182
Churchill, Winston S. 78–9, 81, 176,
  210
Clery, Col. Cornelius 71
Cody, William 40–3; and frontiers-
  men 42
Committee and Physical Deteriora-
  tion 19
Cooper, James Fenimore 35–8, 74;
  and Indians 35–7
Cornford, Leslie 19–20, 164n
Cornwell, Jack 200
cowboy 43–5, 76–7
Crockett, Davy 38
Custer, Gen. George 41, 74–5

Daily Telegraph 9, 191
decadence, fears of 4–5; and
  national efficiency 17–19
*The Decline and Fall of the British
  Empire* 17–18
degeneracy, working class 4, 20–1
Dinuzulu 125, 136
Dodge, Col. Richard 38–9
Dooley, Mr 77
Doyle, A. Conan 127–8
Driscoll, Lt.-Col. Patrick 56, 58

Eastman, Charles 141–2
education, progressive 22–3

First US Volunteer Cavalry. *See*
  'Rough Riders'
Fitz-Gerald, W. Blackburn 20
Fitzpatrick, Percy 49; *Jock of the Bush-
  veld* 50
Forbush, William 133–5, 141
frontier, myth of 5–6, 31–5,
  203–4; African 48–51; American
  37–40; Australian 47–8; Canadian
  45–7; 'Lost Legion' 52–4; New
  Zealand 47. *See also* Cody,
  Kipling
Frontiersman's Pocket-Book 56–8
Fry, Charles B. 24, 139
Frye, Northrop 33–4

Gifford, Hon. Maurice 63
Girl Guides 10, 185, 209
Grootboom, Jan 69, 70
Gross, Dr Hans 128

Haggard, H. Rider 4, 83, 99n, 126;
  King Solomon's Mines 50–1
Hall, G. Stanley 133, 166
Hamilton, Angus 96–7
Hargrave, John 142–3
Hay, Ian [John Beith] 176
hero, image of 89, 112
The Hill 81
history, myth of 169–72
Hobhouse, L.T. 15
Hobson, John A. 15
Hora, Melville 55–6
Hughes, Thomas 171
Hyatt, Stanley P. 206

imperialism 13–16; and adventure
  121; and Boy Scout movement
  168–74
Indians 39, 42; and Cooper 35–7;

and Hargrave 142–3; and North-West Mounted Police 45–6; as scouts 66, 74; and Seton 138–42; Sioux society 141–2; stereotypes 137–8, 142
invasion, fear of 18–19; stories 192

James, William 140–1
Jameson Raid 91
Keary, Peter 166–7
Kibbo Kift 143
Kingsley, Charles 170–1
Kipling, Rudyard: and colonial virility 77–8; *Jungle Book* 149; *Kim* 129; and myth of frontier 34–5, 52–3

Labouchere, Henry 49, 68
The Lanchester Tradition 158
Lawson, Henry 47–8, 147
Legion of Frontiersmen 18, 54–60, 204n
Legion of Scouts 18
Long, William 149
Lonsdale, Earl of 54, 207
Lovat Scouts 81

Mafeking, siege of 91–5; fever 111–12; journalists in 96; Mafeking Boy Scouts, 129–31; relief of 95–6. *See also* Baden-Powell, heroic image
Manual of Military Engineering 127
masculinity, crisis in 16–17
Mason, Charlotte 23
Masterman, Charles C.G. 15
Millais, Sir John 168
Milner, Alfred, Viscount 14

National Service League 18, 182, 183, 184
Natty Bumppo 35–7, 74

nature 21–6; camping 25; and education 22–3; social darwinism 25–6; 'open-air boy' 24–5
Navy League 183
Ndebele 66–7, 68–70
Neilly, Emerson 96, 98
Newbolt, Sir Henry 173–4
Niall, Ian 206
North-West Mounted Police (and Royal North West Mounted Police) 45–7, 58–9, 75

Partridge, Bernard 197
Paterson, Banjo 147
Pearson, Arthur 9–10, 122
Pocock, Roger 51–2, 54–9, 80–1, 207. *See also* Legion of Frontiersmen
Pope, Jessie 188–9
Potts, Jerry 75
Princess Patricia's Canadian Light Infantry 58

race 171–2
races, martial 135
Raffles 81
recapitulation, theory of 132–5, 142–3
Reid, Howard 193–4
Remington, Frederic 44, 64
Riddle of the Sands 19
Roberts, Frederick Sleigh, Earl 18, 113
Roosevelt, Theodore 39–40, 76–7
'Rough Riders' 75–7
Rowntree, Seebohm 163–4
Russell, Bertrand 16n
Russell, Charlie 44

Schreiner, Olive 204
The Scout 10, 122, 156–7, 187–8

scouting, 66–70; on American frontier 72–5; on imperial frontiers 75; and irregular corps 75–81; theories of 70–2. *See also* Baden-Powell, Burnham

Scouting for Boys 6–7, 126–32, 150–3; Mafeking Boy Scouts 129–31; Scouts' chorus 126; Scout Law, 150–3; Scout Oath 150–1

Scouts' Book of Heroes 201–2

Selous, Frederick C. 50, 68

Service, Robert 53–4

Seton, Ernest Thompson 13, 33, 126, 138–42, 179, 207; and ideal Indian 140–2; and instinct 140–1; and obedience 148–9; *Two Little Savages* 138, 140; Woodcraft Movement 13, 139

Sherard, Robert 19–20, 163

Sherlock Holmes 127–8

Smiles, Samuel 162–3, 166

Smith, John 124, 169

Smith, Sir William A. 12. *See also* Boys' Brigade

Sons of Daniel Boone 13, 33

South African Constabulary 113–14

Spanish-American War 76–7

Springhall, John O. 182, 184

Steele, Sam 75, 82, 113

Stelzle, Charles 163

Stigand, Capt. Chauncey H. 127

Strathcona's Horse 80

studies, social 19–20, 163–4

Summers, Anne 183, 184–5

Tom Brown's Schooldays 171

Townshend, R.B. 207

Turner, Frederick Jackson 39

VAD 185

Vane, Sir Francis 180–1, 182

Warren, Allen 183–4

Waugh, Evelyn 206

Wells, H.G. 189

Westward Ho! 170–1

White, Stewart E. 22

'Wild West' 41–3

Wilson, Major Allan 66, 67, 173

Wilson, Lady Sarah 94, 96

Wister, Owen 43–4

Wodehouse, P.G. 167, 193

Wolf Cubs 10, 149, 209

Woodcraft Indians (and Seton Indians, Woodcraft Movement) 13, 139. *See also* Seton

Young England 191

YMCA 184

youth movements 11–13; and obedience 148–9

Zulus 135–6; and Boy Scout movement 136–7

Picture Credits and Sources

Black and White, Newspaper Library, British Library, 6
Bristol Art Gallery, cover
Chums, Osborne Collection, 14
Glenbow Museum, 4
The Graphic, Newspaper Library, British Library, 3, 5
Illustrated London News, National Army Museum, 8
Arthur Mee, *Arthur Mee's Hero Book*, Hodder and Stoughton Ltd, 16
Sir John Millais, Tate Gallery, 10
Museum of Canadian Scouting, Scouts Canada, 9, 13
Notman Photographic Archives, McCord Museum, 1
Punch, 15
Philmont Museum, 11
Royal Canadian Mounted Police Museum, 2
Scouting for Boys, 12
Under the Union Jack, Newspaper Library, British Library, 7

Every attempt has been made to identify and credit sources for photographs. The publisher would appreciate receiving information as to any inaccuracies in the credits for subsequent editions.